THE SOCIAL SELF

INQUIRIES IN SOCIAL CONSTRUCTION

Series editors
Kenneth J. Gergen and John Shotter

Inquiries in Social Construction is designed to facilitate across disciplinary and national boundaries, a revolutionary dialogue within the social sciences and humanities. Central to this dialogue is the idea that all presumptions of the real and the good are constructed within relations among people. This dialogue gives voice to a new range of topics, including the social construction of the person, rhetoric and narrative in the construction of reality, the role of power in making meanings, postmodernist culture and thought, discursive practices, the social constitution of the mental, dialogic process, reflexivity in theory and method, and many more. The series explores the problems and prospects generated by this new relational consciousness, and its implications for science and social life.

Also in this series

Therapy as Social Construction
edited by Sheila McNamee and Kenneth J. Gergen

Psychology and Postmodernism
edited by Steinar Kvale

Constructing the Social
edited by Theodore R. Sarbin and John I. Kitsuse

Conversational Realities
Constructing Life through Language
John Shotter

Power/Gender
Social Relations in Theory and Practice
edited by H. Lorraine Radtke and Henderikus J. Stam

After Postmodernism
Reconstructing Ideology Critique
edited by Herbert W. Simons and Michael Billig

THE SOCIAL SELF

EDITED BY
DAVID BAKHURST
and
CHRISTINE SYPNOWICH

SAGE Publications
London • Thousand Oaks • New Delhi

First published 1995

SAGE Publications Ltd
6 Bonhill Street
London EC2A 4PU

SAGE Publications Inc
2455 Teller Road
Thousand Oaks, California 91320

SAGE Publications India Pvt Ltd
32, M-Block Market
Greater Kailash – I
New Delhi 110 048

British Library Cataloguing in Publication data
A catalogue record for this book is available
from the British Library

ISBN 0 8039 7596 1
ISBN 0 8039 7597 X (pbk)

Library of Congress record available

Typeset by Mayhew Typesetting, Rhayader, Powys
Printed in Great Britain by The Cromwell Press Ltd,
Broughton Gifford, Melksham, Wiltshire

Contents

List of Contributors   vi

1 Introduction: Problems of the Social Self   1
   David Bakhurst and Christine Sypnowich

2 Meaning and Self in Cultural Perspective   18
   Jerome Bruner

3 Wittgenstein and Social Being   30
   David Bakhurst

4 What a Vygotskian Perspective Can Contribute to
   Contemporary Philosophy of Language   47
   Ellen Watson

5 The Soviet Self: A Personal Reminiscence   67
   Felix Mikhailov

6 Death in Utopia: Marxism and the Mortal Self   84
   Christine Sypnowich

7 The Social Self in Political Theory: The Communitarian
   Critique of the Liberal Subject   103
   Stephen Mulhall and Adam Swift

8 The Gendered Self   123
   Diana Coole

9 Becoming Women/Women Becoming: Film and the Social
   Construction of Gender   140
   Helene Keyssar

10 Why Multiple Personality Tells Us Nothing about the Self/
   Mind/Person/Subject/Soul/Consciousness   159
   Ian Hacking

Index   180

List of Contributors

David Bakhurst is Associate Professor of Philosophy at Queen's University at Kingston, Ontario. He is the author of *Consciousness and Revolution in Soviet Philosophy* (1991), and a number of articles on ethics, philosophical anthropology and the philosophy of mind.

Jerome Bruner is Research Professor of Psychology at New York University. He has held the G. H. Mead University Professorship at the New School for Social Research, New York, and the Watts Chair of Psychology at Oxford. He has written widely on questions of language, mind and human development. His books include *Child's Talk* (1983), *Actual Minds, Possible Worlds* (1986) and *Acts of Meaning* (1990).

Diana Coole is Senior Lecturer in Politics at Queen Mary and Westfield College, University of London. She is author of *Women in Political Theory* (1988, 2nd edition 1993). Her research is in the area of contemporary European thought. She is currently writing a book on politics and negativity.

Ian Hacking is University Professor of Philosophy at the University of Toronto. His books include *Rewriting the Soul: Multiple Personality and the Sciences of Memory* (1995), *Le Plus pur nominalisme* (1993) and *The Taming of Chance* (1990).

Helene Keyssar is Professor of Communication at the University of California, San Diego. She has published books on the films of Robert Altman, feminist theatre, black American drama, and (with Tracy Strong) a biography of Anna Louise Strong. She has also edited a collection of essays on feminist drama. She is currently working on a book on the relations between theatre, film and television in American society.

Felix Mikhailov is a member of Moscow's Institute of Philosophy, and Head of the Department of Philosophy at the 2nd Medical Institute, Moscow. He is author of *The Riddle of the Self* (1980), *Obshchestvennoe soznanie i samosoznanie individa* (*Social Consciousness and the Self-Consciousness of the Individual*) (1990), and numerous articles on philosophy and psychology.

Stephen Mulhall is Reader in Philosophy at the University of Essex. He is co-author (with Adam Swift) of *Liberals and Communitarians* (1992), and author of *On Being in the World* (1990), *Stanley Cavell: Philosophy's Recounting of the Ordinary* (1994) and *Faith and Reason* (1994), as well as a series of articles reflecting his interests in Wittgenstein, Heidegger and Kierkegaard. He is currently working on an introduction to Heidegger's *Being and Time*.

Adam Swift is Fellow in Politics and Sociology at Balliol College, Oxford. He is co-author (with Stephen Mulhall) of *Liberals and Communitarians* (1992). He is currently collaborating on two comparative projects with an international focus: a study of social class, social mobility and meritocracy, and a book on popular beliefs about social justice.

Christine Sypnowich is Associate Professor of Philosophy at Queen's University at Kingston, Ontario. She is author of *The Concept of Socialist Law* (1990) and a variety of articles in political philosophy. She is presently writing on the politics of difference and the concept of equality.

Ellen Watson is a Lecturer in Philosophy at the University of Queensland, Brisbane, Australia. She received her Ph.D. in philosophy from the University of California, San Diego in 1992. Her research explores the connections between disparate traditions in their approaches to language and mind.

1

Introduction: Problems of the Social Self

David Bakhurst and Christine Sypnowich

To what extent is the individual a creature of society? This book examines the claim that we owe our status as persons, who think, speak and act as we do, to our inauguration and participation in social forms of life. The idea that we are 'social selves', whose very identities are intimately bound up with the communities and cultures in which we live, is a view that has been propounded by thinkers throughout the human sciences. Moreover, it is usually a position intended to be subversive of received opinion. It is argued that by failing properly to recognize our status as social beings we fall into theoretical confusions that reflect and reinforce a deleterious individualism in our intellectual culture. And this failing is often thought to have political significance, legitimizing views which celebrate individuals' rights to liberty and privacy at the expense of the values of fellowship and community. As a result, arguments about the social self are often made with strong feeling and a sense of urgency, and provoke critical responses that are equally impassioned. The essays in this collection aim to capture the fervour of the debate, while taking a calm and careful look at the central arguments.

The book explores conceptions of the social self developed in a variety of overlapping disciplines, including philosophy, psychology, political theory, film and feminism, and considers the ideas of thinkers as diverse as Marx, Wittgenstein, Foucault, Bakhtin, Gilligan, and MacIntyre. Different disciplinary cultures inevitably produce different visions of our social nature, and as the chapters which follow illustrate, no single view of the way in which the self is defined in society predominates, nor is one likely to be forthcoming. Indeed, while this introduction speaks of selves as socially 'constituted', 'constructed' or 'defined', as if these expressions were interchangeable, many thinkers would distinguish them. Moreover, some prefer not to deploy the concept of the self at all, speaking instead of 'subjects', 'persons' or 'individuals'. Though these terminological differences are often theoretically insignificant, they sometimes reflect differences of substance.

The intention of this book is not to provide a grand synthesis of views, but to clarify the complex, criss-crossing issues at the heart of the debate, as they appear in different fields. It aims to show where there is agreement between those who emphasize our status as social beings despite apparent differences in their positions, and where, in contrast, their seemingly like-minded pronouncements in fact obscure a diversity of ultimately conflicting opinions. Thus we aspire to make clear what is at issue in controversies over the 'social self' and what is at stake in resolving those controversies one way rather than another.

The Cartesian self

Perhaps the best way to grasp what is shared by those who argue that we are social selves is to begin by focusing on, not the similarities between their respective positions, but their common target. Proponents of the social self are usually united in their hostility to a conception of the person that emerged at the beginning of modernity and which has subsequently exercised a profound influence on our intellectual culture. The most vivid expression of this conception is found in the writings of René Descartes, a philosopher whose ideas are often portrayed as central to the development of modern conceptions of the individual and the intellectual projects of modernity more generally.

In the second of his *Meditations on First Philosophy*, written in 1641, Descartes concludes that his philosophical deliberations have so far established the following about himself:

> But what then am I? A thing that thinks. What is that? A thing that doubts, understands, affirms, denies, is willing, is unwilling, and also imagines and has sensory perceptions. (1641: 19; cf. 34)

Here we have the crux of the Cartesian conception of the self: the idea that the individual is, above all else, a thinking thing (*res cogitans*). In the *Meditations* Descartes does more than merely emphasize or privilege the thinking, reasoning side of our natures at the expense of other features of the human condition. For him, each of us 'is in the strict sense only a thing that thinks' (p. 18).

Descartes arrives at this conception on his quest to establish the foundations of knowledge. He pursues this project by retreating from the bodily world that the senses present to us, with all its distractions and invitations to error, into the depths of his mind. He resolves to scrutinize his ideas methodically, setting aside all those he can doubt, until he finds some which are certain and thus fit to serve as the basis for other beliefs. He soon conjectures, however, that no belief is beyond doubt, for it seems possible that all his ideas might have been inculcated in him by a malicious demon who has brought it about that Descartes believes only falsehoods.

It is interesting that Descartes's famous thought experiment already presupposes a particular picture of the mind and its relation to the world, a picture which seems natural and compelling. Descartes assumes that each of us is directly acquainted only with the contents of his or her own mind, so that our knowledge of the 'outside world' is always indirect, mediated by mental representations. He then worries that, if our only access to reality is via mental representations, there will be no way we can compare reality as we take it to be with reality as it really is: all we can do is compare representations with other equally fallible representations. Thus we confront the sceptical possibility, illustrated by the story of the evil genius, that the world might be utterly unlike the way we take it to be.

Descartes's scepticism gets its life from the idea that the mind is a kind of self-contained world of thoughts and experiences, essentially independent of the 'external' world of people and things 'outside' or 'beyond' it. Our selves sit, as it were, at the centre of these subjective worlds, spectators in the theatre of the mind in which they are forever trapped. And Descartes's solution to the evil genius hypothesis – the consoling thought that the demon could not deceive him about the certainty of his own existence – does nothing to undermine this picture. On the contrary, it is Descartes's existence as a mind so conceived that the *cogito* affirms. Moreover, it is natural that given Descartes's methods he should decide that each of us is essentially such a mind. For, using his powers of imagination as the test of logical possibility, he concludes that while he might exist without a body (the evil genius hypothesis has, after all, established that such a possibility is not incoherent), the *cogito* shows that thinking cannot be separated from his existence (1641: 18). Descartes therefore declares that 'absolutely nothing else belongs to my nature or essence except that I am a thinking thing' (p. 54).

Thus the Cartesian self is, in its very nature, disembodied. We are essentially thinking things, but only contingently bodily beings; our bodies are mere vehicles for our minds. This idea Descartes reinforces with his renowned metaphysical dualism which represents mind and body as distinct substances, fundamentally different kinds of stuff. Of course, mind and body interact causally (though Descartes fails to explain how this is possible), but this commerce with the physical is not a genuine expression of our essence. Note that when Descartes mentions sense perception in the statement of his nature, he has in mind not a physical engagement of mind and world, but rather a mode of thought, the apprehension of certain kinds of mental images. Those images may have a causal history which involves the external world, but they are no more physical phenomena than any other mental episode (1641: 19, 21). Moreover, insofar as sense perception is tainted by association with the body, Descartes is quick to devalue it as a mode of acquiring knowledge: the ideas of sense are partial and deceptive, they are nothing without reason. What we say we see and hear 'is in fact grasped solely by the faculty of judgement which is my mind' (p. 21).

It follows from all this that, for Descartes, the self is a profoundly asocial phenomenon. Each self inhabits its own subjective realm and its mental life has an integrity prior to and independently of its interaction with other people. This is because other people are parts of the external world and we know that world only derivatively via the mediation of our ideas. Indeed, the minds of others are even further removed from us than ordinary external objects, for the thoughts and feelings of others are events in private mental worlds which are essentially hidden from us. We know about them, if we do, not by observation, but by inference from the bodily behaviour of others. This picture raises another famous sceptical puzzle: the problem of other minds.

A chorus of voices from different disciplinary perspectives is now to be heard decrying the influence of Cartesian ideas on many aspects of contemporary thought. It might be objected, however, that these criticisms often exaggerate Descartes's influence. After all, by no means all Descartes's contemporaries shared his view of the mind as an immaterial substance, and his conception of the powers of reason and the project of foundationalist epistemology were forcibly challenged by the naturalistic empiricism of Locke and, especially, Hume. This objection has a point. We should certainly not identify Descartes's ideas with the philosophical pre-suppositions of modernity in a way which suggests that Western intellectual culture laboured under Cartesian confusions until the emergence of postmodernism! Nevertheless, Descartes's thought undoubtedly had an enormous effect on the subsequent history of philosophy. Descartes set the agenda for epistemological inquiry, even if his successors did not all agree with the answers he gave or even the questions he put. Henceforth philosophers were intent on discovering how, in the maelstrom that is our engagement with the world and with others, the individual can come to have knowledge. The image of the isolated knower remained intact, particularly in Anglo-Saxon philosophy. Other enduring ingredients of the Cartesian picture are the idea of the mind as a theatre of representations which display (or mirror) the events of the external world, and the related presumption that the self can be seen as the spectator of the mind's show (see Rorty, 1980 and Dennett, 1991). His position encapsulates the ideal of transparency in subjectivity, where a subject can know itself completely, and reaffirms the disavowal of the body central to Western philosophy since Plato, where reason and the mind are posited against unreason and the corporeal.

It is thus not surprising that Descartes figures as an emblem of the individualism or 'atomism' challenged by advocates of the social self. For such thinkers, our social being is not merely some empirical manifestation of a higher, more ethereal essence, but is crucial to our very identity as persons. This point is not easy to make, for it is a testimony to the power of Descartes's ideas that a strong individualism seems so obvious and irrefutable. Nevertheless, once the significance of the social is properly recognized, then it is Descartes's position which seems tendentious, and we are moved to make the following rejoinder to his summation of our natures. What then are *we*? We are beings situated in a cultural environment in community with other such beings. We are things which think, to be sure, but our intellectual powers are nurtured and sustained in that cultural environment and derive their character from it. We are beings who live and act in consort with others and whose lives are structured by our ties to each other, ties which, like the joys and sufferings we experience, we feel and express bodily. Our distinctness consists in the fact that our faces are turned to each other; we can read in each human face a story composed in a social world, and we can read it only because we are members of such a world.

Some conceptual geography

What precisely does it mean to say that we are socially constituted beings? To produce a single answer would be misleading. It is better to let the contributions in this volume jointly serve as a response to that question. Nevertheless, a little conceptual geography may help readers find their way. Let us begin by mapping out, in general terms, some of the contours of the debate.

Varieties of argument

Arguments that we are 'social selves' come in different strengths. A 'modest' or 'weak' argument maintains that we are socially constructed beings because our identities are significantly shaped by social or cultural influences. For example, almost everyone will admit that had he or she been born and raised in a very different culture, or at some other point in history, he or she would have been quite a different person. This is true, it is argued, because the particular mental states of individuals, and the dispositions of their characters, are formed in social interaction. Each of us believes what he or she believes, wants what he or she wants, and so on, as the result of a complex process of education and socialization. We learn the science and myths of our time and place, and we internalize social values and norms. All this makes us who we are. Of course, such a position need not hold that we are just 'stamped out' by society. We are participants in our own construction and exercise some autonomy in the face of the forces of socialization. Nevertheless, on such a view, the influence of social forces is the paramount determinant in the shaping of our identity.

In contrast, 'radical' or 'strong' arguments maintain that we are social selves not just in the sense that what we believe and how we behave are profoundly influenced by the social circumstances of our lives, but because our very capacities to think and act are themselves socially constituted. On such a view, the fundamental powers at the heart of our identity as persons can exist only in social space. Thus Lev Vygotsky, who founded the Russian school of 'socio-historical psychology' in the turbulent decade following the 1917 Revolution, argues that our social being is implicated in the genesis of the intellectual capacities constitutive of consciousness. The human mind is not just shaped by society, it is made in society. Alexei Leontiev describes Vygotsky's position:

> Consciousness is not given from the beginning and is not produced by nature:
> consciousness is a product of society: it is *produced*. . . . Thus the process of
> internalization is not the *transferral* of an external activity to a pre-existing,
> internal 'plane of consciousness': it is the process in which this plane is formed.
> (Leontiev, 1981: 56–7)

Such a position obviously stands in sharp contrast to the Cartesian picture
and represents us as socially constructed in a profound sense. Analogous
radical arguments might be made with respect to the will – i.e. that it is
not just the commitments we make to certain ends, projects and ways of
living that are of social origin, but the very capacity to make such
commitments and to deliberate between them – and to such fundamental
aspects of our identities as gender and sexual orientation (recall de
Beauvoir's claim that women are made, not born [1949]). In all these
arguments, the social serves, not to mould an antecedently present self or
identity, but to bring that self into existence.

We should also observe an important distinction between the kinds of
consideration that are invoked to show that we are social selves. Sometimes the claim is supported by empirical considerations, by appeal to facts
about the nature of social interaction and its influence. Sometimes purely
conceptual, a priori arguments are deployed. The latter are often transcendental in kind; that is, they take some incontrovertible fact of human
experience as their premise and explore what else must be true if human
experience is thus and so. Wittgenstein is sometimes said to have established that no being could possess a language unless it were a member of a
community; and Russian Marxist Evald Ilyenkov attributes the very
possibility of intentionality, of a relation between a thinking subject and
an object of thought, to collective human activity.

Arguments of the modest or weak kind defined above are usually
supported by empirical considerations. Strong arguments, in contrast, are
often either a priori in kind or contain both conceptual and empirical
elements. In the work of Vygotsky or Jerome Bruner (who contributes an
essay to this volume), one sees a close interplay of conceptual and
empirical considerations. These thinkers show a constant readiness to
revise radically a theoretical paradigm in the face of empirical material,
while recognizing the extent to which their empirical theories are informed
and constrained by conceptual commitments. Although this suggests that
we should be careful about absolutizing the distinction between the
conceptual and the empirical, it is useful to discriminate between those
arguments for our status as social selves that rely primarily on empirical
claims and those that seek to establish what human beings must be like if
some undeniable features of the human condition are even to be possible.

Matters of ontology

It is useful to remind ourselves that talk of 'the self', social or otherwise,
can be precarious. What is this familiar expression supposed to denote?

We have spoken of 'the Cartesian conception of the self', but although Descartes's paradigm invites such talk, it is somewhat anachronistic. No term in Descartes's French or Latin obviously invites translation as 'self'; indeed, in the Cambridge edition of his works, the term is used to refer to the combination of mind and body, not an ethereal subject of experience (Descartes, 1641: 56, 61). The term entered English philosophy with Locke's *Essay* (1690: II. xxvii. 9, 17), but it was not long before its appropriateness was challenged. Hume famously argues that since no idea of a 'self' is given in experience (we experience only our mental states, we do not experience ourselves [or our 'selves'] experiencing them), no meaning can be annexed to the term. The very idea of the self is a philosopher's fiction (Hume, 1739: I. vi).

As we noted above, in response to concerns about the artificiality of the concept of the self, some who emphasize our social nature avoid the term (though alternatives like 'subject' or 'person' are scarcely better understood). For all that, however, the concept of the self endures. Our minds are not, as Hume thought, mere 'bundles' of mental states – our mental lives cohere in the experience of a particular subject. It may be that our subjecthood is not presented to us in the way that (many) contents of the mind are. But this does not mean that it is not genuine, an aspect of how things must be if our mental lives are to have unity and coherence at all. (This kind of argument led Hume's great adversary, Kant, to the idea of a 'transcendental ego' that was not given in experience, but which served as a precondition of the possibility of experience.) A metaphor of ownership seems inviting: a self (or person) is that to which mental states belong.

Of course, most thinkers today are anxious not to portray the self as something ethereal and unworldly. We aspire to see the self as fundamentally embodied, situated in the world of material things. Yet even those who share this aspiration are often reluctant to identify a person with his or her physical being. The history of a person does not simply coincide with the history of some body. It is common to invoke the concept of the self to help make this point, and again the metaphor of ownership seems appropriate: we naturally think of our bodies as things we own, a presumption at the centre of debates about rights to self-ownership (see Nozick, 1974 and Cohen, 1988) and feminist discussions of abortion, prostitution and surrogate motherhood (see Thomson, 1974; Overall, 1987). My selfhood or subjecthood is distinct from my body, for from the perspective of the self the body appears as object, not as subject, or as simultaneously subject/object. Of course, if one construes the self in this way, it is crucial not to think of the self as an entity, for that way lies a position as occult as Cartesianism. In contrast, the self might be thought of on the model of a field of force, or centre of gravity: the focus of the events which constitute a life.

Thus, part of the resilience of the concept of the self derives from our need to articulate the idea of a focal point of the life and thought of an individual, and to do so in a way which captures the intimate, subjective space of personal being. It might seem then that the idea that the self is a social phenomenon is from the outset paradoxical, suggesting that the most intimate side of our natures is in some sense part of the public domain. Advocates of the social self are thus often prompted to rethink the very concepts of thought and desire, public and private, subjectivity and the structure of a human life.

It is important to observe that these efforts at reconceptualization usually take one of two quite different attitudes to the ontological status of the self. Some thinkers argue that to understand selves or persons as socially constituted is to attain genuine insight into our nature, a nature which is misrepresented by individualist conceptions. Thus, Marxists such as Vygotsky and Ilyenkov, political communitarians like MacIntyre and Taylor, and feminists like Millett and Gilligan, offer accounts of the social nature of personhood which purport to tell us how things really are. We might call them 'realists' about the self. In contrast, some arguments that the self is a social phenomenon are designed to cast doubt on the reality of the phenomena supposedly picked out by terms like 'self' and 'person'. For Foucault and postmodern feminists like Judith Butler, the self is a fiction of modernity, constructed by discourses such as metaphysical philosophy and psychotherapy and many of the practices of everyday life. As such, selves have no nature or essence, they are not parts of the furniture of the world; they are discursive effects, products of our forms of representation. This kind of 'irrealism' about the self not only challenges the pretensions of Cartesianism, it also calls into question the idea that both subjectivity and the structure of a life presuppose a focus in a single unitary subject. If we think we must see ourselves this way, it is argued, this is not a consequence of the way selves are, or even of the way we must represent them, but a fact about the character of the societies and cultures in which we live: our modes of *self*-representation are themselves socially constructed.

This contrast between realist and irrealist forms of contructivism, like most dichotomies, is not as absolute as it appears at first sight. The two sides tend to move towards one another as their respective positions are developed. In addition, there are thinkers, such as Wittgenstein and Bakhtin, who are difficult to place straightforwardly into either camp. Nevertheless, the distinction is valuable because whether a thinker's sensibilities are realist or irrealist significantly shapes his or her position, and the kind of consequences that are likely to be drawn from it.

Politics

One domain in which controversy has raged over the consequences of understanding the self as a social phenomenon is political theory. Some thinkers have argued that there is no essential link between a conception of the nature of the self and a commitment to some or other political vision: the metaphysical and ethical components of social constructivism and individualism can and should be separated. Admittedly, insight into the nature of personhood may help us better understand the conditions in which human beings may flourish, but it does not follow that a constructivist view of persons directly entails a collectivist politics. One might believe that persons are socially constituted whilst advocating a political theory based on individual rights; just as one might be a methodological individualist who urges the forging of community (see Taylor, 1989b; Mulhall and Swift, 1992).

Nonetheless, whether or not there is any strict logical connection between conceptions of the self and certain political ideas, it is undeniable that there is a strong historical association between the atomistic self of Descartes and other early modern philosophers and the theories of rights, justice and obligation of political liberalism. The view that the person is a kind of psychological 'atom' has an obvious affinity with the idea that the individual is entitled to a sphere of non-interference. And just as there are no earthly authorities higher than the individual in Descartes's epistemology, so political authority derives from the commitments of individuals in the social contract theories of Hobbes and Locke.

The historical association of liberalism with atomistic views of the self has naturally led many thinkers to the idea that an analogous connection holds between views of the self as socially situated and as some kind of political collectivism. Such a connection has long been emphasized in the Marxist tradition, though it is a complicated one. Marx sees communism as a true expression of our natures, but he does not suppose that the recognition of this is in itself sufficient to undermine capitalism. Rather, Marx's claim that the essence of each individual is 'the ensemble of social relations' (Marx, 1845: 29) is supplemented by an account of economic development wherein the realization of socialism is necessitated by specific historical conditions. Some contemporary communitarians, in contrast, argue much more directly that because we are socially constituted beings, who derive our concept of the good from participation in collective cultures and traditions, we should create a political order that recognizes the value of community and nurtures and sustains communitarian institutions. Finally, many postmodern thinkers also see strong connections between representations of the self and political ideas though, unlike Marxists or communitarians, they commonly look to critique to unmask or deconstruct these connections while expressly disavowing a new, substantive politics of community.

In this exercise in conceptual geography, we have considered how the claim that we are social selves can take strong or weak forms and how it may be supported by empirical or a priori considerations, or by some combination of the two. It should be clear that the concept of the self is a resilient one, notwithstanding the controversies about how it is best understood. In addition, while debates about the social self are rich with political themes, their consequences for political action are by no means certain. Let us turn now to consider briefly the substance of the chapters which follow.

Chapter 2, by psychologist Jerome Bruner, explores relations between the concepts of meaning, culture and the self. Bruner was one of the architects of the so-called 'cognitive revolution' in the 1950s and 1960s, which overturned behaviourism in favour of a conception of human minds as storing and manipulating internal representations rather in the way computers do. In recent years, however, Bruner has increasingly distanced himself from the spirit of cognitivism, arguing that its obsession with 'information processing', artificial intelligence and so on has resulted in views no less mechanistic or individualistic than the behaviourism they succeeded. In response, Bruner proposes a 'contextual revolution' which recognizes the way in which culture is constitutive of mind.

Bruner has always applauded the cognitive revolution's desire to place the concept of meaning at the centre of psychology; cognitivism's mistake was to try to see meaning as merely the formal manipulation of symbols. In his contribution to this volume, Bruner suggests that no single theory of meaning can be adequate. He urges us to focus, not on some abstract picture of how language relates to reality, but on how meaning is made in human beings' interactions with each other and their world, a world which is as much a product of their modes of interpretation as it is an antecedent influence upon them. Here Bruner begins to trace the structure of meaning-making, delineating three 'primitive frameworks' in which we, as makers of meaning, situate events (actions, happenings, expressions, etc.): the intersubjective, the instrumental, and the normative. In turn, our descriptions of events so situated are governed by two higher-order systems: the propositional system – the abstract network of symbolic, syntactic and conceptual rules that govern language and commonsense logic – and the narrative system. Narrative has a crucial role in Bruner's scheme of things. We are storytelling creatures. The character of human thought thus cannot be understood as governed exclusively by the formal rules and categories of the propositional system; rather, we must explore the narrative structures human beings employ in their strivings to make sense. Accordingly, we must see the self neither as a kind of metaphysical essence nor as a purely formal subject of thought, but as a creature of narrative. The self is thus as much a product of our culturally mediated ways of making meaning as it is their presupposition.

Ludwig Wittgenstein is often credited with having undermined Cartesian and empiricist visions of the mind as a private realm in favour of a view of thought and language as practices necessarily governed by public standards of correctness. Yet as David Bakhurst observes in Chapter 3, 'Wittgenstein and Social Being', there is a great deal of controversy about exactly what follows from Wittgenstein's famous arguments in the *Philosophical Investigations* (1953). The consequences of Wittgenstein's discussion of rule-following, for example, are hotly contested. Wittgenstein compares a rule to a signpost, and asks how a signpost can direct us when it can be read in any number of ways. It is natural to say that we must give the signpost an interpretation. But this move presents a problem. If we need an interpretation to understand the rule, do we not need a further interpretation to understand the interpretation? We are threatened by an infinite regress.

As Bakhurst notes, Wittgenstein resolves such philosophical puzzles by appeal to human practice. Rule-following rests not on interpretation but on action. It is simply a fact about human beings that we find it natural to engage in the practices we do. Rule-following rests on nothing more nor less than human agreement. That we share the relevant sensibilities is an aspect of our common form of life which stands in no need of philosophical explanation.

Bakhurst considers whether it follows that Wittgenstein believed that our powers of thought and language are essentially social in kind. Some philosophers – such as Saul Kripke and Norman Malcolm – take Wittgenstein's remarks on rule-following to show that membership of a community is essential if a being is to be capable of language and linguistic thought. In contrast, other commentators – such as Gordon Baker and Peter Hacker – insist that although Wittgenstein holds that a logically private language is impossible (i.e. a language which can in principle be understood only by one speaker), he does not deny that there could be a language which only one person happened to know. An entirely solitary language user is perfectly possible. Developing remarks by both Kripke and Malcolm, Bakhurst argues that the 'communitarian' interpretation is strongest where Wittgenstein's celebrated appeal to 'human agreement' is taken not as an empirical criterion of correctness in rule-following, but as a precondition of the possibility of language (Bakhurst calls such a reading 'transcendental anthropocentrism'). He then considers how a communitarian Wittgensteinian can defend the view that a forever solitary language user is impossible against the criticisms of Baker and Hacker. Bakhurst concludes that, whether or not these criticisms can be conclusively rebutted, Wittgenstein's philosophy casts important light on our understanding of ourselves as social beings.

Vygotsky is another thinker who, like Bruner and Wittgenstein, places the concept of meaning at the centre of arguments against individualism. Vygotsky's work has had a growing influence in the West since its first appearance in translation in the early 1960s (Bruner contributed the preface to the first English translation of *Thought and Language*). However, although Vygotsky was a truly interdisciplinary thinker, his influence has largely been confined to radical trends within psychology and education. In Chapter 4, Ellen Watson argues that Vygotsky's ideas could make a fruitful contribution to the philosophy of language. Watson describes two influential approaches in contemporary semantics. The first is the individualistic, 'head-first' semantics exemplified by the work of Jerry Fodor. On this view, the meaning of linguistic expressions is determined by the content of the mental representations they can be used to express. In turn, mental representations derive their content from the causal relations they bear to entities in the world. Such a position focuses almost entirely on relations between the material environment and the heads of individuals (which, for Fodor, contain an innate 'language of thought', the 'machine language' of the brain). In contrast, the 'communitarian linguistics' of Benjamin Lee Whorf holds that no account of the nature of language can take the concepts of thought and world for granted, since each individual's conceptual scheme is structured by the linguistic practices of his or her community. Whorf invokes now famous comparisons between 'standard average European' languages and Hopi to argue that different languages 'carve up' experience in fundamentally different ways.

Watson finds both approaches wanting, arguing that neither is equipped to understand communication. She turns to Vygotsky for inspiration. For Vygotsky, each human child enters the world equipped with elementary mental functions (primitive forms of attention, memory, thought, etc.) which are qualitatively distinct from the higher functions constitutive of human consciousness proper. These higher functions are fundamentally social in kind: they involve the mediation of psychological tools which the child appropriates through the 'internalization' of social forms of activity. Language is the most crucial of these 'mediational means', for with the onset of language, thought becomes linguistic and speech rational, thereby facilitating the interrelation of all the higher mental functions. Vygotsky's view of the internalization of language suggests parallels with Whorf but, Watson argues, Vygotsky has a far more dialectical conception of the relation between language and thought, which appreciates the relevance of our biological endowment as well as the transforming power of culture. Moreover, like Ilyenkov after him, Vygotsky recognizes that as much as culture creates individuals, culture itself remains a human creation. Watson concludes that Vygotsky's insights might be developed into a full-blown 'use-based' theory of meaning which would identify the meaning of a linguistic expression with its functional role in the practices of the community.

The social and political background to Soviet controversies over the self is explored in Chapter 5 by the Russian philosopher Felix Mikhailov. Mikhailov examines the legacy of Marxism in contemporary Russia and argues that we might distinguish between Marx the critical philosopher and Marx the political revolutionary. While the former expounded a subtle philosophy wherein social being is the source of individuality, the latter actively pursued the overthrow of capitalism and its replacement by communism. Although it is tempting to exonerate the philosopher and blame the revolutionary for the disasters of communist practice, Mikhailov insists that the two Marxes, with their respective emphases on theory and practice, are inseparable. Blame is perhaps better cast on a 'third Marx', a legitimizing symbol fabricated by the Soviet order. It is this Marx who repressed human individuality; indeed, there is a sense in which Marx himself was dehumanized for this purpose. Mikhailov relates the poignant story of his mother's narrow escape from execution in the dark days of Stalin's purges to illustrate how terror transformed the autonomous individual into a 'cog' in the state machine.

Philosophy in the USSR was beset by these difficult social conditions, but Mikhailov notes that in periods of 'thaw', important and original work was done. And it was the nature of persons and their relation to society – a matter of such painful political significance – that was the centre of philosophical debate (to which Mikhailov himself contributed; see Mikhailov, 1980). Philosophers such as Ilyenkov returned to the first Marx to expound a social thesis about the self that eschewed mere social engineering. It is not surprising that, as Mikhailov says, Marx the philosopher was seen as something of a dissident by apologists for the official order. It is thus ironic that Marx is now often decried as the source of all Russia's ills. Mikhailov, however, gives good grounds for supposing that Marx the philosopher lives on.

While Mikhailov ponders the death of Marx in the former Soviet Union, Christine Sypnowich examines the significance of death itself in the Bolshevik project. In Chapter 6, 'Death in Utopia: Marxism and the Mortal Self', she argues that the idea of overcoming mortality is central to utopias in general, and to the communist one in particular. Taking up some of Mikhailov's themes about the culpability of Marx for Soviet authoritarianism, Sypnowich argues that an aspiration to overcome finitude is implicit in such Marxist ideas as the commemorative nature of labour, the subsumption of the individual in 'species being', and the aim of an ideal society at the end of history. Moreover, fascinating examples of the rejection of mortality abound in Bolshevik culture, from Bogdanov's science fiction to Mayakovsky's poetry, and in the revolutionaries' commemoration of death itself. The most bizarre case, however, is the cult of Lenin and the embalming of his corpse. Sypnowich argues that the irony of this most daring Promethean project was its role in the decay of Bolshevism, as the creativity and spontaneity of early utopianizing was crushed by Stalinist authoritarianism and a state-directed culture. The imposition of socialist realism, a form that depicts social relations as homogeneous and fixed, represents how the conquest of finitude came to kill the political ideals inherent in its aim. Thus social conditions in the USSR sometimes suggested an indifference to life, rather than the hope of its indefinite prolongation. Moreover, with the purges, camps and forced migrations, the Soviet state committed atrocities against life which made a mockery of the idea of immortality through communism.

The chapter ends with some reflections on the problem of mortality and politics. Sypnowich argues that the mortal self is the impetus for politics, and that political action should be approached in a utopianizing spirit acknowledged to be ultimately unrealizable. Bearing the more modest aim of human betterment in mind, we have reason to be wary of contemporary efforts in both Eastern Europe and the West to ignore the significance of human frailty in the name of new utopias.

The idea that the person is socially constituted, so central to Marxism, has recently become the focus of debate in contemporary political philosophy. Communitarian thinkers such as Alasdair MacIntyre (1981), Michael Sandel (1982), Charles Taylor (1989a), and Michael Walzer (1983) have attacked contemporary liberalism for its atomistic conception of the self. For them, it is not just that this conception depreciates the values of altruism or comradeship; such a view is also theoretically confused. Stephen Mulhall and Adam Swift subject the communitarian critique to careful scrutiny in Chapter 7, 'The Social Self in Political Theory'. They argue that ontological and normative questions in this debate must be distinguished, and that a communitarian view of persons, however persuasive, is not necessarily in conflict with a liberal politics. They maintain that although an appreciation of the dependence of individual upon society may pose problems for a libertarian such as Robert Nozick, it is not incompatible with John Rawls's famous doctrine of 'justice as fairness', which has been the communitarians' constant target. Criticism has focused above all on Rawls's adaptation of the classic metaphor of a social contract, where he imagines individuals deliberating about justice in an 'original position', in which they are ignorant of their identities in the society for which they are legislating. Mulhall and Swift point out that Rawls intends the original position as a device of representation, not a metaphysical picture of the nature of persons. As Rawls now insists, his focus is not the abstract individual, but the citizen of a constitutional democratic polity. It thus seems forced to accuse him of atomism.

Mulhall and Swift note, however, that insofar as communitarians embrace a substantive conception of the good, such as the Aristotelian idea that the best life is one of political action, then they are obviously in conflict with liberalism, particularly Rawls's doctrine which eschews any public commitment to a vision of the good life. They are thus unpersuaded by Walzer's contention that Rawls's abstract approach is inherently undemocratic because it dictates a conception of politics. Finally, Mulhall and Swift observe that political theorists are, like all individuals, social selves who cannot help but express the political values of their milieu. This, they suggest, remains a powerful communitarian insight which may profoundly affect the ways we theorize about politics.

In Chapter 8, 'The Gendered Self', Diana Coole takes up themes central to the liberal–communitarian debate and explores how they bear on discussions in recent feminist theory. She argues that modern political thought is distinguished by three views of persons: the liberal-individualist position, which takes the individual to be autonomous, rational and self-interested; the dialectical-communitarian view, which emphasizes the ways in which selves can find fulfilment only in interaction with others; and finally, postmodern ideas that dispute the integrity of the self in either version, arguing that subjects are fragmented and divided objects of discourse and desire.

Coole notes that feminists have developed arguments for the liberation of women by recourse to all three conceptions. The ideal of the autonomous individual has been important for feminists from Wollstonecraft to Millett as an antidote to the sexist presumption that women are naturally dependent on men while destined to care for them. The idea of a dialogical self, favoured by the dialectical-communitarians, has found favour among feminists such as Gilligan and Chodorow concerned to stress the value of a female identity based on care and relationships. And feminists like Judith Butler, intent on deconstructing the dualism of autonomous male and nurturing female as a product of a masculine order of meaning, have deployed postmodern construals of the subject.

Coole draws the intriguing conclusion that the lessons of postmodernism are inevitable, even if we do not want to subscribe wholly to its politics. That is, the person is a multiplicity of identities, an individual in public contexts, an aspiring self in more personal ones, and a subject in social theory. This complex understanding of the person is particularly important when we consider the gendered self, for whom gendered identity seems both essential and arbitrary, depending on the context at issue. Coole concludes that, however important it may be, the question of gender is inevitably indeterminate.

Feminist debates about the self are given vivid illustration in film, and it is Helene Keyssar's argument in Chapter 9 that this medium is an excellent vehicle for exploring the kinds of changes in the female self essential for women's liberation. Film, Keyssar contends, offers ways of transcending the conundrum of essentialist versus constructivist accounts of the gendered self. She complains that few films have in fact made use of the medium's potential to explore 'women becoming women', but her chapter focuses on one of them: the very successful and controversial *Thelma & Louise*. Keyssar maintains that this film typifies Bakhtin's idea of a literary genre which centres on the emergence of an individual in historical time: it is a feminist version of the Western or 'buddy movie', in which the main characters are women who commit a crime in the course of their pursuit of liberty.

A crucial early moment of the film is the appearance of a revolver, and Keyssar reflects on the sexual politics of guns and weaponry in the movies. As gun-wielding hero-outlaws, Thelma and Louise are much like their male predecessors, but with some significant differences. In contrast to the isolated and enigmatic loners or one-dimensional cowboy partners who populate traditional Westerns, the women's motivations are defined entirely in terms of their friendship, which is essential to their attainment of maturity and understanding. Further, Keyssar contends that the film subverts the usual understanding of the medium as embodying a male gaze which objectifies women, since it is the women's point of view that shapes and distinguishes both the narrative and its cinematic technique.

The ending of *Thelma & Louise* has been a matter of considerable contention among both viewers and critics. Keyssar explores different views of its significance and concludes that it need not be read as a fatalistic comment on the prospects for women's liberation. She suggests that the film's end is not so unlike the more upbeat message of another 'women's film', *Outrageous Fortune*. Indeed, the ambiguous fate of Thelma and Louise is in keeping with Bakhtin's idea of emergence, where the world and the hero change together. There is hope for the ideal of a new woman and a new man, as well as new relations between them.

The final chapter, by Ian Hacking, examines what we can learn about the self from the curious phenomenon of 'multiple personality disorder' (MPD). Philosophical discussions of personal identity, concerned to establish what it is for an individual to persist as the same person over time, are prone to employ outlandish thought experiments. The literature is full of tales of brain transplants, minds stored in computers, brains in vats running bodies by remote control, and so on. These imaginary cases are invoked to test our intuitions about what is logically (even if not physically) possible, and this is supposed to reveal insights into the boundaries of the concept of a person. Such strategies may be entertaining, but they are so distant from reality that their significance is unclear. MPD, in contrast, seems to be a perfect 'real life' experiment, provided by nature itself, into the structure of personhood.

Hacking denies this: MPD, he argues, teaches us nothing direct about the self, mind, or consciousness. He traces the phenomenon from late seventeenth-century cases of 'double consciousness' through to the contemporary fascination with multiple personality which dates from the 1970s. The phenomenon has undergone so many changes in different sociocultural contexts that MPD seems to be no single condition. Indeed, it is difficult to say how a patient from one epoch would have behaved in another.

Hacking reviews what philosophers have made of the phenomenon and argues that where they cite MPD as evidence for their position, their reading of the phenomenon is crucially influenced by the views they are trying to verify. Indeed, the facts of MPD so underdetermine our theories about it that they have been used both to refute the idea of a transcendental ego and to support it. Thus, at best MPD may serve only to illustrate some antecedently held philosophical thesis.

Hacking is careful not to suggest that MPD is unreal, the invention of doctors and therapists. The symptoms, he points out, are real enough: they are ways in which disturbed individuals manifest their disturbance in different settings. MPD thus teaches us about self and mind as figures in our social arrangements, about how our forms of talk, and our medical and scientific practices, contribute to the phenomenon Hacking calls 'making up people'. It is a feature of the social character of the self that this is perhaps all we may aspire to understand, be it in 'normal' or 'abnormal' cases. There is no deeper reality to plumb.

The social self takes many guises. We hope that those who are attracted to the idea that we are socially constituted beings will find much that is valuable in these pages, and that even the most unrepentant atomists will see the seriousness and integrity of the ideas of their opponents.

References

Cohen, G. A. (1988) *History, Labour and Freedom. Themes from Marx*. Oxford: Oxford University Press.

de Beauvoir, Simone (1949) *The Second Sex*, trans. and ed. H. M. Parshley. Harmondsworth: Penguin.

Dennett, Daniel (1991) *Consciousness Explained*. Boston: Little Brown.

Descartes, René (1641) *Meditations on First Philosophy*, trans. John Cottingham. Cambridge: Cambridge University Press, 1986.

Hume, David (1739) *A Treatise of Human Nature*, ed. L. A. Selby-Bigge. 2nd edn revised by P. H. Nidditch. Oxford: Oxford University Press, 1978.

Leontiev, A. N. (1981) 'The problem of activity in psychology', in James V. Wertsch (ed.), *The Problem of Activity in Contemporary Psychology*. Armonk, NY: M. E. Sharpe.

Locke, John (1690) *An Essay Concerning Human Understanding*, ed. P. H. Nidditch. Oxford: Oxford University Press, 1975.

MacIntyre, Alasdair (1981) *After Virtue*. London: Duckworth.

Marx, Karl (1845) 'Theses on Feuerbach', in Karl Marx and Frederick Engels, *Selected Works in One Volume*. London: Lawrence & Wishart, 1968.

Mikhailov, F. T. (1980) *The Riddle of the Self*, trans. Robert Daglish. Moscow: Progress.

Mulhall, Stephen and Swift, Adam (1992) *Liberals and Communitarians*. Oxford: Blackwell.

Nozick, Robert (1974) *Anarchy, State and Utopia*. Oxford: Blackwell.

Overall, Christine (1987) *Ethics and Human Reproduction*. Winchester, MA: Allen & Unwin.

Rorty, Richard (1980) *Philosophy and the Mirror of Nature*. Oxford: Blackwell.

Sandel, Michael (1982) *Liberalism and the Limits of Justice*. Oxford: Blackwell.

Taylor, Charles (1989a) *Sources of the Self*. Cambridge: Cambridge University Press.

Taylor, Charles (1989b) 'Cross purposes: the Liberal–Communitarian debate', in N. Rosenblum (ed.), *Liberalism and the Moral Life*. Cambridge, MA: Harvard University Press.

Thomson, Judith Jarvis (1974) 'A defence of abortion', in M. Cohen, T. Nagel and T. Scanlon (eds), *The Rights and Wrongs of Abortion*. Princeton, NJ: Princeton University Press.

Walzer, Michael (1983) *Spheres of Justice*. New York: Basic Books.

Wittgenstein, Ludwig (1953) *Philosophical Investigations*, trans. G. E. M. Anscombe. Oxford: Blackwell.

2

Meaning and Self in Cultural Perspective

Jerome Bruner

I

A close analysis of the search for the 'meaning of meaning' leads inexorably to the suspicion that there is something inherently misconceived about the quest. Each theory of meaning that has been proposed has turned out to be not so much wrong as limited, useful in some ways but vain or empty in others. It is not simply that theorists of meaning are like blind men describing an elephant, each failing to observe all the features of the great beast. Rather, the search for an all-encompassing 'meaning of meaning' seems to be blighted by the Rule of Perspective. What something means is always a function of the perspective in which the thing in question is placed. Context is inevitably an issue. 'Cup' means one thing in the context of drinking, another in the religious setting of Holy Communion, and yet another when related to concepts of inclusion in set theory. If we take the three meanings to a more abstract level, seeing them as all pertaining to *containers*, thereby creating a superordinate class divisible into 'drinking', 'Communion' and 'set-theoretic' sub-classes, we only mask incommensurable perspectives. Cups contain water in a different sense than they contain the Host in Holy Communion, or substitutable equivalents in set theory. This is not to say the creation of such a set of nesting categories may not be useful for some purposes. But it would be a mistake to overlook what such an abstract exercise rules out of court. What we have left out of account is that 'container', in our example, is being used as a trope in some unspecified way to conceal the fact that drinking cups, Communion cups and set-theoretic cups figure in three ways of life and that their abstract kinship as containers fails to capture the different senses of those ways of life. The cost of the achievements of abstraction is paid for dearly by a loss in particularity. We have captured 'meaning' in only the barest sense. Context, perspective and use have been jettisoned in a way that might satisfy some logicians, but would surely leave the glass-blower, the priest or the mathematician unrequited.

Image, denotative, causal, translational, verificationist and use theories of meaning all serve different purposes or intellectual functions and gain their sense from different philosophical perspectives or metaphysical stances. For that reason, they are even more difficult to combine or reconcile than the cups in our example. For each of them rests on presuppositions about what 'the world' really is and how we come to know it. And so long as we live within the constraints imposed by those presuppositions, the theory of meaning espoused suits the purposes announced. Thus a reductive general theory of meaning would be possible if and only if there were universal agreement on a once-and-for-all metaphysics that could generate both a reductive ontology and a reductive epistemology. Even if that philosophical miracle were achieved, it would still leave unexplained the nature of 'meanings' as the anthropologist, historian, literary critic or moralist might conceive them. And it should certainly not satisfy the psychologist who, as I shall try to show, can only proceed from a notion of somebody's perspective.

There are difficulties, however, in holding that meaning is always and everywhere relative to perspective and context, that there is no fundamental 'meaning in the abstract' from which the particular sense of things may be derived. Such contextualism is often taken to be in peril of relativism, if not solipsism. But, curiously, the peril never seems quite to materialize. We are able to stay out of harm's way by negotiating the particular sense of things through quite ordinary, more or less loosely rule-governed conversational exchanges. Occasionally, we engage in specialized inquiries into what something 'means', and reduce what has been said to a propositional form that permits either logical analysis or empirical verification. This is ordinarily referred to as 'doing science' and is rarely confused with the 'folk psychological' negotiation of meaning. In commonsense meaning-making, we typically keep our epistemic aspirations modest, trying to 'understand' just enough to 'get on with things'. There is even a taboo against pushing the quest for meaning too hard lest we offend. This is not so, of course, in science and philosophy, for in these domains the interrogation of meaning, once sanitized and decontextualized, should not be 'taken personally'. For it no longer concerns those aspects of meaning-making that relate to the domain of ordinary living.

II

We experience the world because we understand it in certain ways, not vice versa. Meaning is not *after* the fact; it is not something we experience, as it were, after a first exposure to nature in the raw. Experience is already an interpretation. And we act in furtherance of our interpretations or construals. Moreover, interpretation is not private, locked inside a single mind; it is premised on an intersubjective exchange with others in turn premised on the belief that we share a common world. This is the foundation of what we speak of as *culture*. Even the simplest sharing of attention is based upon some appreciation of other minds. When we construe a meaning, we 'read' another's mind or place what we encounter according to cultural conventions, expectancies and norms. These readings or construals constitute our understanding of others' understandings, beliefs, desires, intentions, and reflect our own understandings of the world we share with them.[1]

Such understandings, however, may in some sense be 'detached' from the world. 'Common sense' finds it irresistible that there is a world 'out there', independent, autonomous, aboriginal. However much we may hear, read and reason to the contrary, we always feel that everything starts out there. This sense of externality has virtually ineluctable phenomenal immediacy. It has deep ontogenetic and phylogenetic roots, and its elaboration into adult folk psychological conceptions is promoted by cultural beliefs and a language that preserves the distinction between facts, on the one hand, and beliefs and opinions, on the other. We are 'reality junkies'. In consequence, we are susceptible to the belief that meanings lie in things themselves, that meaning inheres in getting a close look at things, in being a witness, in referentiality. This is why – in spite of Nietzsche's perspectivalism[2] in one generation and Nelson Goodman's (1978) in another, and in spite of the demise of positivism – perspectival views of meaning-making are always open to popular suspicion and, as I observed above, resisted by slippery slope arguments that warn of a slide into relativism at the first step towards constructivist theories of meaning.

As Stephen Toulmin (1990) has noted, the sharpest turning point toward 'objective meaning' occurred in the mid-seventeenth century. Charles Taylor describes how this thirst to disenchant the world influenced conceptions of language:

> One of the principal concerns of both Hobbes and Locke was to ground our picture of the empirical world in the firm foundations provided by clear unequivocal definitions of basic terms. But doing this meant demystifying language, showing it to be a pliant instrument of thought, very important, but still an instrument. It was perverse to seek in language a domain of authority for our beliefs. (1985: 249)

This effort after demystification is what led to the (then) scientifically useful fiction of meaning as a tool for the (correct) representation in the mind of what existed in the world. As many philosophers and historians of ideas have since noted, this involved a delusive game of putting into the world those ideas and meanings that *ex hypothesi* fitted the requirements of the specialized ontology of science (see, e.g., Rorty, 1979). Such demystification was doubtless fuelled by a rationalistic desire to overcome projection, to separate our intuitions of meaning and relevance from objective reality (see Taylor, 1985: 249). Since words signify things or ideas, you capture the nature of meaning if you can trace what (and how)[3] they stand for their designata.

Such doctrines had the effect of marginalizing the essentially inter-subjective nature of human meaning-making. Designative theories of meaning gave such pride of place to the achievement of objectivity that only opprobrium could be left for subjectivity with its potential for self-deception and folly. This was all part of the battle against enchantment being waged by science. But science, for all its great promise, was only one among many perspectives. As Henry Adams put it two centuries later, 'All the steam in the world could not, like the Virgin, build Chartres' (1918: 388). And while Newton's *Opticks* unlocked the secret of white light as a mixture of all spectral colours, the young Jonathan Edwards preached to his parishioners in Northampton, Massachusetts that Newton's discovery should encourage Everyman to unlock God's secrets on his own, that self-reliance would serve them better than John Winthrop's Puritan devoutness. Edwards's 'meaning' had, it might be argued, as powerful an effect on the conduct of real life as Newton's (see Bruner, 1993).

III

Let us turn now to develop an account of meaning that will help us understand how ordinary people make sense of the world in cultural contexts, and, further, how the making of meaning is profoundly interwoven with the nature of our 'selves'.

It seems self-evident that meaning-making involves situating expressions, events and acts in structured frameworks. In so situating them, we relate them to what we already know. There are three primitive forms of contextualizing that make this possible, all of them with deep biological and evolutionary roots, though they are culturally elaborated in language. The first is the framework of *intersubjectivity* – the situating of events, interactions and expressions in the 'symbolic space' that human beings define as shared by them with others. At the simplest level, intersubjectivity is mediated by our universal capacity to recognize that we share minds and their intentional states, at first by mutual gaze, gesture or contact, and soon after, at a somewhat more elaborated level, by recognizing that we are jointly attending to a common target. We come equipped with (or very soon acquire) theories about the beliefs, desires and intentions of other people (see Bruner, 1995). Much meaning-making depends upon developing increasingly elaborate notions about what is sharable with others. Indeed, language use would be impossible without these notions, and the acquisition of language is the cultural means by which elaboration is effected. Doubtless, this acquisition relies upon innate biases in the human genome, but there are many different ways through which these innate biases find expression. As Judy Dunn has shown (1988), even young children learn quickly to tailor their messages, and their construals of the messages of others, according to how they expect others to construe the situation.

Intersubjectivity is both the basis of and the means for the elaboration of deixis in language (i.e. those grammatical and lexical features, such as personal and demonstrative pronouns and tense, which define the spatio-temporal co-ordinates of an utterance), for understanding meanings from the perspective of parties in an exchange – that *here* and *this* are close to *me* when I speak; closer to *you* when you speak. As John Lyons has argued, deixis plays an even larger role in reference than once suspected (1977: ch. 5). An intersubjective deictic space is what makes possible the rich system of indexicals in natural languages. Intersubjectivity thus provides the vehicle for locating the perspective from which meaning is to be taken. Without this perspective we would be helpless in attaching meaning to such primitive vocatives as 'Oh look!' or 'Watch this!' Nor would there be a basis for deciding what is being foregrounded in an utterance, and what backgrounded from a *speaker's* point of view. Without it we would be unable to construe possessives like *mine, yours, his, theirs.*

Instrumentality provides the second framework for meaning-making – the means–ends structure of human action: who does what under whose control to whom and with what end. Instrumentality finds linguistic expression in the framework of case grammar: agents performing actions directed at recipients involving objects and instruments, all aimed at a goal and taking place in aspectual time defined by progress toward that goal, and so on. Charles Fillmore (1968) was right to conjecture that case grammar is a communicative realization of the child's early grasp of the arguments of action, a grasp probably assisted by preadaptation. Early holophrastic speech may be a compressed or elliptical version of developing case grammar – as in such early expressions as 'All gone!' for a task completed on target (see the excellent discussion in De Laguna, 1927; also Bruner, 1978). And in addition, as I have argued elsewhere (Bruner, 1990: ch. 3), the child's precocious grasp of the arguments of action facilitates her early command of narrative, which, as we shall see, is of critical importance.

The third framework of meaning-making is the *normative*, where events and expressions are situated in the ordered framework of obligations and commitments that lie at the heart of human culture. Much meaning-making involves placing events in a framework of expectancy: what we can count on, what constitutes a deviation from the expected. Not only do our habits take on the force of functionally autonomous motives (see Allport, 1937), but we assess whether a given happening is pleasant or unpleasant on the grounds of its habitual appropriateness. And, of course, the culture exploits this 'conservatism' in establishing commonsense notions about legitimacy. The child quickly picks up the normative sense of acts, events and intentions (see Bruner, 1983). Speech acts in J. L. Austin's (1962) or John Searle's (1969) sense are linguistic-cultural formalizations of the deontic frame. They 'package' obligations and expectancies of appropriateness in linguistic exchange, and raise them to the level of cultural performance. For they have not only a conventional expressive form; their deployment requires that a set of 'felicity conditions' be met. Each type of speech act, as Austin intimated in his William James Lectures (1962), constitutes a kind of mini-culture. Promising entails having a belief that one is in a position to deliver; requesting entails that what is asked for is in short supply for the speaker, that she sincerely wants what is being requested, and so on. This is surely tantamount to being inside a culture as well as within the domain of intentional states.

It is on developmental and evolutionary grounds that I refer to these three frameworks as 'primitives' in meaning-making: three parallel modes for placing or locating events in order to understand them. The first has to do with the human need to relate to others in a meeting of minds. The second involves placing things in a context of goal-directed activity within a framework of means—ends relations. The third deals with how to place events into the structure of the expected, reliable, and thus seen to be legitimate, course of things.

IV

The three primitive frameworks — the *intersubjective*, the *instrumental* and the *normative* — operate under powerful second-order systems that make it possible to extend meaning-making beyond the compass of immediate precipitating events and, just as importantly, to allow the frameworks to operate in parallel with each other. This assures against a crippling short time perspective in meaning-making, and allows us to construct complex meanings that combine the three primitive modes in distinctive ways. The number of such higher-order systems is a matter of conjecture. But there are certainly two. One is the *narrative* system. It combines the three modes into the structure of a temporally extended story. Intersubjective, instrumental and normative meanings, once imbedded in a narrative, take on translocal meanings. The second is the *propositional* system. It achieves higher meaning by abstraction: by sacrificing temporality, personalization and context. It operates by the placing of particular instances into larger, and more general, category systems.

While the narrative system depends on rules of mimesis, the propositional is governed by what might be called a 'logical calculus'. They serve different functions, though they are in no sense autonomous one from the other. The narrative system orders experience temporally to represent an initial canonical state that has been breached in some fashion, recounts means—ends actions of an agent or agents who seek to restore it, and terminates with an implied assessment of the outcome. It traffics in the subjective states of the protagonists, and in the intersubjective link between narrator and hearer. The story as a whole has a meaning or 'gist', and it is constituted in such a way that the constituents that comprise it — characters, settings, acts, and the like — take their meaning from the place that they occupy in the story as a whole. The comprehensibility of a narrative is its mimicry of what the listener or reader takes to be possible in life. Narratives thus provide an *interpretation* of events, rather than an explanation. (For a detailed discussion of the structure of narrative, see Bruner, 1990: esp. 43–65.)

The propositional system shapes meaning-making by the structured network of symbolic, syntactic and conceptual rules that govern language and commonsense logic. The system is large and complex, and must be partitioned − perhaps into a semiotic and a conceptual component − to be manageable for analysis. It includes the lexical operations by which we impute attributes to wholes, divide wholes into parts, order subordinates into superordinate categories − attributive, metonymic, hyponymic and antonymic rules of considerable complexity. It also, by grammatical rule, defines what is to be taken as topic and what as predicate or comment. We must be wary of treating grammatical considerations too formally. Roman Jakobson convinced me long ago that syntax is soaked in semantic presuppositions and that meaning-making is a form of translation. George Miller's work also suggests that the lexicon is full of covert but powerful grammatical presuppositions that place what is expressed into a meaning framework (Beckwith et al., 1991).

As for the conceptual rules by which we assign meanings, they seem to be something of a mixed case of the propositional and the narrative systems. I had originally thought that here in the 'logic of thought' we see formalization in the propositional mode par excellence (Bruner et al., 1956). But I was mistaken. The history of the study of concept formation is instructive on this point. As Douglas Medin has recently noted (1989), research has gone through several rescue-intended paradigm shifts since the Bruner−Goodnow−Austin work of 1956. My colleagues and I proposed then that many categories and category systems were composed by formal rules for combining the defining attributes of class exemplars. Making sense or meaning had to do with placing events in categories according to such rules (which even a machine could follow). Rosch and her colleagues (1978), however, noted that natural-kind categories were not constructed that way, but were organized around the similarity of instances to a good prototype exemplar (a sparrow is a better prototype bird than an awk, and a creature makes it more easily into the bird category by being more similar to the former than the latter). So placing or situating things became a matter of making normative similarity judgements. But then Smith and Medin (1981) demonstrated that categories were not defined just by a single basic-level prototype, but by prototypical exemplars that could serve in different common contexts (say, garden birds and birds of prey). So it became clear that context was crucial to meaning-making. Finally, both Keil (1979) and Carey (1985) showed that what held together a category, or category system, were neither attribute rules, base-level prototypes nor context-sensitive exemplars, but *theories*. For example, if a paramecium is to count as an animal, it has to have ways of sensing its environment, eating, taking up oxygen, and eliminating waste in order to function, and so on. These are the ways an animal stays alive, and it is this theory of animal life that dictates the category's properties, not a formal conjunction of attributes or some exemplifying prototypes. A categorial placement, then, is based on a theory, not on a similarity match or on following attribute rules.

So we have returned to a better square zero. Categories, part-whole rules, entity-attribute rules, oppositional contrast are abstract spin-offs from case grammatical or even narrative descriptions of the world. The conceptual-grammatical framework for meaning-making, then, can be expected to show a certain derivative kinship with the narrative system. For theories, albeit naive theories, are couched in agent–action–goal language and constrained by norms of appropriateness. This may account for why meaning-making is so often expressed anthropomorphically and riddled with normativity. Indeed, perhaps it is the wish to overcome this 'fault' that makes us so prone to mechanomorphism in describing the rich complexity of human action. The anthropomorph says the paramecium ingests carmine particles 'because it likes to eat and will eat anything', while the mechanomorph, eager to climb to epistemic purity, says the wearied television watcher has been turned off by 'reactive inhibition', like a laboratory rat after too many maze trials. Neither is false from a certain perspective, but both risk category errors through over-generalization.

The three primitive frameworks and the two higher-order systems that we have described are all constrained by our biological capacity for symbolic action, but for all that, they are doubtless culturally elaborated. How we situate acts, expressions and events in order to give them meaning is more like a *bricoleur* fixing a broken car with whatever is at hand than Mendeleyev constructing the Periodic Table of the Elements. We go from narratives in the agentive frame to causal theories in the epistemic as and if needed; but there is no shame in this – so too did Darwin in developing the theory of evolution, as Misia Landau's enlightening book reveals (1991).

There is, however, one crucial relation between all the forms of meaning-making that is uniquely human and cultural, and I want to end this chapter by commenting on it. It relates directly to the topic of this volume – the nature of the self.

V

The 'self' is a baffling concept and its growth and transformation has provoked wonder among philosophers, psychologists, social scientists, literary theorists, linguists and moralists for two millennia. And there is no telling where new insights will show up, whether in literary or social theory, studies of the comparative ethology of the 'mind reading' of animals (see Whiten, 1991), or in speculations about the self as the marked protagonist in personal narratives (see Polonoff, 1987).

My object now is somewhat speculative. I want to explore how the self-concept represents a focal intercept of all meaning-making frameworks. Its origin (as George Herbert Mead [1934] noted many years ago) is probably inherent in intersubjectivity, particularly at the point where the human infant differentiates its own sphere from the sphere of its caretakers, an accomplishment usually marked by the appearance of pointing, joint attention, first-person pronouns, and even what is called 'infantile negativism' (see Moore and Dunham, 1994; Neisser, 1993; Messer, 1994). Indeed, many have argued – most recently Paul Ricoeur (1992) – that Self consists precisely in differentiation from Other. At that crucial point there begins a developmental cascade into which two streams flow. One is motoric: the young child insists on initiating her own acts, particularly when she begins to master walking and various manipulatory skills. This is followed by a great stream of word learning, of mastering both expressive speech and denotative labelling (see Messer, 1994). This burst of word learning seems to be precipitated principally by situations where objects come to have relevance to the child's own self-initiated activities. But the child governs not only her own agentive sphere, her locus of control, but begins to master expectable regularities in her intimate environment – what comes before and after what, what merits use of the causative *because*, who can be counted upon as a interlocutor, and so on. And these expectancies soon take on a normative character: not only *do* we have corn muffins at Sunday breakfast, it is a source of distress when we do *not* (the example is drawn from the well-known studies of 'narratives from the crib' presented by Nelson, 1989; see the article by Bruner and Lucariello in that volume).

In this development, we see a connection established between the young child's frameworks for dealing with deixis, agency, deontics, and conceptual-grammatical relations. This is greatly aided by the child's gift of narrative understanding and narrative telling. Indeed, narrative comes to be used even before the third year as a way of framing problem-solving tasks – as Carol Feldman (1989) showed in her study of narrative as a form of problem-framing (also in the Nelson volume), where the child turns back to ask 'how come?' something happened as it did in a narrative account of events. The normative linguistic framework also enters the scene before the end of the third year. A three-year-old (after mastering the differentiation of past and present tense marking) begins using the unmarked present tense for indicating expected or desired events (e.g. 'On Sundays we have corn muffins'). And it is just around this time, to cite Judy Dunn's pioneering study (1988), that the child begins to tell rhetorically designed stories (usually in the form of excuses). By now, the child's genius as a *bricoleur* of meaning is well established.

But note one important point. Self, as it were, is the centre of gravity of all the systems of meaning-making (if I can use Daniel Dennett's [1991] metaphor in a sense somewhat different from his). She is an origin point in intersubjective space; she is the invariant protagonist in accounts of the world; she is the beneficiary and victim of norms; and she is the logical operator and unmarked case in the conceptual-logical domain. That she becomes 'egocentric' is not so much a comment on her stage of development, as earlier theorists would have it, as it is testimony to the start of a lifelong quest to co-ordinate the various forms of meaning-making strategies she employs. It is not child's play to make meanings that relate self to other subjectivities, to be the fulcrum of control, to be bound by commitment to norms and yet remain autonomous, and to be self in a world of causes beyond one's control.

VI

Let me conclude by adopting the perspective from which I began, that of the anthropological meta-theorist looking at theories of meaning. You will already have sensed my own view. It is that human beings are what they are not by virtue of their genetic inheritance alone, but by dint of being participants in a culture that provides them with bases for meaning. Cultures obviously have different ways of aiding their members toward the realization of meaning. But all cultures have one universal feature that is indisputable: they always respect the centrality of self in the meaning-making enterprise. All cultures take as the mark of having achieved meaning that the individual says an equivalent of 'I understand', that achieving meaning is marked by a unique subjective state that will be understood as such by others who share a culture.

All that we can say about *understanding* itself is that it is a *reportable* subjective state. Its phenomenology seems to have deftly eluded us – whether it is an *'aha'-Erlebnis*, a 'sense of recognition', or whatever. Its epistemological status is moot, and it is ontologically unprivileged. But mostly, we experience meaning and strive to do so, feeling distress when we fail, particularly if others report that *they* understand. But the status of *expressed* understanding as an interpersonal phenomenon is virtually without compare. Once we say to another, 'Yes, I know what you mean', or 'I understand what's going on', or even 'It's not what it seems', then we assume social obligations of the most binding and serious kind. We become liable in law. We become committed to act in a manner appropriate to our reported grasp of something. Indeed, we put our reputations as intelligent beings at stake by stating or withholding that we know what something means. And, in the event we are *unable* to report that we have achieved a meaning, we trigger highly complex behaviour in others who are involved in the transaction: expanded restatement in the event that the non-understood matter is an utterance, tutelage where it is some instrument we failed to grasp, and so on. 'Advanced societies' expend enormous sums of money to reduce incomprehension, for misunderstanding leads to friction as well as incompetence. In natural conversation, for example, expressions of *non*-understanding are as likely to be taken as mock or real opposition as they are as 'ignorance'. For comprehending along with others what something means is a matter of some considerable moment, assuring intersubjectivity to each party involved. 'I don't understand' is an expression that takes priority over all others; it stops things dead. Comprehension is the most primitive and important precondition for human solidarity.

What all this suggests is that culture and individuality converge in the process of meaning-making. 'To grasp a meaning' and to be recognized as doing so is the sine qua non for human beings attempting to live together in a symbolically regulated, negotiated system. In this sense, meaning-making is as crucial to maintaining a culture as it is to individual adaptation. Acts of meaning, I believe, serve both functions at once. We can conceive of self, then, as an intersection of culture and individual identity. That meaning-making should be so dependent upon intersubjectivity, instrumentality and normativity, all three serving as constituent processes in narrative and in propositional thinking, should come as no surprise.

Notes

An earlier version of this chapter was presented in the Sesquicentennial Lecture Series, 'The Frontiers of Philosophy', at Queen's University, Kingston, Canada in April 1993.

1. For an excellent account of how the psychologist looks at the problem of other minds, see Astington, 1994.
2. For a particularly cogent exposition of Nietzsche's views, see Nehamas, 1985.
3. I include the 'how' to take account of Peirce's classic distinction between the three modes of 'standing for' – icons, indexes, and signs.

References

Adams, Henry (1918) 'The dynamo and the virgin', in *The Education of Henry Adams*. Boston and New York: Houghton Mifflin.
Allport, Gordon (1937) *Personality*. New York: Holt.
Astington, Janet (1994) *The Child's Discovery of the Mind*. Cambridge, MA: Harvard University Press.
Austin, J. L. (1962) *How to do Things with Words*. Oxford: Oxford University Press.
Beckwith, R., Fellbaum, C., Gross, D. and Miller, G. (1991) 'WordNet: A lexical database organized on psycholinguistic principles', in U. Zernick (ed.), *Using on-line Resources to Build a Lexicon*. Hillsdale, NJ: Erlbaum.
Bruner, Jerome (1978) 'Learning how to do things with words', in J. Bruner and A. Garton (eds), *Human Growth and Development*. Oxford: Oxford University Press.
Bruner, Jerome (1983) *Child's Talk*. New York: Norton.
Bruner, Jerome (1991) *Acts of Meaning*. Cambridge, MA: Harvard University Press.
Bruner, Jerome (1993) 'Explaining and interpreting: two ways of using mind', in Gilbert Harman (ed.), *Conceptions of the Human Mind: Essays in Honor of George Miller*. Hillsdale, NJ: Erlbaum.
Bruner, Jerome (1995) 'From joint attention to the meeting of minds', in Moore and Dunham (1995).
Bruner, Jerome and Lucariello, Joan (1989) 'Monologue as narrative recreation of the world', in Nelson (1989).
Bruner, J., Goodnow, J. and Austin, G. (1956) *A Study of Thinking*. New York: Wiley.
Carey, Susan (1985) *Conceptual Change in Childhood*. Cambridge, MA: MIT Press.

De Laguna, Grace (1927) *Speech. Its Function and Development.* New Haven: Yale University Press.

Dennett, Daniel (1991) *Consciousness Explained.* Boston: Little Brown.

Dunn, Judy (1988) *The Beginnings of Social Understanding.* Cambridge, MA: Harvard University Press.

Feldman, Carol (1989) 'Monologue as problem-solving narrative', in Nelson (1989).

Fillmore, Charles (1968) 'The case for case', in E. Bach and R. Harms (eds), *Universals in Linguistic Theory.* New York: Holt, Rinehart and Winston.

Goodman, Nelson (1978) *Ways of Worldmaking.* Indianapolis: Hackett.

Keil, Frank (1979) *Semantic and Conceptual Development: An Ontological Perspective.* Cambridge, MA: Harvard University Press.

Landau, Misia (1991) *Narratives of Human Evolution.* New Haven: Yale University Press.

Lyons, John (1977) *Semantics,* in two vols. Cambridge: Cambridge University Press.

Mead, George Herbert (1934) *Mind, Self and Society.* Chicago: University of Chicago Press.

Medin, Douglas (1989) 'Concepts and conceptual structure', *American Psychologist,* 44 (12).

Messer, David (1994) *The Development of Communication: From Social Interaction to Language.* New York: Wiley.

Moore, C. and Dunham, P. (eds) (1995) *Joint Attention: Its Origin and Role in Development.* Hillsdale, NJ: Lawrence Erlbaum.

Nehamas, Alexander (1985) *Nietzsche: Life as Literature.* Cambridge, MA: Harvard University Press.

Neisser, Ulric (ed.) (1993) *The Perceived Self.* Cambridge: Cambridge University Press.

Nelson, Katherine (ed.) (1989) *Narratives from the Crib.* Cambridge, MA: Harvard University Press.

Polonoff, D. (1987) 'Self-deception', *Social Research,* 54.

Ricoeur, Paul (1992) *The Self as Other.* Chicago: University of Chicago Press.

Rorty, Richard (1979) *Philosophy and the Mirror of Nature.* Princeton, NJ: Princeton University Press.

Rosch, Eleanor and Lloyd, Barbara (eds) (1978) *Cognition and Categorization.* Hillsdale, NJ: Lawrence Erlbaum.

Searle, John (1969) *Speech Acts.* Cambridge: Cambridge University Press.

Smith, Edward and Medin, Douglas (1981) *Categories and Concepts.* Cambridge, MA: Harvard University Press.

Taylor, Charles (1985) *Human Agency and Language. Philosophical Papers, vol. 1.* Cambridge: Cambridge University Press.

Toulmin, Stephen (1990) *Cosmopolis: The Hidden Agenda of Modernity.* Chicago: University of Chicago Press.

Whiten, Andrew (ed.) (1991) *Natural Theories of Mind: Evolution, Simulation, and the Development of Everyday Mindreading.* Oxford: Blackwell.

3

Wittgenstein and Social Being

David Bakhurst

Those who maintain that we owe our status as persons, and as subjects of thought, to participation in a human community, sometimes draw inspiration from Wittgenstein.[1] This is not surprising, for such notions as human agreement, custom and form of life clearly have a special place in Wittgenstein's thought. Nevertheless, to see Wittgenstein as some kind of 'epistemic communitarian' is controversial. Readings which privilege the concept of community in his thought have long drawn criticism, and the present orthodoxy among Wittgenstein scholars is that the customs and forms of life of which he spoke are not essentially social phenomena. My aim in this chapter is to consider what contribution, if any, Wittgenstein makes to our understanding of ourselves as social beings.

The private language argument

A natural starting point is the 'private language argument', which is sometimes taken to show that a being who is not a member of a community could not have a language. At *Investigations* §243, Wittgenstein asks us to imagine a language someone might invent to record his 'inner experiences'. Wittgenstein has in mind a language which is logically private: one in which the words refer to phenomena known only to the speaker. The language is thus not one another person could understand, since no one but the speaker has access to the objects by which the words are defined (i.e. the private linguist's experiences) (cf. 1953: §267). How, Wittgenstein asks, could such a language be established? Suppose that the private linguist tries to name his sensations. Confronted with a certain sensation, he resolves to call sensations of this type 'S' by giving himself a kind of ostensive definition. How is he subsequently to tell that he is employing 'S' correctly? If he doubts that he remembers the definition of 'S', he cannot appeal to memory, for he has no means to check that he remembers aright. (In Wittgenstein's striking figure, he is in the position of someone who buys several copies of a newspaper to assure himself that what it says is true [§265].) This point about memory illustrates the private linguist's general predicament: since he has no recourse to any external check, he cannot distinguish what seems right from what is right, and this,

Wittgenstein concludes, 'only means that here we can't talk about "right"' (§258). Since nothing can be a language if it lacks standards of correctness, a logically private language is impossible.

What would follow from this argument, were it valid? First, it would discredit the influential conception of language that emerged in the early modern period, particularly in the writings of Hobbes and Locke. On this view, words are conceived primarily as names of sensations and ideas, these being entities revealed directly only to the mind that experiences or 'possesses' them. Language is portrayed as an aid in the classification and organization of thought and as the means by which each solitary mind may convey its contents to others. The idea that meaning ultimately relies on the association of signs with private experiences was long a fundamental tenet of empiricist thought, appearing, for example, in many twentieth-century notions of a 'sense-datum language'.

Second, and more generally, Wittgenstein's argument attacks the conception of the mind that accompanies this view of language – the idea of the mind as a self-contained world of thoughts and experiences, of which the subject alone is directly aware (see Chapter 1 above, pp. 2–5). If Wittgenstein is right, such a subject of thought could not operate concepts. Thus the Cartesian project in epistemology – the idea of the solitary *res cogitans*, supremely confident in its own subjectivity, yet desperately trying to establish that it is embodied, that there are other minds, external objects, and so on – is radically misconceived. Moreover, Wittgenstein's philosophy suggests we should not see mental lives as constituted by events in some hidden 'inner' realm; our minds are sometimes 'on the surface', present in our behaviour (see Wittgenstein, 1953: §§284, 420). Thus, when someone speaks there are not (or not necessarily) two processes occurring, an 'outward' process of the articulation of signs, and an 'internal' process of thinking, concealed from public view; rather, we confront a single process of the manifestation of thought in speech (see Wittgenstein, 1958: 148). Our mental lives are lived, at least in part, in public space.

These are powerful conclusions. Yet they do not obviously reveal a central place in Wittgenstein's philosophy for considerations about membership in a community. Such considerations enter the picture when commentators claim that the standards of correctness lacked by the private linguist may be elucidated only by appeal to the practices of a community. Whether, and in what sense, this is true, has provoked bitter dispute. We shall consider two contrasting versions of the 'community view': that of Saul Kripke, and that of Norman Malcolm.

Kripke's Wittgenstein

In his controversial *Wittgenstein on Rules and Private Languages* (1982), Kripke locates the core of the private language argument in Wittgenstein's celebrated discussion of rule-following (Wittgenstein, 1953: §§138–242), which Kripke takes to pose a sceptical paradox about meaning. Kripke illustrates the paradox with a mathematical example – the meaning of the 'plus' function – but the paradox is intended to apply to the application of any concept. Suppose I am doing a calculation for the first time involving numbers larger than I have hitherto employed, say (for ease of exposition) '68 + 57'. I arrive at the answer '125', which I am sure is arithmetically correct and conforms to the way I have used 'plus' in the past. Kripke imagines a sceptic who questions the second of these certainties. What, he asks, determines that the answer '125' conforms to my past usage of 'plus', in a way that, say, the answer '5' does not?

Since this is a new calculation for me, I cannot reply that '125' is the answer I usually give. But can I not say that I am doing just what I always do when I add? '125' is the answer my past mathematical behaviour dictates here, '5' is not. But what about my past behaviour dictates this answer rather than some other? My past usage is, after all, compatible with indefinitely many different ways of continuing. The sceptic points out that nothing about my past behaviour determines that I was adding as opposed to 'quadding', where the 'quum' of two numbers is the same as their sum if their sum is less than 120, and 5 otherwise. So we need to find some fact that constitutes my meaning 'plus', 'a fact as to what I meant that would show that only "125", not "5", is the answer I "ought" to give' (Kripke, 1982: 11).

It is tempting to say that when I learnt the plus function, I grasped a rule that dictates appropriate answers over an infinite number of cases. The rule somehow contains its extension, as it were, coiled up inside it like a spring (see Wittgenstein, 1953: §188). However, there seems no way to construe this understanding that will silence the sceptic. It would be a mistake, Kripke argues, to represent understanding the rule as a disposition to give certain answers. Talk of dispositions might explain why I am caused to answer '125', but not why I ought to give that answer if I am to be consistent. A dispositional account fails to capture the normativity of rule-following – the sense in which only certain answers 'accord' with the rule (see Kripke, 1982: 22–37).

Another alternative is to construe grasp of the rule as some kind of mental state, which constitutes meaning 'plus' and not 'quus'. But if the supposed mental state requires interpretation for it to guide my behaviour, then an obvious regress threatens, for the sceptic's arguments will apply equally to it. But if the claim is simply that there is a primitive mental state of meaning 'plus', then such a state seems utterly mysterious. How is it to be distinguished from, say, the feeling that one is applying the rule consistently? The presence of such a feeling cannot constitute what it is to apply the rule consistently. Moreover, as Kripke remarks (1982: 40–8), Wittgenstein undertakes an extensive phenomenological analysis to show that there simply is no particular, special experience which accompanies acts of meaning and understanding.

Kripke concludes that there is nothing about the subject's behaviour, or her mental life, which constitutes her meaning 'plus' rather than 'quus'. Since his argument is supposed to apply to any concept the result is global scepticism about meaning: there is no such thing as meaning. Kripke writes:

> there is no fact about me that distinguishes between my meaning a definite function by 'plus' (which determines my responses in new cases) and my meaning nothing at all. . . . It seems that the entire idea of meaning vanishes into thin air. (1982: 21–2)

Kripke reads Wittgenstein as proposing a 'sceptical solution' in Hume's sense; that is, one which concedes that the sceptic's argument is irrefutable, but maintains that our practices do not require the kind of justification the sceptic shows to be impossible (pp. 62–8). For Wittgenstein, as Kripke portrays him, which concept some individual is applying is not determined by any fact about her; it can be elucidated only by appeal to the community of which she is part (pp. 89–113). Kripke argues that since there are no 'superlative facts' about meanings, a sentence like (*S*) 'By "plus" Sarah means addition' has no 'truth conditions' (i.e. there are no facts which make such sentences true). (*S*) does, however, have 'assertibility conditions' or 'justification conditions'. We are justified in asserting *S* where Sarah's usage of 'plus' is in harmony with our own, where her way of adding agrees with the way other members of the community add. Thus, the assertibility conditions of attributions of meaning essentially 'involve reference to a community' (p. 79).[2]

Kripke maintains his reading is in harmony with Wittgenstein's use of the concepts of 'criteria', 'agreement', and 'form of life' (pp. 96–9). The criterion by which we judge whether an individual is following some rule is whether the individual agrees with the practices of the community. Here 'agreement' means something like 'sameness of response' (Kripke does not mean to imply that the community, in some overt process, comes to agree on what is to count as correct). 'The set of responses in which we agree, and the way they interweave with our activities, is,' Kripke writes, 'our *form of life*' (p. 98). Appeal to our community's form of life is the place where all questions of justification come to an end. Forms of life cannot be explained (cf. Wittgenstein, 1953: §192).

Kripke's reading of Wittgenstein raises many questions. One thing, however, is clear: for Kripke's Wittgenstein, the concept of a language user is essentially tied to the concept of membership of a community. We can think of a physically isolated individual as following rules only if we take him 'into our community and apply our criteria for rule following to him'. An individual '*considered in isolation*' cannot be said to follow rules (Kripke, 1982: 110).

Malcolm's Wittgenstein

In *Nothing is Hidden*, Malcolm praises Kripke's '"social" interpretation' (Malcolm, 1986: 171, 157). He objects, however, to Kripke's claim that

Wittgenstein's argument is sceptical in kind. At *Investigations* §201, Wittgenstein sets out the paradox Kripke seizes upon: how can a rule determine some course of action, when any course of action can, on some interpretation, be shown to conform to the rule? However, as Malcolm points out, Wittgenstein immediately dismisses the paradox as a confusion. It is not that there are no standards of correctness in rule-following, but that the paradox is resolved by appeal to action rather than interpretation. As Wittgenstein puts it: 'What this shows is that there is a way of grasping a rule which is *not* an *interpretation*, but which is exhibited in what we call "obeying a rule" and "going against it" in actual cases' (1953: §201).

In Malcolm's view this appeal to action in no way diminishes the significance of the community's role, for:

> When Wittgenstein says that following a rule is a *practice* . . . he means that a person's actions cannot be in accord with a rule unless they are in conformity with a common way of acting that is displayed in the behaviour of nearly everyone who has had the same training. This means the concept of following a rule implies the concept of a *community* of rule-followers. (Malcolm, 1986: 156)

Thus, in contrast to Kripke, Malcolm holds that there are facts about meanings and that 'what fixes the meaning of a rule is *our customary way of applying the rule in particular cases*' (1986: 155). Without communal agreement there would be no right or wrong way to proceed. There are, of course, indefinitely many ways of responding to the question 'What is the sum of 57 and 68?', but only one response counts as following the rule of addition. It is conceivable that someone might follow rules for addition in a deviant way, but since this way of acting departs from our practices, we see it as a failure of understanding, not as an alternative form of addition. The deviant must be 'retrained' by the community. Appeal to our common training is where explanation of rule-following terminates: 'We go on, all agreeing, following rules and applying words in new cases – without guidance. Other than the past training, there is no explanation. It is an aspect of the form of life of human beings' (Malcolm, 1986: 181).

Malcolm's use of the concept of training marks a difference between his approach and Kripke's. While Kripke says little about the origin of our language capacities, arguing only that if we are to see an individual as a rule-follower we must treat her as a member of our community, Malcolm holds that it is only through training that we acquire the ability to follow rules at all. A language can be possessed only by a being who is, or once was, a member of a community.

The 'community view' criticized: Baker and Hacker

It seems we have a choice between two species of Wittgensteinian communitarianism, one (Kripke's) that denies there are genuine facts about meaning and appeals to community to explain the 'appearance' of such facts, another (Malcolm's) that insists that genuine facts about meaning exist and do so in virtue of the real activity of social beings.[3] However, for Gordon Baker and Peter Hacker, both positions are fundamentally unsatisfactory.

Baker and Hacker maintain that Kripke's 'sceptical' reading is not just unfaithful to Wittgenstein's texts; the supposed sceptical paradox is nonsensical. They argue that a rule and what accords with it are 'internally related'; that is, what it is to follow the rule for addition is to get the answer '125' when summing 57 and 68, what it is to follow the rule 'add 2' after 1,000 is to proceed 1,002, 1,004, 1,006 . . . etc. No other answers will do, because no other answers amount to following the rules in question. No wedge can be driven between the rule and its application so that we can ask whether its 'usual' extension is really correct. Kripke asks: how do I know that I am now adding? But this question is empty. The way I apply the rule now, like the way I did yesterday, *just is* what following the rule for addition amounts to. There is no logical guarantee that I will continue to 'go on in the same way', but this just means that nothing guarantees that I will not lose the ability to add. Baker and Hacker write:

> To understand a rule is to grasp an internal relation between the rule and its (potential) extension. . . . Given that there is such-and-such a rule, then whether [someone's] doing so-and-so with the intention of following that rule *is* acting in accord with the rule depends only on what the rule is. . . . Correctness and incorrectness are determined by the internal relation between the rule and what counts as accord with it. It is not a *discovery* that '1,002' follows '1,000' in the sequence of even integers. Rather getting this result is a *criterion* for following the rule of this series. (Baker and Hacker, 1984: 76–7)

Baker and Hacker concur with Malcolm that Wittgenstein took rule-following to rest ultimately on action, not interpretation. Following a rule is a practice, and the ability to do so is the mastery of a technique. But nothing Wittgenstein says suggests that following a rule is essentially a social practice. Having prised rules apart from their extensions, Kripke appeals to communal agreement to explain why our rules have the extensions they do. But once we recognize that rules are internally related to their extensions, then the appeal to community loses its point: we can take the sensible position that 'whether a person is following a rule, does not depend on what others are or might be doing' (Baker and Hacker, 1984: 76). This puts paid, not just to Kripke, but to any communitarian reading of Wittgenstein, Malcolm's included.

Baker and Hacker acknowledge, of course, that human beings are social animals and our common language practices depend on agreement; what they deny is that rule-following demands a plurality of subjects. For them, rule-following simply requires practices which exhibit regularity, and there is no reason why a solitary subject should not establish such practices alone. From the incoherence of a logically private language it follows that any language must in principle be learnable by other subjects, but not that language is possible only where there exists a community.

The role of community

To decide how the communitarian position can be defended, let us consider what exactly the appeal to the community is designed to do. Communitarian Wittgensteinians are often regarded as taking the practices of the community to define the standard of correctness in rule-following. What makes one way of following a rule correct, and another incorrect, is that the former has the community's stamp of approval. It is as if, as I continue the series '1,002, 1,004, 1,006 . . .', the community's tacit approval at each step makes it the case that I am 'adding 2' correctly. This position provokes predictable objections. It seems to make assertibility, and even truth, a matter of social fiat. It puts the practices of the whole community beyond criticism, thereby inviting relativism. And it conflates following a rule correctly and just 'doing what everyone else does'. This, so the objection goes, is conceptual democracy gone mad.

It is important, however, that neither Kripke nor Malcolm actually defines correctness in terms of what the community does or might do. Kripke explicitly eschews identifying correctness in rule-following with getting the answers, whatever they might be, that the community arrives at, or is disposed to arrive at (1982: 110–13; contrast Dancy's reading: 1985: 75). Such an approach would represent a 'straight' solution to the sceptical paradox. In contrast, the 'sceptical' solution recognizes that agreement with the community is not a necessary and sufficient condition for correctness in concept application. Thus, Kripke writes, it is not 'that the answer everyone gives to an addition problem is, by definition, the correct one, but rather the platitude that, if everyone agrees upon a certain answer, then no one will feel justified in calling the answer wrong' (1982: 112).

Kripke's position may now seem puzzling. For if the appeal to agreement is merely platitudinous and fails to define a genuine standard of correctness, then it seems Kripke has no account of correctness whatsoever. But if this is so, how can Kripke do justice to the normativity of rule-following?

One might respond like this. The attraction of defining correctness in terms of community responses is the prospect of giving a substantive analysis of normativity in non-normative terms. However, the point of the sceptical solution is to concede that no such explanation can work. No specification of 'facts' will suffice to capture the normativity of meaning. As Kripke mentions in a note, defining correctness in terms of agreement simply begs the question against the sceptic (1982: 146; cf. Wittgenstein, 1978: §392). For how are we to determine what counts as 'agreement' between speakers? A similar sceptical paradox can be constructed for the concept of 'agreement' as for the concept 'plus'. There is no primitive notion of 'sameness' to which we can appeal. The moral is, or ought to be, that the notion of agreement is irreducibly normative.[4] It is for this reason that we must give the sceptic a different kind of answer, one which, as

Kripke puts it, illuminates 'the role and utility in our lives of assertions about meaning' (1982: 112). Of course, someone looking for a substantive philosophical analysis of what correctness 'consists in' will find such an alternative platitudinous (cf. Blackburn, 1984: 87).

Admittedly, what Kripke says about the place of assertions about meaning in our lives is weak (1982: 90–3). He maintains that I judge that someone is adding when she gives answers that agree with those I am inclined to give. However, this is a poor description of our practices: I judge another to be adding when she goes through procedures and arrives at answers I take to be appropriate, regardless of whether those are the answers I am 'inclined' to give (if I know I am hopeless at maths, then I know I am inclined to get the wrong answers). Kripke goes on to say that the making of judgements about meanings is of obvious importance to us, since it is useful to know when we can rely on others to behave in a way we expect. But this is absurdly utilitarian. It is as if Kripke adopts the view of an alien anthropologist who, sure that our judgements of correctness in rule-following have no real substance, provides a crass functionalist explanation of why we behave as we do.

Let us improve Kripke's account. Although he focuses on 'assertions about meaning', consider what he should say about straightforward empirical statements like 'The log is on the fire.' Kripke maintains that his account of meaning in terms of justification conditions applies generally and is distinguished by asking not just 'under what circumstances are we allowed to make a given assertion', but also, 'granted that our language game permits a certain "move" (assertion) under certain specifiable conditions, what is the role in our lives of such permission?' (1982: 74–5). This could be taken to mean that a grasp on formally specified assertibility conditions must be supplemented by an understanding of the place of such assertions in our life-activity. Supplementation is necessary because any specification of assertibility conditions is prey to attack from Kripke's sceptic. But while any specification of justification conditions leaves meaning indeterminate, the indeterminacy ceases to be problematic when we take into account the 'form of life' of those who use the language. This is not because considerations about forms of life represent some fact which resolves the indeterminacy; rather, to grasp the role an expression plays in the life of some linguistic community is to see why it should be used this way rather than that, to see a pattern of similarities and consistencies. This perspective – which we might call 'the perspective of use' – cannot be 'codified' and incorporated into the assertibility conditions of the utterance in question, for any attempt at codification opens the door to the sceptic. It must simply be appreciated, recognized. Hence, adopting the perspective of a member of a community – recognizing the nature of its form of life – is essential if we are to grasp the patterns of similarity and difference which underlie its linguistic practices. Invoking this perspective is designed not to explain meaning away (which is the effect of Kripke's functionalist explanations), but to restore the vantage point from which judgements of correctness, consistency and rationality make sense, and from which the sceptical paradox, while formally irrefutable, fails to carry conviction.

Does the communitarian Wittgensteinian have anything to say about what correctness 'consists in'? Here we can perhaps draw inspiration from Malcolm's discussion. Malcolm attacks what he takes to be Kripke's conflation of truth and justification (Malcolm, 1986: 163–7). Wittgenstein urges us to attend to how language is used. It is ironic, Malcolm observes, that some Wittgensteinians proceed to construct use-based theories of meaning that threaten to undermine how we actually employ words like 'meaning' and 'truth'. Malcolm reminds us that as we use the word 'truth' in our 'language games', we clearly distinguish a claim's being true from its being justified or assertible, and from its being held to be true in some community. The suggestion, it seems, is that we must elucidate the meaning of such concepts as 'truth', 'objectivity' and 'consistency' by looking at how they are employed within our language games. From that perspective, however, it is clear that we generally do not treat what is true, consistent or objective as a matter of communal agreement or convention. This is why, of course, it is a mistake to define truth, consistency and objectivity in terms of agreement or convention.

Where does this recognition that our judgements of truth and reality are 'internal' to our language games leave the concept of community in Wittgenstein's philosophy? Questions of truth and reality are decided within our language games according to their criteria for the determination of the true and the real. For the most part, these criteria make no reference to communal agreement (Wittgenstein, 1967: §§430–1). However, if judgements of truth and reality are to be elucidated by appeal to our language practices as lived, and if those practices in turn presuppose a background of shared activity, then our social being is implicated in the very possibility of our entering a conceptual relation to the world. On such a view, it is not that communal agreement determines truth or consistency, or that the world our concepts reveal to us is a 'social construct' or a product of agreement (as revealed to us the world is independent of us in so many ways). However, the concepts we deploy have life only in language, and language has a life only in society. We might say that Wittgenstein, thus understood, offers us a species of empirical realism and 'transcendental anthropocentrism'. That is, what Wittgenstein calls 'agreement in judgement' is not an empirical criterion of correctness or truth; rather, it is a precondition of the possibility of a discourse in which judgements of truth, correctness, consistency, and so on, have a place.

Defending the transcendental reading

In my view, the position at which we have arrived offers the best chance of giving a central role to the concept of community in a Wittgensteinian framework. The position is some distance from the spirit of Kripke's text; however, there are hints of such an interpretation in Malcolm. In an interesting exchange in the journal *Philosophy*, Malcolm objects to Baker and Hacker's insistence that 'the rule and nothing but the rule determines what is correct'. For him, this represents a kind of rule-fetishism:

> Baker and Hacker do not seem to give sufficient recognition to Wittgenstein's insight that a rule does not determine anything *except* within a setting of quiet agreement. If you imagine *that* no longer existing, you become aware of the *nakedness* of the rule. The words that express the rule would be without weight, without life. A sign-post would not *be* a sign-post. A rule, *by itself*, determines nothing. (Malcolm, 1989: 9)

For Baker and Hacker, Malcolm's objection presupposes that a rule and what accords with it are externally related. Malcolm talks as if we can identify something as a rule and then wonder why it has this extension rather than some other. He then appeals to communal agreement for the answer, but the question is empty since '*Given that there is* a certain rule, then nothing *other than* the rule constitutes the standard of correctness' (Baker and Hacker, 1990: 170).

This response seems to miss Malcolm's point. The communitarian can agree that, given the rules, the rules determine what is correct. (Though, as Malcolm stresses, one must not lose sight of Wittgenstein's emphasis on the 'open-textured' nature of language, that we frequently encounter hard cases where the rules do not deliver neat answers about what to say, where we feel that the extension has to be constructed.) Malcolm, however, is interested in the question of how it is possible for there to be rules at all. He is concerned with the issue Wittgenstein raises at the opening of the *Blue Book*: what breathes life into the signs of our language? What transforms some arrangement of matter into a sign which has meaning? (Wittgenstein, 1958: 1–5; cf. 1953: §§432, 454). It is in answer to this question that the appeal to community has a role. The sign is 'given life' in virtue of its employment by a community of speakers engaged in the practices constitutive of their form of life. This is the sense in which the appeal to community has transcendental significance; it figures as part of an elucidation of the conditions of the possibility of language, of the animation of the 'brutely natural' into the meaningful. For Malcolm, it takes a plurality of beings to bring meaning into the world.

To this, Baker and Hacker might reply that the communitarian is wrong to suppose that, when it comes to the question 'How is meaning possible?', there is anything substantive the philosopher can say. The philosopher yearns for a vantage point beyond language from which to explain its possibility. He asks us to see our speech as mere 'noise-making', and then find the ingredient which turns this meaningless racket into meaningful signs. It is this kind of alienation that rule-scepticism engenders. The rule-sceptic has us treat our behaviour '"from an external point of view" as odd noises, curious inscriptions possibly governed by an as yet unknown rule'. But this is confused, since we 'can no more view [our] own speech as evacuated of any meaning than [we] can view the ceiling of the Sistine Chapel as covered with meaningless blotches of paint' (Baker and Hacker, 1984: 22).

It seems to me, however, that there is a sense in which we can view the ceiling of the Sistine Chapel as a collection of blotches of paint, in which we can hear our words as 'mere noise'. We can, I believe, legitimately puzzle about how some mere collection of marks or sounds can be meaningful, about how the world can contain significance. This puzzlement can, and should, weigh with us, and it is a virtue of meaning-scepticism that it makes us wonder about how meaning is possible. Wittgenstein's philosophy rightly denies that we should respond to this wonder with a substantive philosophical theory that explains how a brutely physical world supplemented by human activity somehow bursts forth with meaning. But to say this is not to say that wonder is illegitimate or inappropriate. The point of the communitarian's strategy is to acknowledge the puzzlement and recognize the perspective from which it ceases to be real: the perspective of our social being, framed by our common human nature. We might say that there is a sense in which our shared activity 'enchants' the world, and that the philosopher's task is to make us alive to this enchantment. This is a difficult task, to be sure, since the enchantment is a feature of everyday things as they usually are, and it is hardest of all to see what is always before one's eyes (cf. Wittgenstein, 1953: §129). Here the rhetoric of enchantment is designed, not to gesture towards a substantive account of meaning as a 'non-natural' phenomenon, but simply to serve as what Wittgenstein calls 'a reminder for a particular purpose' (1953: §127); in this case, to resist the spell of that one-dimensional species of naturalism that would construe the natural world, as it 'really' is, as austerely physical – bereft of value and meaning – as disenchanted in Max Weber's sense. The point is to see meaning as a genuine constituent of the natural world, albeit one that cannot be rendered intelligible without recourse to the perspective of a certain form of life.[5]

However, a powerful objection remains. Baker and Hacker might grant that Wittgenstein is engaged in an exploration of the conditions of the possibility of language. Indeed, they themselves discuss what 'breathes life' into the signs of our language (1985: 141) and 'yields' normativity (1984: 42). However, Wittgenstein says in the *Blue Book* that 'if we had to name anything which is the life of the sign, we should have to say that it was its *use*' (1958: 4). Why should we suppose that use demands community, rather than simply the existence of regular practices of sufficient complexity to warrant description in normative terms? It still remains uncertain whether, and in what sense, Wittgenstein's position entails that an entirely solitary being could not have a language.[6]

The puzzle of the solitary language user

Malcolm is adamant that a person who had never had contact with a community of language users could not have a language. We can, of course, imagine a sole survivor of a holocaust speaking a language, but here the speaker owes her skills to prior participation in a community. Baker and Hacker, in contrast, argue that the origin of a person's skills are irrelevant to whether their present behaviour constitutes language use. It is, they say, a 'grammatical proposition' that 'the criteria for having an ability lie in present performance not in the original mode of acquisition' (1990: 177). Hence, if a solitary being who was once a member of a community can speak a language, then a forever solitary language user is a conceptual possibility.

This debate is harder to assess than it appears. It is unclear that Baker and Hacker can help themselves to the supposed 'grammatical proposition' (i.e. conceptual truth) they mention. It seems incompatible with the spirit of Wittgenstein's philosophy to invoke grammatical propositions to decide in advance what considerations are relevant to assessing a problematic imaginary case. A Wittgensteinian should concede that any details are relevant that might affect our linguistic intuitions, and considerations about the origin of the solitary individual's supposed language skills might do just that. Thus Baker and Hacker cannot invoke their 'grammatical proposition' as a context-neutral standard of logical possibility that dictates how we must describe the imaginary case, for the grammatical proposition is itself tested by our intuitions about the imaginary case (cf. Wittgenstein, 1969: §98).

It is anyway uncertain how much thought experiments can help us here. That we can tell a seemingly coherent story about solitary language users does not show that what we describe is logically possible: consider stories about time travel. What we are inclined to accept as coherent depends on our culturally contingent practices of storytelling. At issue is whether the stories are coherent when we scrutinize them. But this just returns us to the question of what the private language argument actually shows. We construct the imaginary cases to test our theories, but we need our theories to tell us what we are imagining.

What, then, is the communitarian's case? Malcolm sometimes seems to be making an epistemological argument. A forever solitary individual could never know if she was following rules correctly, since she would be in the same position as the private linguist in *Investigations* §258. She would have no criteria by which to distinguish what seems right from what is right. One might object, however, that the predicaments of these two solitary beings are relevantly different. For while the private linguist is, as it were, trapped in the specious present of a purely phenomenological world, the forever solitary individual is, like you and I, a participant in a world of enduring objects, which are in principle, if not in practice, open to public scrutiny. Why can the solitary individual not associate signs with these 'public' objects? If I can achieve this alone on a desert island, why is it beyond a forever solitary individual?

In fact, at the centre of Malcolm's case is a developmental argument. At *Investigations* §258, we are asked to suppose that the private linguist can think; we are then shown that he cannot construct a medium for the expression of thought because he is beset by sceptical problems about identification and consistency. The argument, however, is a *reductio* of the idea that a private linguist can possess concepts and hence can think. We thus cannot represent the private linguist as having a conception of the world waiting to be put into language. It is in this respect that the private linguist and the forever solitary individual share the same predicament: the solitary individual, like the private linguist, lacks the wherewithal to invent a first language from scratch. This is why Malcolm insists that the issue turns on the origins of the solitary linguist's skills. Once we grant the forever solitary individual a perspective on the world, we will not be able to resist the idea that she can operate a language. And this is why thought experiments about forever solitary individuals are misleading; in constructing them we find ourselves granting the solitary individual a conception of the world, but this gives the game away.

For Malcolm, then, a forever solitary individual could not acquire a language. Language must be learnt. Moreover, a language cannot be learnt by a process of hypothesis formation by the individual, since the individual lacks the means to construct or confirm the necessary hypotheses. Among the reasons here is that an individual is able to form such hypotheses only if she has conceptual skills possessed by beings who already have a language. Hence the significance of training. To learn a language the child must therefore appropriate a pre-existing set of language practices. These practices could only reside in the activity of other subjects who train the child to behave as they do.

This developmental point is central to Malcolm's thinking.[7] Why, though, should we assume that language must be learnt?[8] Can we not imagine a being springing into existence *ex nihilo* speaking a language? Again there is no simple answer, for the question turns on whether the imagined being's 'words' are meaningful as opposed to mere noise. For Malcolm, acts of meaning are possible only in the right kind of context. Crucial to this context are certain social practices: practices of responding to what is said, of correcting mistakes, of teaching and learning expressions, and so on. These practices, one might say, give sense to our 'utterances'. It is our words' surroundings that give them their significance (cf. Wittgenstein, 1953: §§583–4). Our common life is the medium of the meaningful.

This brings out what, for Malcolm, is wrong with Baker and Hacker's insistence that it is use, rather than social practice, which animates the sign. For what is involved in some behaviour constituting the use of a sign? Appeal to regularity here is not enough, since judgements of regularity presuppose that we can identify the behaviour as meaningful (i.e. that the word is used in the same way from case to case). Behaviour counts as a regular use of a word only in the right kind of context, and this, for Malcolm, demands a plurality of subjects. This idea strengthens Malcolm's view of development: since the possibility of language use requires the existence of a context of social practice, nothing can be a language user until it is inaugurated into this context – until, one might say, it has acquired the perspective of use.

This argument, however, will not sway Baker and Hacker, who will simply insist that the solitary speaker can construct the necessary context herself. Here the debate reaches an impasse where both sides see the other as begging the question. For Baker and Hacker, Malcolm begs the question by refusing to admit any practice as linguistic unless a community is suitably implicated in its possibility; for Malcolm, Baker and Hacker beg the question by depicting the forever solitary individual in a way that assumes the characteristics that must be explained if we are to appreciate how language is possible.

Can the communitarian win this argument? She has, I think, two possible strategies: one ambitious and one modest. The first is to try conclusively to defeat Baker and Hacker by supplementing the considerations we find in Malcolm. For example, we might argue that the very possibility of my distinguishing myself from my world, so that I can conceive of myself as standing in a relation to the world which differs from the relations in which other subjects stand or might stand, requires the existence of perspectives other than my own. If I am to have a perspective on the world I recognize as mine, I must be able to make sense of the possibility of perspectives other than my own. But I can grasp this possibility only if I actually encounter the minds of others.

Inspiration might be sought here from Wittgenstein's enigmatic remarks about other minds in the *Investigations* (e.g. 1953: §302; which Dancy [1985: 69] interestingly develops in the spirit of Malcolm, 1954 and 1958). Attacking the Cartesian and sense-datum theorist, Wittgenstein suggests that we cannot acquire knowledge of the possibility of other minds by projection from our own case – by, say, my imagining that there is some other subject of experience who has what I have when I am in pain. Likewise, even on Wittgenstein's anti-Cartesian view of the mental, there remains a problem about how a second-person perspective could be constructed by a supremely solitary being. For Wittgenstein, while my ascriptions of subjective states to others are governed by criteria, this is not so in the case of first-person ascription (I don't assert that 'I am in pain' on the basis of evidence). How, then, is a forever solitary being to construct the idea of mental states the presence of which is to be determined evidentially? We acquire knowledge of the possibility of other minds because we live in a world where we confront their actuality, where the minds of others are manifest to us in their activity. There are some things that argument or inference will not settle for us, and the possibility of other minds is one of them. We need to encounter the possibility of the other, and this can be done only by encountering the other's actuality. (For another approach, more loosely inspired by Wittgenstein, see Davidson, 1992: 262–4.)

This argument is hardly conclusive; it merely suggests a way the communitarian might proceed. It could be argued, however, that to try to see off Baker and Hacker with ever more ambitious arguments is to succumb to the kind of intellectual temptation Wittgenstein's philosophy warns us against. In contrast, a more modest communitarian approach might concede that Wittgenstein's arguments show only that a shared language presupposes the existence of a community. This concession is smaller than we might think. For Wittgenstein's insight that nothing holds our language practices together save for agreement – which is not compelled or underwritten by 'the world' – is undiminished by the recognition that a solitary language user is logically possible. Once Wittgenstein's insight is combined with his critique of epistemological individualism we are left with a clear recognition of our social being. It is typical of the philosopher, of course, to try to represent how things are with us as how things must be for any possible being (cf. Wittgenstein, unpublished manuscript, quoted in Kenny, 1984: 44). But the point of Wittgenstein's philosophy is to direct attention away from philosophical abstractions to the actual character of our lives. That Wittgenstein's work explores the possibility of our form of life is enough. We should not want more.

Indeed, the modest communitarian might argue that preoccupation with abstract questions about solitary linguists has directed energy away from interesting issues which Wittgensteinian communitarians might fruitfully pursue. For example, Wittgenstein is renowned for his diagnosis of the origin of philosophical puzzlement: philosophical issues derive from 'the bewitchment of our intelligence by means of language' (1953: §109). By misunderstanding the character of our language we fall into confusion, posing questions that can have no answers and constructing explanations of phenomena that cannot or need not be explained. Wittgenstein, however, seems to treat this bewitchment as a matter of purely linguistic confusion. He points out, for example, that we draw false analogies between forms of expressions: since the question 'What is gold?' has an answer, we assume the same must be true of 'What is time?' However, if we take seriously Wittgenstein's idea that 'to imagine a language is to imagine a form of life' (1953: §19), we must recognize that our propensity to fall into philosophical delusion cuts deeper than a susceptibility to make mistakes of this kind. Why do some linguistic confusions occur and not others? Why do some philosophical pictures, such as the Cartesian conception of the mind, exercise a powerful grip on our intellectual culture, while others are easily dispelled? These questions cannot be answered simply by appeal to our mistaken understanding of linguistic forms; they need to be pursued in a richer exploration of our form of life in its historical evolution. Philosophical anthropology needs to turn to cultural history. While such an interest in the genealogy of philosophical questions may seem remote from Wittgenstein's approach to the discipline, I believe that, properly pursued, it is an essential part of what Wittgenstein called 'one of the heirs of the subject which used to be called "philosophy"' (1958: 28).

I leave it open whether Wittgensteinian communitarians should adopt the ambitious or the modest strategy. Either way, I hope I have shown how we can read Wittgenstein's philosophy as a genuine contribution to our understanding of ourselves as social beings.

Notes

I am grateful to audiences at the University of Toronto, Queen's University at Kingston, and the University of California, San Diego, for helpful suggestions and criticisms. I am also indebted to Jonathan Dancy, Hanjo Glock, Stephen Leighton, Mark MacLeod, Hanna Pickard and Michael Tippett for fruitful discussions of the themes of this chapter.

1. As I have done in my work on Vygotsky and Ilyenkov (see Bakhurst, 1991).

2. Kripke invokes the distinction between 'truth conditions' and 'justification conditions' (so central to philosophy of language in the 1970s and early 1980s) to suggest that we see the development of Wittgenstein's thinking about meaning as a shift from a truth conditional view in the *Tractatus* (1917) to an assertibility conditional approach in the later philosophy (Kripke, 1982: 71–7). However, Kripke's discussion is misleading, misconstruing the *Tractatus* view of truth conditions and their relation to facts, and implying that the later Wittgenstein embraced an anti-realist theory of meaning. The later Wittgenstein was not an anti-realist, nor had he any *theory* of meaning. Kripke has been soundly criticized on this score (see e.g. Baker and Hacker, 1984: 47–9; Malcolm, 1986: 163–7).

3. In fact it is unclear whether Kripke's and Malcolm's stances should be so sharply distinguished. Kripke sometimes portrays Wittgenstein as denying that there are any facts about what we mean (e.g. 1982: 70–1). However, he also suggests that Wittgenstein is simply attacking mistaken philosophical conceptions of meaning (e.g. Platonism) and that once those conceptions are displaced we may continue speaking 'with perfect right' of facts about meanings (1982: 69). This more modest formulation is less obviously in conflict with Malcolm, whose appeals to 'training' and 'action' anyway do not serve to establish facts about meaning that would silence Kripke's sceptic. In addition, Kripke, no less than Malcolm, responds to Wittgenstein's paradox by appeal to *practice*, to what we do when we follow rules and take others to be doing so (commentators sometimes wrongly imply that Kripke turns to the community for a definitive *interpretation* of the rule [Baker and Hacker, 1984: 66–70]). Thus, there is a sense in which, for all their differences, both Kripke and Malcolm invoke our practices as part of an answer designed to sidestep rule-scepticism.

4. This shows there is no hope of giving a non-circular account of meaning by appeal to agreement understood as 'sameness of response'. We can understand the notion of agreement only if we invoke other normative notions (e.g. responses agree when they accord with one another) and if we can see the respondents as meaning the same thing. We need a richer notion of agreement than most Wittgensteinians have countenanced: since two people may 'agree' in the use of some concept even if they apply it differently – so long as they agree on the kinds of considerations relevant to its application – it is best to elucidate agreement in terms of sameness of sensibility, rather than sameness of response.

5. I have been influenced here by John McDowell. Unfortunately, his book, *Mind and World*, which contains a valuable discussion of naturalism and 'disenchantment', appeared only as this text was going to press (see McDowell, 1994, esp. pp. 70–86, and 92–9, where he discusses readings of Wittgenstein).

6. This question has preoccupied Wittgenstein's commentators since the publication of the

Investigations. See, for example, Strawson, 1954; Ayer, 1954; Winch, 1958: 33–9; and more recently, McGinn, 1984: ch. 4 and Pears, 1988: ch. 14.

7. David Pears argues that the developmental point is merely 'a speculative thesis in developmental psychology' and that Wittgenstein was 'the last person to draw a philosophical conclusion from a premiss which would be, at best, only contingently true' (1988: 365). This response, however, begs the question against Malcolm, whose point is that certain matters that seem to be contingent are not so. (We can imagine someone responding to *Investigations* §258 by arguing that whether a solipsistic mind can categorize sense-data is 'a purely contingent matter'. This would be to miss Wittgenstein's point in the way Pears misses Malcolm's.)

8. Sometimes Wittgenstein writes as if he has no problem with the idea of an innate mastery of language. At the same time, he frequently warns against the 'mistake' of supposing the child learning her first language already possesses a language 'of thought' (see 1953: §32; 1958: 104–5; cf. Pears, 1988: 376–81).

References

Ayer, A. J. (1954) 'Can there be a private language?', *Proceedings of the Aristotelian Society*, Supplementary Vol. XXVIII.

Baker, G. P. and Hacker, P. M. S. (1984) *Scepticism, Rules and Language*. Oxford: Blackwell.

Baker, G. P. and Hacker, P. M. S. (1985) *Wittgenstein: Rules, Grammar and Necessity*. Oxford: Blackwell.

Baker, G. P. and Hacker, P. M. S. (1990) 'Malcolm on language and rules', *Philosophy*, 65.

Bakhurst, David (1991) *Consciousness and Revolution in Soviet Philosophy*. Cambridge: Cambridge University Press.

Blackburn, Simon (1984) *Spreading the Word*. Oxford: Oxford University Press.

Dancy, Jonathan (1985) *Introduction to Contemporary Epistemology*. Oxford: Blackwell.

Davidson, Donald (1992) 'The second person', in P. A. French, T. E. Uehling and H. K. Wettstein (eds), *Midwest Studies in Philosophy, Vol. 17: The Wittgenstein Legacy*. Notre Dame: University of Notre Dame Press.

Kenny, Anthony (1984) *The Legacy of Wittgenstein*. Oxford: Blackwell.

Kripke, Saul (1982) *Wittgenstein on Rules and Private Languages*. Oxford: Blackwell.

McDowell, John (1994) *Mind and World*. Cambridge, MA: Harvard University Press.

McGinn, Colin (1984) *Wittgenstein on Meaning*. Oxford: Blackwell.

Malcolm, Norman (1954) 'Wittgenstein's *Philosophical Investigations*', in Malcolm (1963).

Malcolm, Norman (1958) 'Knowledge of other minds', in Malcolm (1963).

Malcolm, Norman (1963) *Knowledge and Certainty*. Ithaca, NY: Cornell University Press.

Malcolm, Norman (1986) *Nothing is Hidden*. Oxford: Blackwell.

Malcolm, Norman (1989) 'Wittgenstein on language and rules', *Philosophy*, 64.

Pears, David (1988) *The False Prison*, Vol. 2. Oxford: Oxford University Press.

Strawson, P. F. (1954) 'Wittgenstein's *Philosophical Investigations*', in *Freedom and Resentment*. London: Methuen, 1974.

Winch, Peter (1958) *The Idea of a Social Science*. London: Routledge & Kegan Paul.

Wittgenstein, Ludwig (1917) *Tractatus Logico-Philosophicus*, trans. D. F. Pears and B. F. McGuinness. London: Routledge & Kegan Paul, 1961.

Wittgenstein, Ludwig (1953) *Philosophical Investigations*, trans. G. E. M. Anscombe, 2nd edn. Oxford: Blackwell, 1967.

Wittgenstein, Ludwig (1958) *The Blue and Brown Books*, 2nd edn. Oxford: Blackwell, 1969.

Wittgenstein, Ludwig (1967) *Zettel*, trans. G. E. M. Anscombe. Oxford: Blackwell.

Wittgenstein, Ludwig (1969) *On Certainty*, trans. Denis Paul and G. E. M. Anscombe. Oxford: Blackwell.

Wittgenstein, Ludwig (1978) *Remarks on the Foundations of Mathematics*, trans. G. E. M. Anscombe, revised edn. Oxford: Blackwell.

4

What a Vygotskian Perspective Can Contribute to Contemporary Philosophy of Language

Ellen Watson

Contemporary semantics, or the study of meaning, contains two contrasting schools of thought regarding the relationship between language and thought. One, exemplified by the philosophy of Jerry Fodor, holds that thought is primary, and that language gets its meaning because it expresses thought. The other, exemplified by the work of the linguist Benjamin Lee Whorf, holds that language is primary, and that thought is shaped by it. The question that divides the two schools concerns the correct description of the relationship between language and thought: do meanings originate in the autonomous individual mind or in the individual's community? The difference that emerges in their respective answers to this question mirrors a more general distinction between individualistic and communitarian approaches to language and mind.

According to Fodor, it is sufficient for a semanticist to study the relationship between a single individual's mental representations and the objects in that single individual's environment. Fodor's position ignores both the social and the communicative dimensions of language. In Whorf's approach, on the other hand, the social nature of language is so fundamental that the language spoken in an individual's community is claimed to structure his or her very identity, thought, mind and environment. This approach avoids the narrow perspective of Fodor's individualistic semantics; however, as we shall see, it does little better at accounting for the communicative function of language.

The Soviet psychologist Lev Vygotsky presents a more balanced view of the relation between thought and language, in works written during his brief but productive career from 1924 to 1934. Vygotsky's discussions of thought and language could contribute much to contemporary debates in semantics. In this chapter I will show how Vygotsky's research on language and thought contains insights that might be incorporated into a new approach that is neither exclusively individualistic nor exclusively communitarian, and thus might resolve some of the current dilemmas of semantics.

Jerry Fodor – an individualist semantics

Jerry Fodor's semantic theory exemplifies a strategy that has been prominent in analytic philosophy of language for several decades, and has its roots in the classical empiricist tradition. The strategy concerns itself primarily with analysing the meaning of mental representations (thoughts, beliefs, fears, etc.) rather than expressions of natural language. The theory of mind is therefore of paramount significance for these philosophers of language, and the theory of mind they have inherited from the empiricist tradition is an extremely individualistic one.

The classical empiricists (including Thomas Hobbes, John Locke and David Hume) wrote during the seventeenth and eighteenth centuries, at a time when the natural sciences were gaining influence in European culture. They sought to make the human mind a subject of scientific scrutiny. In the opening sections of *Leviathan*, for example, Hobbes tries to formulate a theory of the mind that was in keeping with Galilean theories of motion. According to Hobbes, sentience is a result of motion inside the body: perceptual sensations result when an external body presses on the sense organs and causes reverberations and counter-resistance inside the body, and memory consists of retained motion which persists due to principles of inertia (see Hobbes, 1651: sections 1–3).

In the empiricist tradition, if perception and memory are just the residue of impressions made by external objects, then the mind is like a canvas, a passive recipient of images produced by an outside source, or perhaps like a filing cabinet, a store of representations collected and rearranged but still fairly static. David Hume is famous for holding that the mind is essentially no more than a bundle of ideas, and that there is no separate spirit or consciousness that underlies and unifies the mind's experience (Hume, 1739: I. iv. 6).

One can find echoes of the empiricists' assumptions throughout the work of contemporary computationalist philosophers of mind, including that of Jerry Fodor. The technique of using the most prominent scientific technology of the day as a model to explain the human mind continues in this work in a very literal way. Inspired by attempts in artificial intelligence to model human cognitive processes, they take the digital computer to be a very powerful metaphor for the human mind. If our minds are purely physical machines that process information, they argue, what better model could there be than a computer to help us find out how we do it? Fodor is so moved by these considerations that he cannot imagine a superior theory of mind. His landmark work, *The Language of Thought*, begins: 'The only psychological models of cognition that seem even remotely plausible represent such processes as computational' (Fodor, 1975: 27).

Fodor's commitment to computationalism yields a theory of the nature of mental representations that he calls the Representational Theory of Mind (see Fodor, 1987). He argues that computational machines cannot process information unless they are equipped with some internal system in which to represent that information to themselves – a machine language. If human beings process information in ways analogous to computers, we too must come with a machine language, a language of thought. Fodor calls this hypothetical language 'Mentalese'. His argument is that, without such a language, we could not represent even primitive perceptions to ourselves, and certainly could never go on to learn a natural language such as English (see Fodor, 1975: ch. 1).

For that reason, Fodor argues that the language of thought must be innate. In this he differs from the empiricist philosophers. Locke and Hume argue that human beings have no innate concepts; each of us when born is a *tabula rasa*. Fodor, on the other hand, accepts as a consequence of his computationalism that *all* concepts must be innate. Specific *beliefs* may be added on the basis of experience (such as 'The lights are on'), and new inferences may be drawn from sets of beliefs, but the basic conceptual building blocks of those beliefs are present from the start and remain unchanged (see Fodor, 1975: ch. 2).

Fodor's analysis of the structure of mental representations is derived from a later philosophical tradition, twentieth-century analytic philosophy of language, specifically its concept of the propositional attitude. Mental representations such as beliefs, desires and fears are called 'propositional attitudes' because the sentences we use to ascribe them have a common structure: each state can be analysed as a different attitude of a subject to a proposition. For example, the sentence 'John believes that he left the stove on' says that a subject *John* has the attitude of *belief* to the proposition that *he left the stove on*; the sentence 'John fears that he left the stove on' says that the same subject holds a different attitude (fear) to the same proposition. In contrast, mental states such as pain or hunger do not represent attitudes to propositions; the states in question are said to lack 'propositional content'.

In keeping with his Representational Theory of Mind, Fodor analyses a propositional attitude as a relation in which a human being stands to a sentence that is literally inscribed in that person's head in the language of Mentalese. John's belief that it is cold outside is therefore a particular relation between John and the sentence 'It is cold outside', as it is written in the language of John's thought. Again, this language is supposed to function as the 'machine language' of the brain. As the ones and zeroes that make up machine code are instantiated in a computer as electrical activity across chip circuitry, the symbols of Mentalese would consist of something like patterns of neuronal activity.[1]

How do these mental sentences in the language of thought get put into play as representations? For an explanation, Fodor relies on a causal theory of perception that again owes much to the empiricists. This theory was drafted into service for semantics by Dennis Stampe, in his paper, 'Toward a causal theory of linguistic representation' (1977). Stampe points out that one can explain the natural representational relationships that obtain between phenomena such as tree rings and the number of years of a tree's age, or the moon and its reflection in a pond, by citing the causal and 'covariational' relations that hold between them. These natural meaning relationships depend solely on causal relationships between the entities involved, and do not depend on human interpretation (see Stampe, 1977: 87).

The sentences of Mentalese gain semantic content in a related way. In his book *Psychosemantics*, Fodor argues, as a crude first pass, that a symbol expresses or represents a particular property 'if it's nomologically necessary that *all* and *only* instances of the property cause tokenings of the symbol' (1987: 100). In other words, my thought, 'There is a cat' means that there is a cat because it gets put into play as a belief in the functional architecture of my mind – gets 'put into my belief-box', as Fodor says (1987: 17) – when and only when a cat is present to me. The meaning of this longer mental token is, in turn, made up recursively from the meanings of its components; the concept 'cat' means *cat* because its tokening covaries with all and only cats.

The causal relations that underlie the meaning of mental representations are determined by laws that hold in the natural world. Fodor writes:

> The Crude Causal Theory [of meaning], together with psychophysics, provides a plausible sufficient condition for certain symbols to express certain properties: viz., that tokenings of those symbols are connected to instantiations of the properties they express *by* psychophysical law. ... For example: Paint the wall red, turn the lights up, point your face toward the wall, and open your eyes. The thought 'red there' will occur to you; just try it and see if it doesn't. (1987: 112–13)

This story resembles the empiricist theory of perception described above. According to both Fodor and the empiricists, the world impresses itself upon our minds automatically and the corresponding perceptual beliefs occur to us unbidden. Fodor and Stampe found their theory of meaning on this automatic, purely physical process.

Fodor uses the concept 'red' in the above example because he believes that all presentations of red things will cause us to token the concept in a perceptual belief. However, the story is more complicated for higher-level concepts. For example, some presentations of cats may fail, for various reasons, to produce a tokening of the concept 'cat' (for example if it is dark), and sometimes someone might token the belief 'There is a cat' when he or she is actually being confronted with another object, for example a ring-tailed possum. Therefore, a crude causal theory that relies only on psychophysics is not sufficient. A more accurate statement of the causal covariational semantic theory should read as follows: 'A symbol expresses a property if it is nomologically necessary that all and only instances of the property *would* cause tokenings of the symbol, other things being equal' – in other words, would cause them were the subject presented with an object displaying the property, would if perceptual conditions were ideal, would as long as the subject's perceptual system were not damaged, etc.

This, roughly, is how Fodor's causal semantics accounts for the semantic content of mental representation; how does it account for the semantic content of spoken or written representations? According to Fodor and the other writers in the covariational tradition, expressions in natural language get their meaning derivatively from the thoughts they are used to express.[2] Therefore, these philosophers take a 'head-first' approach to semantics.

Again, this view has its philosophical roots in the work of the empiricists. Hobbes, in a chapter entitled 'Of Speech', declares:

> But the most noble and profitable invention of all other, was that of SPEECH, consisting of *names* or *appellations*, and their connexion; whereby men register their thoughts; recall them when they are past; and also declare them one to another for mutual utility and conversation. (1651: 33)

And Locke writes in his *Essay Concerning Human Understanding*:

> Man . . . had by nature his organs so fashioned, as to be fit to frame articulate sounds, which we call words. But this was not enough to produce language; for parrots, and several other birds, will be taught to make articulate sounds distinct enough, which yet, by no means, are capable of language.
>
> Besides articulate sounds, therefore, it was further necessary, that he should be able to use these sounds, as signs of internal conceptions; and to make them stand as marks for the ideas within his own mind, whereby they might be made known to others, and the thoughts of men's minds be conveyed from one to another. (1690: III. i. 1–2)

In these passages, one gets a clear statement of the head-first approach to language; thoughts are the things with content, and language is a vessel for conveying those thoughts from one head to another. This view is reflected in statements made by contemporary semanticists such as Gilbert Harman, who begins a paper with the claim, 'The meanings of linguistic expressions are determined by the contents of the concepts and thoughts they can be used to express' (Harman, 1982: 242).

Fodor says very little more than this about natural language, and says even less about its communicative function. What he does say suggests that he, like Hobbes and Locke above, holds an 'envelope theory' of the communicative function of linguistic utterances, according to which spoken or written words are vessels containing the contents of the thoughts they express, and in communication those words convey their contents from one head to another. In Fodor's theory, an exact match is required between the concepts in two subjects' heads for communication to be achieved. He writes that 'communication actually *consists in* establishing a certain kind of correspondence between [speaker's and hearer's] mental states' (1975: 108).

Fodor's semantic theory is driven by the same deeply held assumptions about the nature of the mind and its relationship with objects in the external world as were the theories of the empiricists. Both Fodor and the empiricists look to current trends in the physical sciences for a model of the mind as a cognitive engine, although the difference in available technological models leads to a difference in their positions on innate concepts. Both Fodor and the empiricists look to the physics of their day to explain perception, the process by which objects in the outside world make their impressions on the mind, although Hobbes's story depends on laws of Galilean physics, while Fodor's depends on laws of psychophysics. In adopting this explanatory strategy from the empiricists, Fodor inherits their tradition of individualism.

Empiricists since Locke have had trouble countering scepticism about the external world. The external world may causally impinge on the mind via the senses, but is always remote from it. Since the human subject is separated from the objects that impress ideas upon it, the subject can never be certain whether those impressions are accurate. Fodor's work embraces this scepticism and calls it 'methodological solipsism'; he argues that one need not, when doing psychology, even suppose the existence of an external world that resembles the subject's beliefs about it; it is enough to consider a subject's mental states in isolation (see Fodor, 1980). Further, the only access the human subject has to other people is through this same, isolating perceptual process. We can have surface impressions of other people, but can never really know them. As in classical empiricism, the thinking self is alone in its confrontation with the physical world.

The speaking self is similarly alone in both philosophies. Utterances and inscriptions that encase one's thoughts may be sent out, but one can never be sure whether they are being correctly decoded by the recipient. In addition, communicative practices and linguistic conventions in the speaker's community can never have any impact on fundamental meaning relationships, since these are wholly determined by primitive facts about the physical world. Fodor's semantic theory thus leaves no room for conceptual change or for the social construction of semantic categories. The causal relations that yield meaning in Fodor's theory are fixed relations that hold between rigidly individuated entities. The basic tokens of Mentalese are present in the mind from birth, and are predisposed to be triggered by certain perceptual inputs without alteration over time. The objects in the environment must be similarly rigidly individuated into kinds *in nature*, in order to do the triggering. Otherwise, the causal covariational relation between object and concept could not take place in the automatic way that Fodor's causal theory requires.

In the next section we will examine a theory that makes just the opposite claim about the relation between convention and conceptual categories. It thus escapes some of the deficiencies of causal semantics, but in doing so runs into a number of problems of its own.

Benjamin Lee Whorf – a communitarian linguistics

As we saw in the previous section, contemporary head-first semanticists find the metaphysical ground of meaning in the causal relations that hold between objects in the world and the individual's perceptual system, causal relations that result in mental representations in the individual. We observed that one finds almost no mention of culture or society and only quick and inadequate accounts of the communicative function of natural language in these writers' discussions of meaning and language. In this section I will examine the work of a linguist who emphasizes everything the head-first semanticists leave out, and who reverses the metaphysical priority of language and thought.

Although Benjamin Lee Whorf spent all of his adult life employed as a fire inspector for the Hartford Fire Insurance Company, he distinguished himself in his avocation of linguistics, most notably for his work comparing the grammar of what he called 'Standard Average European' (or SAE) languages to the grammar of native American languages such as Hopi, Shawnee, Mayan and Nootka. Whorf's ideas continue to influence the work of thinkers such as Clifford Geertz (1974), Stephen Levinson (1983; Brown and Levinson, 1987), and Helen Watson-Verran (1993). Through comparative analyses of the grammars and vocabularies of these languages, Whorf found a number of connections between the grammar of a language and the metaphysical presuppositions embedded in the conceptual schemes of those who speak it. He concluded that a culture's metaphysics and values reside in its language and determine the character of individual thought. Whorf presents certain facts about language that purport to show that our metaphysical views might be more parochial than we previously believed.[3]

In his paper, 'The relation of habitual thought and behaviour to language' (1956: 134–59), Whorf shows how metaphysical presuppositions are reflected in the cultural practices of the linguistic community (turning his anthropological eye on both Hopi and West European/Anglo-American rituals). He is careful not to say that either the metaphysical views or the cultural practices are *implied* or *entailed* by the features of the language, only that there are 'traceable affinities' between them (1956: 138). He states:

> I should be the last to pretend that there is anything so definite as 'a correlation' between culture and language, and especially between ethological rubrics such as 'agricultural, hunting', etc., and linguistic ones like 'inflected', 'synthetic', or 'isolating'. (1956: 138–89)

Whorf also argues in a number of places that language and perception, and language and culture, have a dynamic relationship, and that influence flows back and forth between them (see 1956: 156).

Nevertheless, Whorf claims that language has a strong influence on thought and on culture, stronger than either has on language in return. In several passages, he explicitly denies the view advocated by head-first semanticists that language is used purely to express thought. His characterization of that view nicely summarizes the head-first position on the priority of thought:

Talking, or the use of language, is supposed only to 'express' what is essentially already formulated nonlinguistically. Formulation is an independent process, called thought or thinking, and is supposed to be largely indifferent to the nature of particular languages. Languages have grammars, which are assumed to be merely norms of convention and social correctness, but the use of language is supposed to be guided not so much by them as by correct, rational, or intelligent THINKING.

Thought, in this view, does not depend on grammar but on laws of logic or reason which are supposed to be the same for all observers of the universe. (1956: 207–8)

Whorf argues that this view is actually an illusion, derived from the facility in using language that human beings display and observe in themselves: 'The fact that every person has talked fluently since infancy makes every man his own authority on the process by which he formulates and communicates' (1956: 207). Since human speakers do not *notice* language structuring their thoughts, they conclude that it does not happen. Whorf would presumably find Fodor guilty of this same kind of naive presupposition.

Whorf's claim that language has a strong influence on thought is supported by his comparative analyses of grammatically diverse languages. One significant example concerns the relationship between nouns and concepts of form and matter. Whorf points out that English contains both individual and mass nouns (1956: 140). The distinction is marked grammatically – mass nouns lack plurals and drop articles (for example, we do not say 'the butters', except to indicate more than one type of butter). Mass nouns often appear in what Whorf calls 'container-formulas' – for example, 'glass of water', 'cup of coffee', 'bag of flour' (p. 141). These container-formulas get metaphorically extended to individual bits of matter that are in some particular form but not literally in a container – for example 'lump of dough', 'stick of wood'.

Because of the existence of mass nouns and the corresponding use of container-formulas in English, Whorf suggests that

the 'lumps, chunks, blocks, pieces', etc., seem to contain something, a 'stuff', 'substance', or 'matter' that answers to the 'water', 'coffee', or 'flour' in the container formulas. So with SAE people the philosophical 'substance' and 'matter' are also the naive idea; they are instantly acceptable, 'common sense'. It is so through linguistic habit. (1956: 141)

Whorf's point is that the Platonic metaphysics of form and matter is embodied in and perhaps inspired by the grammar of SAE languages, and that a language that lacks mass nouns and container-formulas would presumably be less hospitable to this metaphysics.

Another important example concerns the relationship between verb tenses and concepts of time. Whorf points out that while English divides the reporting of events into three tenses – past, present and future – Hopi distinguishes instead between various modes of validity. While English distinguishes between past and present occurrences, Hopi treats these as the same, because both serve to report events that have already manifested themselves in physical actuality. Hopi speakers group together in a different grammatical category all events that have not manifested themselves in physical actuality. This group would include events described using the English future tense, as well as all mental or spiritual matters. A third validity marker concerns events that have just begun, in other words, events that are just on the edge of passing from unmanifested to actual.

In a related example, Whorf points out a difference between Hopi and English that concerns cardinality and ordinality in describing the passage of time. English treats units of time as distinct segments of some greater line, 'time', which is passing. This shows that 'time' functions as one of English's mass nouns. Thus, English expressions such as 'five days' are on a par with expressions such as 'five hats' or 'five boxes'. Hopi does not segment time in this way. Whorf suggests that, given the range of words to which Hopi plurals and cardinals can apply, cardinality of time, as expressed by a sentence like 'He left after the tenth day', is not possible in Hopi (1956: 140, 216). Whorf interprets Hopi descriptions as embodying the view that the arrival of 'day' is another arrival of the *same* day. He says that a Hopi speaker therefore might not understand our expression, 'Tomorrow is another day' (p. 148). According to Whorf, the Hopi experience is more cyclical than segmented, and rather than *length* of time, Hopis experience a subjective recognition of growing-later. Whorf argues that in this case the English-speaker's description is more abstract, for human experience only yields subjective perception of *one* day, and of its growing-later. The other nine are always necessarily remote to experience.

Whorf's claim is that the differences between Hopi and English cause Hopi-speakers and English-speakers to have different understandings of time itself; grammar manifests itself in metaphysics. He makes a number of anthropological observations to support this claim. Hopi culture is filled with elaborate ceremonies to announce and prepare for future events. Whorf explains that these ceremonies are better understood if one remembers that, according to the principles of Hopi grammar, the arrival of a future day is understood as the return of the *same* day; it thus makes sense to try to effect changes to that day by making changes in this one. Whorf remarks, 'This is the way the Hopi deal with the future – by working within a present situation which is expected to carry impresses, both obvious and occult, forward into the future event of interest' (1956: 148). In contrast, Western cultures, whose languages contain cardinality of time, put more emphasis on measuring units of time, keeping historical records of past days which will never return, and allocating 'pro-rata values' to time, in the form of institutions such as time wages, rent, credit, interest, depreciation charges, and insurance premiums (1956: 153). Whorf does not claim that these cultural practices are entailed by Standard Average European grammar:

No doubt this vast system, once built, would continue to run under any sort of linguistic treatment of time; but that it should have been built at all, reaching the magnitude and particular form it has in the Western world, is a fact decidedly in consonance with the patterns of the SAE languages. (1956: 153–4)

On the basis of the above examples, Whorf draws the following general conclusions about the relationship between the structure of language and the structure of thought. Of the differences between Hopi and Standard Average European languages, he writes:

I find it gratuitous to assume that a Hopi who knows only the Hopi language and the cultural ideas of his own society has the same notions, often supposed to be intuitions, of time and space that we have, and that are generally assumed to be universal. (1956: 57)

Elsewhere, he states his conclusion more generally:

Concepts of 'time' and 'matter' are not given in substantially the same form by experience to all men but depend upon the nature of the language or languages through the use of which they have been developed. (1956: 158)

In the next passage, Whorf describes his general theory of the relationship between thought and language:

We are inclined to think of language simply as a technique of expression, and not to realize that language first of all is a classification and arrangement of the stream of sensory experience which results in a certain world-order. (1956: 55)

In this passage, we can see that Whorf's views are diametrically opposed to Fodor's. Whorf here explicitly rejects both the envelope theory of communication and the priority of thought. For Whorf, language is prior even to individual perceptual experience.

Whorf sometimes talks as if certain concepts are inexpressible in a language and therefore are unthinkable for a monolinguistic speaker of it. On the basis of these claims, many followers and critics have taken Whorf to hold that languages whose structures vary to a certain degree are incommensurable with each other (see Davidson, 1974). This means that it would be impossible to translate the (relevant) expressions in one language into expressions in the other. Given the link Whorf makes between language and thought, it also means that speakers of the one language would never be able to *think* the (relevant) thoughts that are commonsense intuitions for speakers of the other.

However, this criticism misses an important aim of Whorf's work. As commentator John Lucy points out:

Whorf realized that the very variety among languages posed serious problems for the comparison of linguistic classifications. Contrary to the popular image of Whorf as an absolute relativist, he firmly believed in the possibility of meaningful comparison of and generalization across languages. However, he insisted that the frames of reference used in such comparisons be independent of the particularities of any given language. (Lucy, 1985: 7)

The frames of reference of which Lucy speaks would have to concern some innate and essentially human properties shared by all speakers.

Importantly, Whorf believes that the shared frames of reference are *sublinguistic*. In his paper 'Language, mind, and reality', Whorf maintains that human beings share a basic need to communicate (1956: 251–2), and a fundamental drive to find patterns in experience (p. 257). He writes:

> It is as if the personal mind, which selects words but is largely oblivious to pattern, were in the grip of a higher, far more intellectual mind which has very little notion of houses and beds and soup kettles, but can systematize and mathematize on a scale and scope that no mathematician of the schools ever remotely approached.
>
> And now appears a great fact of human brotherhood – that human beings are all alike in this respect. (1956: 257)

The urge to pattern experience is universal, but the particular patterns that human beings construct to interpret the world may vary, even widely, from culture to culture (and also, as Whorf points out, between various scientific disciplines [1956: 220–32]).[4]

Whorf not only recognized but also valued both the universal and the diverse in humankind. Nonetheless, despite these aims, his work does not in itself contain the arguments to defeat charges that he advances a radical incommensurability thesis. Whorf is a linguist, and philosophers might complain that his account lacks an explanation of exactly how metaphysical views are embodied in language, and, more importantly, how they are transmitted to the members of the linguistic community. Without a Language of Thought hypothesis like Fodor's, Whorf owes the semanticist an account of how speakers of one language could ever learn the concepts embodied in another, or even in their own. Whorf does not deny that communication is possible, as his critics sometimes charge, but he does not give an account of *how* it is possible, given the degree of difference he finds between languages.

Whorf's work has been severely criticized on both empirical and theoretical grounds, especially by those in the head-first tradition. He is vulnerable on both fronts. Linguists such as Eric Lenneberg have called Whorf's facts into question (Lenneberg, 1953), and if Whorf has got the facts wrong, then he can hardly support the metaphysical implications he draws. On the theoretical side, philosophers have questioned both the consistency (Davidson, 1974) and the significance (Rosch, 1977; Devitt and Sterelny, 1987: 173) of Whorf's conclusions regarding the relation between thought and language.

For our purposes, the most important shortcoming of Whorf's work is that he only considers one direction of causal relation between language and thought. If Fodor leaves no room for the impact of communicative practices on the thought of the individual, Whorf, in placing priority on language instead of thought, omits an account of how an individual speaker can adopt the concepts embodied in language and how individuals can communicate across linguistic paradigms. Whorf's thoroughgoing communitarianism ultimately results in an inadequate theory of the relationship between language and thought.

Vygotsky – a dialectical approach

Contemporary semanticists can look to the work of Vygotsky for a middle way between the approaches of Fodor and Whorf. Fodor is motivated by a theory about the mind and perception inherited from the empiricists and inspired by science and scientific inquiry. He argues that thoughts are the primary bearers of meaning, and that natural language gets its meaning because it expresses thoughts. Whorf believes that people's metaphysical pictures of the world come from their culture via the language they speak. He proposes that language is primary and that thought, mind, identity and world-view are shaped by it. Vygotsky takes both a scientific, empirical perspective and a sociocultural one. He believes that language gets its nature as a meaningful sociocultural activity from the use to which individuals put it, and also that language shapes and transforms the mind of the individual who learns to use it.

The first major difference between Vygotsky and the writers above concerns his view of the reciprocal relationship between thought and language. He criticizes those who, like Fodor and Whorf, emphasize one part of the relationship at the expense of the other (Vygotsky, 1986: ch. 1), and prefers a strategy that examines the development of *both* language and thought in the individual, and the influence each domain has on the other. Like Whorf, Vygotsky considers language a mechanism for the transmission of cultural conventions, conceiving of language as a sociocultural artifact, but he does not neglect the contribution of the individual's cognitive capacities to the development of language use.

Metaphysical foundations – Ilyenkov and the ideal

The ideas on which Vygotsky based his views were later crystallized by the philosopher E. V. Ilyenkov in his paper 'The concept of the ideal' (1977). Ilyenkov gives an analysis of properties formerly considered 'ideal', properties such as monetary value, religious value, morality, legality, propriety, and, most importantly for our purposes, semantic value (see Ilyenkov, 1977: 77, 89; Bakhurst, 1991: ch. 6). Because such properties are not based solely on the material constitution of the objects that bear them (one cannot discover the monetary value of a gold coin through an analysis of its chemical constitution [see Ilyenkov, 1977: 89]), philosophers have typically argued that they must originate in the mind of the individual beholder.

However, Ilyenkov follows Marx in rejecting this analysis. He dismisses theories that take the ideal to exist purely in individual consciousness and the real to be everything 'out there', and maintains that those who believe that all properties must either be objective parts of the material world or ideas in the mind hold a 'crudely naive', 'vulgar', 'superficial' and 'silly' materialism (1977: 73, 96).

Hegel makes the ideal a product of the *collective*, rather than individual, consciousness. Ilyenkov describes collective consciousness this way:

> social consciousness is not simply the many times repeated individual consciousness . . . but is, in fact, a historically formed and historically developing system of 'objective notions', forms and patterns of the 'objective spirit', of the 'collective reason' of *mankind* . . . all this being quite independent of individual caprices of consciousness or will. (1977: 77)

Ilyenkov follows Hegel to the extent that he gives a distinctly social analysis to ideal properties:

> [Ideal] objects are, in their existence, in their 'present being', substantial, 'material', but in their essence, in their origin, they are ideal because they 'embody' the collective thinking of people, the 'universal spirit' of mankind. (1977: 81)

Ilyenkov's use of Hegel gives the ideal an essentially historical character; ideal objects are the products of collective activity over a long period of time.

Ilyenkov distinguishes ideal properties such as monetary value from subjective reactions to one's environment, and from subjective illusions or imagination. There is an objective value that a gold coin or a dollar bill possesses within a particular economic community, which is clear from the fact that an individual might mistake this value or imagine it wrongly. Ilyenkov says that 'the form of value . . . exists outside human consciousness and independently of it' (1977: 72).

This is not to say that individuals play no role in the development of ideal properties. Ilyenkov follows Marx in giving a material foundation to Hegel's social analysis of the ideal, one based on the actions of individuals over time. Value, for both Marx and Ilyenkov, is not grounded in the brute material constitution of the valuable object, nor in the mind of the beholder, but rather in the *activity* that has produced the object. And for Ilyenkov:

> Ideality is a characteristic of *things*, not as they are determined by nature but as they are determined by *labour*, the transforming and form-creating activity of social man, his *purposeful*, sensuously objective activity. (1977: 97)

Once subject to this transformative historical process, objects such as dollar bills or the sounds, inscriptions or gestures we call 'language' come to embody certain conventional patterns of activity.

Ilyenkov makes several comments concerning the effect that ideal properties have on the individual human beings who grow up in their midst. In these comments, we see Ilyenkov echo Whorf in claiming that cultural artifacts such as language can shape the human individual. Thus:

> The child that has just been born is confronted . . . by a very complex system of culture, which requires of him 'modes of behaviour' for which there is genetically (morphologically) 'no code' in his body. Here it is not a matter of *adjusting ready-made patterns of behaviour*, but of *assimilating* modes of life

activity that do not *bear any relationship at all* to the biologically necessary forms of the reactions of his organism to things and situations. (Ilyenkov, 1977: 93)

Acculturated human beings do not merely satisfy biological drives such as hunger; they channel those drives through the use of idealized artifacts such as knives, forks and spoons, which embody conventional table manners. Human beings are thus not 'natural' beings, but are themselves shaped by the environment which the actions of previous human beings have shaped before them. As Ilyenkov writes:

> The consciousness and will that arise in the mind of the human individual are the direct consequence of the fact that what he is confronted by as the object of his life activity is not nature as such, but nature that has been transformed by the labour of previous generations, shaped by human labour, nature in the forms of human life activity. (1977: 94)

Ilyenkov's work expresses a general metaphysical description of the dialectical relationship between a human individual and that individual's linguistic community. We will see below how, informed by similar conceptions, Vygotsky describes the specific dialectical relationship between language and the development of thought.

Vygotsky, thought and language

The two main principles which underlie Vygotsky's view of language are that language is a tool and that language is a vehicle for the mediation of thought. I will consider these principles of Vygotsky's theory in turn.

Tools   Vygotsky studied the use of tools both as a model for language use and as a psychological process in itself. Tools are significant for Vygotsky because he found that when human subjects begin to use them, language and thought begin to coalesce. While very young children exhibit some capacity to use tools before they learn to use language (about the same level of tool use that animals exhibit), older children use what Vygotsky calls an 'alloy' of language and the use of tools (Vygotsky, 1978: 25, 30). He writes:

> Children confronted with a problem that is slightly too complicated for them exhibit a complex variety of responses including direct attempts at attaining the goal, the use of tools, speech directed toward the person conducting the experiment or speech that simply accompanies the action, and direct, verbal appeals to the object of attention itself. (1978: 30)

This combination of activities is an alloy because no part can be separated out; Vygotsky claims that when children were told to perform the task silently, they either would fail to achieve the goal or would 'freeze up' (1978: 25). From these observations, he concluded that there was an intimate connection between language and the use of tools in the cognitive development of the child.

Vygotsky shows how tools and language begin to differentiate, in his observations of children's interactions with toys. He argues that very young children's cognition is rooted in the concrete, and therefore their activities are constrained and motivated by the objects in their immediate environment. He says that '*things* dictate to a child what he must do: a door demands to be opened and closed, a staircase to be climbed, a bell to be rung' (1978: 96).

As children begin to engage in play, they are escaping the external constraints of their environment, and are beginning to be constrained instead by the internal rules of the imaginary situation. Vygotsky observes:

> Children, in playing at eating from a plate, have been shown to perform actions with their hands reminiscent of real eating. . . . Throwing one's hands back instead of stretching them forward toward the plate turned out to be impossible for such an action would have a destructive effect on the game. (1978: 100)

Toys are not yet fully symbolic objects, though, because certain properties of the objects still constrain activities performed with them. Vygotsky points out that 'any stick can be a horse . . . but a postcard cannot be a horse for a child', although a postcard could easily stand for a horse for an adult (1978: 98). Toys are not themselves semantically meaningful objects, but they are important *pivots* for detaching meaning from objects and attaching it to the symbols that take their place (see Vygotsky, 1978: 97).

Mediation   Both the use of tools and play are activities that require external objects. Vygotsky calls activity that is organized in part by external objects 'mediated activity'. Mediation proceeds through a number of different developmental stages. Vygotsky illustrates this process by describing the role of mediation in memory (1978: ch. 3).[5] 'Natural memory' is similar to eidetic imagery, and it is akin to perception, in that it involves a direct response to a stimulus. 'Mediated memory' involves interposing a second stimulus, such as a knot in a string, to remind a subject of the first stimulus: 'In higher forms of human behaviour, the individual actively modifies the stimulus situation as a part of the process of responding to it' (Cole and Scribner, 1978: 13–14). When human beings reach the developmental stage at which they employ signs to mediate memory, two transformations take place. First, their minds are now able to operate with mediated memory. Second, objects in their environment are given new 'identities' to serve mediation and help them produce proper responses. This recalls the description Ilyenkov gives of the effects of the ideal on the human individual.

According to Vygotsky, after subjects develop the ability to operate with mediated memory, the next stage is for them to internalize the mediating objects, and start to use internal signs. Internalization is especially crucial for Vygotsky's theory of the development of language use because for him, words and signs start out as *external* objects, not internal ones, as in Fodor's language of thought. Language is first a possession of the child's community, society or culture. Children master language only by internalizing what is at first an operation performed with external objects.

Vygotsky draws an analogy with the internalization of pointing as a meaningful gesture (1978: 56). First, a child makes a natural, grasping gesture toward an object. Adults around the child *read* the grasping gesture as an act of pointing. The child then internalizes the significance accorded to the gesture by adults, and performs it again *for them*. According to Vygotsky's analysis, the gesture is transformed from an object-oriented action to an action aimed at another person (see Bakhurst, 1991: 76–9).

The same process occurs with speech, but after it achieves a social function, speech is internalized once more, and changes from a fundamentally communicative practice to one designed to help order the subject's *own* thinking.[6] Vygotsky maintains that 'every function in the child's cultural development appears twice: first on the social level, and later, on the individual level; first *between* people (*interpsychological*), and then *inside* the child (*intrapsychological*)' (1978: 57). Elsewhere, he writes that:

> When children develop a method of behaviour for guiding themselves that had previously been used in relation to another person, when they organize their own activities according to a social form of behaviour, they succeed in applying a social attitude to themselves. This history of the process of *the internalization of social speech* is also the history of the socialization of children's practical intellect. (1978: 27)

Because internalization is the turning inward of some process that formerly had a social function, the internalization of social speech equals the socialization of the intellect. In going through the stages of natural psychology, mediated activity and internalization, the child's mind is transformed.

Vygotsky, Fodor and Whorf: similarities and differences

Fodor and Whorf represent respectively the individualistic and communitarian extremes in the study of language and thought. Fodor's theory starts with a set of individualistic assumptions about the mind – that it is computational and contains an innate language of thought, that it perceives the world through automatic, fixed and physically determined causal processes, that it is sufficient to study it solipsistically – and what he says about meaning and language follows from those assumptions. According to Fodor, the human mind produces meanings by reflecting the external world. These meanings are communicated via language but are not affected by language. For Whorf, on the other hand, language contains meanings which construct both the mind and the world it occupies.

Vygotsky's work presents a middle way between these positions. First, a Vygotskian semantics can incorporate some of the good points of Fodor's view, while avoiding its problems. Vygotsky recognizes that the self is a social and contextualized creature living in an interactive network with others, but he does not ignore the contributions the physical sciences can make to understanding the human individual. Vygotsky studied the neurological bases of human behaviour, and his interest in the psychological effects of neurological damage shows that he acknowledged that there are innate neurological similarities shared by all human beings (for examples, see Vygotsky, 1978: 19–20, 45 and 55; Luria, 1979: 121–2). Vygotsky would agree with Fodor that children come to language-learning with certain innate cognitive abilities and certain natural motivations. Therefore, Fodor and Vygotsky share the assumption that it is appropriate to look to science when studying the individual.

However, Vygotsky would not agree with Fodor that biology alone endows children with a full set of concepts in their 'Mentalese' language, nor would he accept the view that these are never subject to change during the child's life.[7] Vygotsky believed that innate abilities and motivations are transformed when a child engages in activity and interaction with others. This belief underlies his research on the transition between the concrete and abstract stages of human cognitive development. What starts out as biological becomes social, in Vygotsky's theory.

A Vygotskian semantics will therefore avoid the problems that confront Fodor's semantic theory. Neither objects nor concepts need be rigidly individuated from the outset; indeed, the point of Ilyenkov's discussion of idealization is that objects are transformed by participating as part of a human social form of life. While for Fodor there was a passive, purely representational relation between the individual and objects in the environment, for those in the Vygotskian tradition the two domains are in a dynamic relationship – human beings transform the objects in the environment (into tools, toys, mediators or signs), and those objects transform human beings as well, turning them into the kinds of creatures that can inhabit a world of Ilyenkovian ideal properties.

A Vygotskian semantics can also improve upon Whorf's view. While Vygotsky's work is not tied solely to mental representation and the stark explanatory resources of 'psychophysics', he is not forced to embrace as the only available alternative the idea that the mind is wholly socially constructed. Whorf emphasizes only one side of the dynamic relationship between individual and culture. A Vygotskian theory that incorporates the transformative nature of labour will include an account of the way in which human beings transform their cultural environment as well as the way in which that environment affects them. As John Lucy and James Wertsch have argued, Whorf gives us only a synchronic analysis of language and culture; Whorf does not consider the development of cultural practices or the *dynamic* relationship between culture and language as it changes over time (Lucy and Wertsch, 1987: 75–8).

More importantly, unlike Whorf, Vygotsky's works do include explanations of, or at least hypotheses about, the '*hows*' of these processes. As a psychologist, he studied the actual stages children undergo as they learn language, and the ways children's thought processes and use of objects are transformed at different developmental stages. By looking at the actual development of concepts and language skills, Vygotsky aspires to a better and more balanced picture of language and culture, *with* the 'hows'. A Vygotskian perspective will preserve the social and cultural element of Whorf's theory, while also incorporating a recognition of the innate contribution of the individual recognized in Fodor's theory, and providing explanations of the *means* by which between individual thought, language and society influence each other.

Beyond Vygotsky – a social theory of meaning

Vygotsky was not himself a semanticist, but in his work and the work of his successors, particularly Ilyenkov, one can find the principles of a semantic theory that grounds word-meaning in the social realm. Ilyenkov's theory of ideal properties gives a metaphysical foundation to such a theory. Semantic value is a property which artifacts (such as spoken or written words) gain on the basis of their being employed in conventional patterns of human activity. Words, as artifacts, gain meaning on the basis of their history of use. A Vygotskian semantic theory will thus be a kind of 'use theory', sharing company with other use theories of meaning, including those of J. L. Austin (1962), John Searle (1969), and Ludwig Wittgenstein (1953).

A Vygotskian theory also shares a metaphysical basis with functionalist theories, those which identify meaning with functional role. A prominent semantic theory of this kind is conceptual role semantics, advocated by Gilbert Harman (1982), Ned Block (1986), and Hartry Field (1977). Conceptual role semantics identifies the meaning of a mental representation with its role in a subject's overall cognitive economy. In contrast, a Vygotskian semantic theory would concentrate on the functional roles of representations in natural language, which are external and publicly observable. Nonetheless, the basic idea behind both semantic theories is the same.

Most important, a Vygotskian semantic theory would be able to provide a robust theory of the communicative function of language, while not neglecting the individual and the individual's innate capacities. As we saw, communication is generally ignored by individualistic, 'head-first' semantic theories.

While a Vygotskian theory of meaning would avoid the problematic individualism we found in Fodor's semantic theory, it does not do so by embracing a radical social constructivism such as Whorf's. A Vygotskian theory of meaning in no sense need suggest that human understanding is prevented because of the radical incommensurability of the world's languages. It therefore provides a better account of communication than either Fodor or Whorf can.

Philosophers of language could benefit a great deal from looking to Vygotsky's work for inspiration. Traditional empiricist assumptions about the mind, self and language might begin to be questioned, and some of the problems in contemporary philosophy of language might eventually be resolved. One can only hope that future scholars will pay attention to Vygotsky's insights and principles in building new theories of language and thought.

Notes

1. However, see Novak, 1992 for an interpretation that identifies Fodor's language of thought with genes rather than synapses.
2. Others in the tradition include Gilbert Harman (1974, 1982), Hartry Field (1977), Dennis Stampe (1977), Fred Dretske (1981), and Ned Block (1986).
3. Thanks to André Gallois for this formulation.
4. Helen Watson-Verran's work with Yolngu children bears out Whorf's claim. Contrary to traditional assessments made by white Australian schoolteachers, Yolngu children are not fundamentally incapable of mastering a patterned formal system such as Western mathematics. Their system of kinship relations is equally formal and patterned (Watson-Verran, 1993). Whorf might understand their system as a comparable but different expression of the universal human urge to formalize.
5. Vygotsky reports an experiment by Leontiev in which the experimenters studied the progressive development of mediated memory in children in Vygotsky, 1978: 40–5.
6. In arguing that social speech precedes egocentric speech, Vygotsky is quite self-consciously contradicting the conclusions drawn by Piaget concerning childhood language development and the nature of egocentric speech; see Vygotsky, 1986: ch. 2.
7. These issues are targeted in Fodor's review of the 1962 translation of Vygotsky's *Thought and Language* (Fodor, 1972).

References

Austin, J. L. (1962) *How to Do Things With Words*, ed. J. O. Urmson and Marina Sbisa. Oxford: Oxford University Press.

Bakhurst, David (1991) *Consciousness and Revolution in Soviet Philosophy*. Cambridge: Cambridge University Press.

Block, Ned (1986) 'Advertisement for a semantics for psychology', in P. French, T. Uehling and H. Wettstein (eds), *Midwest Studies in Philosophy, Vol. 10. Studies in Contemporary Semantics*. Minneapolis: University of Minnesota Press.

Brown, Penelope, and Levinson, Stephen C. (1987) *Politeness: Some Universals in Language Usage*. Cambridge: Cambridge University Press.

Cole, Michael and Scribner, Sylvia (1978), Introduction to Vygotsky (1978).

Davidson, Donald (1974) 'On the very idea of a conceptual scheme', *Proceedings and Addresses of the American Philosophical Association*, Vol. 47, reprinted in his *Inquiries into Truth and Interpretation*. Oxford: Oxford University Press, 1984.

Devitt, Michael, and Sterelny, Kim (1987) *Language and Reality*. Cambridge, MA: Harvard University Press.

Dretske, Fred I. (1981) *Knowledge and the Flow of Information*. Cambridge, MA: MIT Press.

Field, Hartry (1977) 'Logic, meaning and conceptual role', *Journal of Philosophy*, 74.

Fodor, Jerry A. (1972) 'Some reflections on L. S. Vygotsky's *Thought and Language*', *Cognition*, 1(1).

Fodor, Jerry A. (1975) *The Language of Thought*. Cambridge, MA: Harvard University Press.

Fodor, Jerry A. (1980) 'Methodological solipsism considered as a research strategy in cognitive psychology', *Behavioral and Brain Sciences*, 3(1), reprinted in his *Representations*. Cambridge, MA: MIT Press, 1981.

Fodor, Jerry A. (1987) *Psychosemantics*. Cambridge, MA: MIT Press.

Geertz, Clifford (1974) 'From the native's point of view: on the nature of anthropological understanding', *Bulletin of the Academy of Arts and Sciences*, 28(1).

Harman, Gilbert (1974) 'Meaning and semantics', in M. K. Munitz and Peter Unger (eds), *Semantics and Philosophy*. New York: New York University Press.

Harman, Gilbert (1982) 'Conceptual role semantics', *Notre Dame Journal of Formal Logic*, 23(2).

Hobbes, Thomas (1651) *Leviathan*. New York: Collier Books, 1962.

Hume, David (1739) *A Treatise of Human Nature*, ed. L. A. Selby-Bigge. 2nd edn, revised by P. H. Nidditch. Oxford: Oxford University Press, 1978.

Ilyenkov, E. V. (1977) 'The concept of the ideal', in *Philosophy in the USSR: Problems of Dialectical Materialism*, trans. Robert Daglish. Moscow: Progress.

Lenneberg, Eric H. (1953) 'Cognition in ethnolinguistics', *Language*, 29.

Levinson, Stephen C. (1983) *Pragmatics*. Cambridge: Cambridge University Press.

Locke, John (1690) *An Essay Concerning Human Understanding*, in two volumes. New York: Dover, 1959.

Lucy, John A. (1985) 'Whorf's view of the linguistic mediation of thought', in E. Mertz and R. J. Parmentier (eds), *Semiotic Mediation: Sociocultural and Psychological Perspectives*. New York: Academic Press.

Lucy, John A. and Wertsch, James V. (1987) 'Vygotsky and Whorf: a comparative analysis', in Maya Hickmann (ed.), *Social and Functional Approaches to Language and Thought*. New York: Academic Press.

Luria, A. R. (1979) *The Making of Mind*, ed. Michael Cole and Sheila Cole. Cambridge, MA: Harvard University Press.

Novak, Milos (1992) 'Mental symbols'. PhD dissertation, University of Queensland.

Rosch, Eleanor (1977) 'Linguistic relativity', in P. N. Johnson-Laird and P. C. Wason (eds), *Thinking: Readings in Cognitive Science*. Cambridge: Cambridge University Press.

Searle, John R. (1969) *Speech Acts: An Essay in the Philosophy of Language*. Cambridge: Cambridge University Press.

Stampe, Dennis W. (1977) 'Toward a causal theory of linguistic representation', in P. French, T. Uehling, and H. Wettstein (eds), *Midwest Studies in Philosophy, Vol. 2. Contemporary Perspectives in the Philosophy of Language*. Minneapolis: University of Minnesota Press.

Vygotsky, L. S. (1978) *Mind in Society: The Development of Higher Psychological Processes*, ed. and trans. Michael Cole, Vera John-Steiner, Sylvia Scribner and Ellen Souberman. Cambridge, MA: Harvard University Press.

Vygotsky, L. S. (1986) *Thought and Language*, revised edn., ed. Alex Kozulin. Cambridge, MA: MIT Press.

Watson-Verran, Helen (1993) 'Mapping logics with clotting reason: mixing metaphors from Aboriginal and Western traditions', Paper delivered at the International Working Conference on Non-Formal Foundations of Reason, 1–6 August, Newcastle, New South Wales, Australia.

Whorf, Benjamin Lee (1956) *Language, Thought and Reality*. New York: Wiley.

Wittgenstein, Ludwig (1953) *Philosophical Investigations*, trans. G. E. M. Anscombe. 2nd edn. Oxford: Blackwell, 1967.

5

The Soviet Self: A Personal Reminiscence

Felix Mikhailov

I

My appointed topic is the idea that human individuals are 'socially constituted beings' as it found expression in twentieth-century Russian Marxism. This is by no means a straightforward subject, for Soviet Marxism is a peculiarly complex phenomenon. Just as philosophers at the end of the nineteenth century pondered whether God is dead, so at the time of writing philosophers of the former USSR are preoccupied with the question: is Karl Marx dead in Russia? When I hear this question, I want to ask 'Which Karl Marx?', for I know at least two, and both are quite real, not imaginary (imaginary Marxes are, of course, many more in number). Moreover, the two got along together admirably while co-habiting the body of a single living individual. It was with this duality, this ambiguity, that the man named Karl Marx influenced more than a century of human history, appearing for some as the prophet of the triumph of justice, and for others as a harbinger of totalitarianism. Accordingly, after the collapse of 'Russian socialism', two distinct voices can be heard above the general din. One cries, 'Marx is dead at last in Russia and thank God for that!', while the other responds that Marx died in Russia long ago; Russians hardly knew him at all.

In my view, it is the very duality of Marx himself that is to blame for this dispute. Let me begin by describing the first Marx. This is the Marx of *Grundrisse*, of *Capital*, of the early *Economic and Philosophical Manuscripts* and the very late works on the history and economics of Russia, China and India. This Marx conducted careful research on the differences between the natural philosophies of Epicurus and Democritus, and on Hegel's *Philosophy of Right*. Hegel is perhaps the most important influence on this Marx. Indeed, some time ago, at the plenary session of an international Hegel conference in Salzburg, Russian philosopher Evald Ilyenkov brought his paper to a close somewhat abruptly with the words: 'I think that contemporary Marxists will sooner or later find the courage to admit that Marxism is just Hegelianism in the twentieth century'. Ilyenkov's declaration created something of a stir, coming as it did from a Soviet thinker, but in fact his words were actually close to a banal truth. The great edifice of Hegelian philosophy was the family home from which

Marx set out on his intellectual journey. He never lost sight of the light from its windows, and that light illuminated Marx's road to the crucial idea of human beings as workers.

We should observe that, in Russian translations, the multiple meanings of the German word for work, *die Arbeit*, are reduced to one, *labour* (*trud*), and *der Arbeiter* is translated exclusively as 'worker' (*rabochii*) in the sense of industrial labourer or proletarian. This obscures the fact that, for all his emphasis on industrial labour, Marx, in both the early and late writings, intends the concept of work to embrace any activity, including intellectual activity, concerned with the purposeful (*tselesoobrazno*) transformation of the objective (*ob"ektivno-predmetnye*) conditions of human life. This broad conception of work forms the basis of a distinctive philosophical anthropology. It is a vision of human beings creating themselves through labour. Human beings act on the world to satisfy their needs. In so doing, they change the very character of their world, for the results of human activity endure. Human beings create artifacts, signs and symbols, and other material embodiments of culture, which stand before them in the environment as 'objectified' forms of activity. Thus, the world with which we engage is not brutely natural in kind, but one 'humanized' by social labour. As we change the world, so the world confronts us anew with new demands for action. As we create and recreate our environment so we change our horizons, making circumstances which force us to remake ourselves. It is not just that the material transformation of the world generates new desires which provoke further transformations, and so on. More than this, each member of each new generation attains personhood by coming to appropriate (and perhaps even transcend) those forms of social activity which constitute our world. Thus, we each become who we are through assimilating the objectified activity of previous generations. It is in this sense that we are 'socially constituted beings'; that in Marx's words, 'the human essence is no abstraction inherent in each single individual. In its reality it is the ensemble of social relations' (Marx, 1845: 29).

This philosophical anthropology is crucial to Marx's understanding of communism. It may be true that human beings create themselves by creating their world. But throughout history, human beings have been unable to control, or to understand, the forces their collective activity unleashes. On the contrary, those forces have often been a source of enslavement. Hence the life-activity of the wage labourer under capitalism is subordinated entirely to the socioeconomic relations which define him or her. Nevertheless, for Marx, the development of capitalism promises to create the circumstances in which human beings can master the powers with which they make their lives and establish a revolutionary new form of social life – communism – in which those powers can self-consciously be harnessed to issue in conditions in which universal human flourishing is possible.

History makes us what we are and, accordingly, Marx's works must be read in their historical context. Centuries of intellectual labour – the labour of human self-understanding – culminated in the philosophical culture of the nineteenth century. First, the Greek understanding of man as a 'microcosm', who has within him the measure and meaning of Chaos ordered by the gods but who is powerless before fate; then Christian humility, where human beings are so tragically dependent on freedom of choice and responsibility for their own life; then the Renaissance understanding of human beings as rivals to God in their creative and active capacities; and finally, individuality as Protestantism understood it, particularized and free from personal dependence. The human essence, which in Kant and Hegel became a premise for the very cognition of the world, of scientific knowledge of natural phenomena, remains today the focus of uncompromising controversy. The first Marx made a weighty contribution to this controversy, which has subsequently been deepened by the work of many others. Marx's focus on the history of human community was an anticipation of, and to some degree an unrecognized precondition for, those searchings for 'the secret of human existence' undertaken in the twentieth century by Freud, the French ethno-sociologists, the American pragmatists, and others. Indeed, if we exclude naturalistically minded exponents of natural-scientific mechanism, those 'last Mohicans' of Robinson Crusoe epistemology (the logic of which was already toppled at the turn of the nineteenth century by classical German philosophy), then in this century there have been no serious thinkers exploring the human essence who have not focused on the history of relations between people. That man is a political animal was already clear to Aristotle. But the twentieth century is distinguished by inquiry into the character of our communal existence and how the unceasing reproduction of our forms of community directly and immediately influences the realization of the intimate, personal characteristics of individuals. Regardless of whether such research is pro- or anti-Marx or indifferent to him, the fact that twentieth-century thought is preoccupied with the inter-determination of individual and society has a lot to do with Marx's influence.

We are still speaking of our first Marx, of Marx the theoretician, whose works magnificently articulate humanity's historical self-realization, the forces behind the human essence's taking root in Being and its development in a multiplicity of specific, concrete forms. On his view, the historical process is a result of the powers of human beings, who are required not so much to appropriate the necessary means of life as to *produce* them in an end-oriented and purposeful way, to produce in such a way that everybody creates something necessary to others and only thereby receives what is necessary for himself, and hence all together create and recreate the means of their community with each other, the forms of their common being. Moreover, this Marx maintains that there is a historical tendency, implicit in the social division of labour, towards the direct expression of the social essence of all individual types of labour, the tendency towards the immediate revelation of the necessity and value of each type for all others (and, hence, the necessity and value of each acting individual). At the beginning of history – that is, in the so-called 'primitive-tribal' community – the division of labour was made on the basis of sex and age and the exchange of necessary labour and its products was really carried out immediately ('within the family', so to speak). Later – in agriculture, animal husbandry, crafts, trade, industrial production, and so on – all the increasingly fragmented and specialized types of labour remained, as Marx demonstrated, socially necessary.

These are important theoretical achievements, but they are only part of the story. The twentieth century has been, for both individuals and their societies, a century of tragic ordeals. The terrible reality of the Fascist dictatorships made the ideal of harmonious relations between individual people and collectivizing humanity seem awfully remote in practice. And it is a great irony that one of the most all-pervasive tyrannical systems, penetrating the souls of four generations of people, is associated with Marx himself, who sought a happy interdependence of social being and unique individuality. Precisely this system – the system of socialism once 'victorious on one sixth of the planet' – is called 'Marxist'.

The irony is compounded by the fact that Marx can be read as a critic of the very kind of communism that eventually came to be. As a Hegelian of materialist orientation, Marx was one of the first Western thinkers (in Russia there was Dostoevsky some time later) who decried the idea that private property as such was the principal cause of poverty, hunger, hatred and greed, and should be abolished in favour of 'equal shares for all'. For Marx, such a view was both utopian and reactionary. In 1844, Marx wrote prophetic lines about the kind of communism in which the abolition of private property is nothing other than a manifestation of the envy of those who have not yet attained the level of private property (Marx, 1844: 94–6). Where that envy is given free rein, everyone is reduced to the lowest common denominator, to the position of the poorest and most destitute. Such a society throws itself and its members back into the pre-feudal era. Later, Marx anticipated the possibility of revolution in Russia and the subsequent emergence of 'barrack-room communism'. Indeed, he was mindful of this kind of communism throughout his life, not allowing his comrades in the Workers' International a single concession to the regressive principle: 'Seize everything and divide it equally.'

Marx was not opposed to the term 'communism', of course, and appropriated it with a dialectical twist for his own position. It is as if he said to his opponents: 'You want communism, the sharing (*obshchnost'*) of all goods (and perhaps women too, whom you conceive of as goods), the universal equality of all working people. But communism is something else; the communal, comradely uniting of owner-workers cannot be achieved by an act of will by impatient and envious people. Communism must await the full realization of capitalism, wherein production is fully mechanized, the exchange of commodities universal, and diverse forms of labour rendered equivalent. In short, only when the development of industry necessitates the socialization of labour – then and only then will the conditions for the socialization of property be ripe, so that property may lose its primitive form and give rise to a system of human relations where each person will be first and foremost an owner of the reified (*oveshchestvlennyi*) labour of all – an owner of the earth, and that which labour prospects from its depths and builds upon its surface. It follows that only the freedom of each person is the condition of the freedom of all. But for you it is precisely the other way around.

'Moreover,' Marx would continue against his vulgar communist opponents, 'you assume that freedom can be achieved by the fiat of a free people's government. But freedom cannot be imposed externally by a "people's administration", rising like a *deus ex machina* out of the ruins of the government you hope to sweep away. All that will result is "freedom" heavily dependent on administrators and petty bureaucrats, the agents of those who control the apparatus of administration and coercion – the "new owners" of "state property".'

It would be naive, however, to focus entirely on the words of Marx the theoretician in an effort to absolve Marx from responsibility for the strange reality of communism as it actually came to be. It is time we spoke about a second Marx – the Marx who was immersed in the political controversies and upheavals of the second half of the nineteenth century. We must consider the Marx who wrote for Chartist newspapers in England and who, before that, was an opponent of Prussian absolutism and French reaction. This is the Marx who led the International, the author of brilliant political pamphlets and scathing polemics, the Marx who charted empirically the development of the socialization of labour and the influence of the hidden (and at that time little recognized) economic interests of social classes, strata and groups. This Marx was himself a utopian, hastily equating the socialization of labour with the progress of the industrial proletariat, in contradistinction to fundamental tenets of his own theory which pertain to the socialization of *all* forms of labour (spiritual, as well as material). Moreover, Marx's suspicion that crude communism would breed authoritarian politics sits uneasily in his work alongside the idea of the dictatorship of the proletariat, the class whose historical mission is to sweep aside by force the old conditions of production (Marx and Engels, 1848: 53). In the *Communist Manifesto* and the political articles and brochures of the later period, Marx the politician always saw the struggle for the victory of communism as a case where 'the end justifies the means', sadly oblivious to the notorious law by which such means quickly become ends in themselves.

Our second Marx continues to see the human essence as 'the ensemble of social relations', but this idea finds rather different expression than in the high theory of the first Marx. Human history is represented primarily as a history of class struggles (Marx and Engels, 1848: 35) and individuals figure in this conception in so far as they are representatives of particular classes. Our position in the social order makes us what we are and determines our objective interests. Moreover, as history progresses, so the social order becomes more clearly polarized, and in the modern era 'two great hostile camps' directly face one another: the bourgeoisie and the proletariat, the oppressors and the oppressed (Marx and Engels, 1848: 36). Our identity as individuals is defined by the camp in which we find ourselves.

Should we conclude, then, that when Russian democrats blame Marx for what the Russian people endured at the hands of the leaders of the Revolution and the dictators of the post-revolutionary period, it is in fact the second Marx who is the legitimate target of their criticisms? This view has something to recommend it, but it is also naive. I believe the situation is more complex. First, the two Marxes are really inseparable from one another. The publicist and politician, for all the passion in his soul, needed the abstract and reasoned analysis of the theoretician, and vice versa. Without the concept of the proletariat and its historical mission (and Marx identified the role of the working class in the socialization of labour when he was still a Young Hegelian), Marx would never have uncovered the secret of surplus value. Moreover, Marx's deployment of the concept of class is compatible with the philosophical anthropology of the first Marx. The image of an antagonistic struggle between hostile classes is not at odds with the idea of human beings creating themselves in and through activity; the class struggle is, for Marx, part of the history of human self-transcendence, for that struggle is to issue in the abolition of all classes in favour of 'an association, in which the free development of each is the condition for the free development of all' (Marx and Engels, 1848: 53).

A second complicating factor is that it is by no means clear that we should portray either Marx as the principal inspiration for Bolshevism. We should not represent the first principles of the Bolsheviks as the idea, generalized from the experience of the Paris Commune, that the bourgeois governmental machine be destroyed in favour of the self-rule of the armed masses, nor as an attempt to adapt Marxism to Russian conditions by, for example, creating armies of workers from the peasantry after the proletariat's victory in the cities. Rather, the tragic strategy of revolution and dictatorship of the party-cum-government had its core in the Russian peasant-lumpen movement (see Mikhailov, 1990). Notably, at the time of the revolution and civil war, Marxists like Plekhanov, former Marxists such as Berdyaev, and members of the intelligentsia, such as Korolenko and Gorky, who had a keen sense of the historical self-consciousness of the people, did not for a minute identify the ideology and practice of the Bolsheviks with the theory, or even the political proclamations, of the founders of Marxism. On the contrary, what they saw in Bolshevism was *Nechaevism*.[1]

However, neither in Russia nor anywhere else where 'Asiatic despotism' dressed itself up in twentieth-century garb and promised a 'thousand-year reign', was a Nechaev made an icon on the red flag of revolution. It was Marx who was given that role. This is because Marx could be portrayed simultaneously as a respectable scholar and as leader of the world proletariat, the uniting of which promised the transformation from the realm of necessity to the realm of freedom. Marx was a world authority who had revealed the sources of exploitation and showed the path to communism. As such he was a suitable prophet and teacher to light the Party's way, providing its leaders with the 'scientific' foresight necessary for flawless social and economic planning. Thus Marx was given to the masses as a charismatic leader of leaders, as a new god incarnate. To this end, the leadership and its swarm of ideologists carefully 'prepared' the texts of Marx and Engels for some eighty years. They published them in many forms from collected works to slender brochures, reproducing and representing their words in such combinations as to create an uncomplicated compendium of symbols for the new era. With this a third Marx was born: the paper Marx of Soviet ideology.

As is well known, long before the Bolsheviks, Marx responded to such appropriations of his work with the words, 'If that is Marxism, then I am no Marxist.' But who among the peddlers of 'scientific communism', who knew Marx only from ideological primers of 'Marxism-Leninism', could appreciate the bitter irony of their teacher's rejoinder? This irony was at the expense, not of Marx himself, but of history, which has seen the creation of ever more subtle mechanisms for controlling the lives of ordinary people in the service of the interests of more powerful others.

This third Marx also brings with him a conception of the person as socially constituted. For this Marx, the person is simply a function of the social structure. Or as Stalin succinctly put it, the individual is a 'cog' in the social mechanism.[2] I shall not dignify this conception by giving it an exposition in a theoretical voice. Let me instead illustrate with a personal anecdote what it is to see a human being as a cog.

My mother was a paediatrician and by all accounts an excellent one. She was a good diagnostician and a caring, self-sacrificing doctor. I remember that, as a young child, I would often awake to find that Mother had brought some sick child back to our home, where she could keep an eye on his or her progress. And in those years, we lived in conditions typical of the majority of Muscovites: home was a single room in a crowded apartment shared with other families. Mother worked for thirty years in district secondary school No. 175. The school drew its pupils largely from the neighbouring buildings. However, for some reason the school was held in high regard by the party leadership and in 1933 Stalin's children, Vasilii and Svetlana, began to study there. Soon thereafter other leading lights in the government transferred their children to the school: Molotov's daughter, Beria's son, the children of Bulganin, Mikoyan and other People's Commissars. Naturally, the well-being of Vasilii and Svetlana Stalin was deemed to be paramount among the school doctor's concerns. After all, as the people sang in those days, Stalin was 'Lenin today!'

The years between 1933 and 1938 were terrible times. Indeed, my mother had lost her brother in one of the purges. One day, Svetlana Stalin came to school unaccompanied. (Interestingly, the daughter of the General Secretary, as if to demonstrate the democratic nature of her father, made the trip from the Kremlin with her bodyguard by trolleybus, although the children of other prominent parents arrived at the school steps in limousines.) My mother examined her and sent her off to class. Mother then went to the vestibule to observe the other children as they arrived. Suddenly, Svetlana's bodyguard dashed into the school. He was pale, his hands were shaking, and his voice trembled almost beyond control:

'Is Svetlana here? Has she arrived?' he gasped.

When he learnt that Stalin's daughter was already in class, he reached into his pocket and, in open view, took out his pistol and reset the safety catch.

'If you'd said she wasn't here,' he confessed, 'I would have shot myself.'

This incident was only one among many. A few days later, my mother was urgently summoned to the Principal's office. The Principal was an experienced teacher with the unfortunate surname of Groza ('danger' or 'terror'), though there was nothing terrible about her: she was a kind, calm and self-assured woman. My mother arrived to find the following scene. The Principal was reclining in an armchair, quite overcome. There were two men in the room, unmistakably members of the secret police. On the Principal's desk lay a plate covered with a napkin.

'Doctor,' one of the secret policemen snapped, 'did you taste the food in the school refectory today?'

'Of course,' Mother replied. Sampling the school food was one of the duties of the school doctor.

'Did you taste *this*?' The interrogator dramatically snatched the napkin from the plate, revealing a piece of meat somewhat green in hue. 'That's what our leader's daughter was given for breakfast! Collect your things, you are under arrest.'

My mother was taken to the renowned Lubianka prison. After two or three days in solitary confinement, she was brought to interrogation. She was asked to sign a 'voluntary confession' which the investigating officer began to dictate: 'I, so-and-so, admit that I sought revenge on Comrade Stalin for the arrest of my brother; I entered into an agreement with the cook at the school refectory, a Trotskyite and enemy of the people, with the aim of poisoning the daughter of our leader.' Mother refused to put her name to such nonsense. They did not beat or torture her, but simply took her back to her cell. She assumed, however, that she was finished, and passed the days waiting to be shot. (It is interesting that she described herself as awaiting, not trial, but death, as if·by some sixth sense she knew that trials by this time had become a mere formality, a kind of prelude to execution.)

Suddenly, however, she was brought back before the investigating officer. His manner had changed; he invited her to sit down.

'We've taken another look at your case. You are innocent. The cook was working without accomplices. You can go home and tomorrow you can go back to work as usual.'

At first, Mother did not immediately understand what the investigator had said. Noticing this, he leaned towards her and, as if revealing a secret, said,

'Light a tall candle in Yelokhovskii Cathedral for Polina Semyénova Zhemchuzhina [Molotov's wife and Commissar for light industry]. She saved you. Now go, and not a word to anyone about what you have seen or heard here.'

Zhemchuzhina-Molotova was profoundly grateful to my mother, whose early diagnosis had caught a potentially disfiguring disorder of her daughter's spine. To this day, however, I do not know how she succeeded in this rescue, for her influence was not enough to save the person she cared about most, her husband, from long years in prison.

My mother had many other dark memories of life at the school. Yet throughout those years – and, indeed, throughout her whole life – she sincerely believed in her work for the country and for the state. It was to her, if not a blessing, then a sacred duty. She was not a political person. She was never a member of the Party; she never read Marx, Lenin or Stalin. She was simply an honest doctor, true to her profession. Here's the paradox: neither the arrest and murder of her brother, nor the tragic fate which befell others close to her, nor her own arrest and interrogation, could shake her faith in the historical mission of the Soviet Union. Only after Stalin's death, in the 'thaw' of the early Khrushchev years (so called after a famous story by Ilya Erenburg), did she begin to reflect upon the terrible tale that was the history of our common life. And then it became clear that her belief in 'the true path of the Soviet people' was combined in her soul in the most remarkable way with a constant *terror*, which she kept secret even from herself. At the end of her life, when Gorbachev's perestroika brought further powerful revelations, she was still extremely afraid for me.

'You're right,' she would say. 'Everything is as you say it is, only by God and all the saints, don't speak to anyone about it.'

Terror – this is the lot of the human cog turned by fate in the mechanism of the state machine. Knowing that my mother was incapable of indifference to any human suffering, I find her terror especially harrowing. Moreover, to live a myth, to dissolve oneself in it, is precisely the lot of the 'partial man', as Karl Marx himself described cogs like us.

The third Marx of the Bolsheviks has long had a place in Russian radicalism, though he often went by other names. He is the shadow of Dostoevsky's Grand Inquisitor, a man who thought he understood human nature so deeply that, pitying our weakness before our own freedom, he was prepared to burn even Christ as a heretic (Dostoevsky, 1880). And this Marx inspired another of Dostoevsky's heroes, Peter Verkhovensky of *The Devils* (1871), one of the most terrible symbols of the Russian 'liberation movement'. Today, the third Marx is alive and well in the platforms of those Russian political parties which campaign for order and discipline, and thirst for the return of strong centralized power to re-establish an empire that can threaten the whole world.

II

So far we have explored the character of three Marxes – two real and one fictional – and examined the conception of the person associated with each. I want now to take up a different, though related, topic: the controversy surrounding the concept of personhood in Soviet intellectual culture, and the role of philosophy within it.

Philosophers were given an important role in the Soviet Union. They were commissioned to present philosophical issues clearly and comprehensibly to society, to 'reflect life'. In the 'Newspeak' of the Bolsheviks this increasingly meant that philosophers were to make lofty pronouncements that endorsed the texts of the founders of Marxism and speeches of the party leadership. Naturally, under such conditions, the number of philosophers (and social scientists in general) diminished. (After all, as Plutarch observed, philosophers typically become either apologists or critics, and whereas the apologists cease to be philosophers, the critics are usually exiled.) Nevertheless, this did not mean that philosophical works were unavailable. After all, we were supposed to be Marxists, and hence philosophers, and philosophers cannot get away with not reading philosophical works. Thus although the establishment recognized that it had to keep an eye on the philosophers, the general view was that they should read what they wanted (within certain prescribed limits), so long as they wrote and spoke in a way that could be understood to endorse the general line. Hence the third Marx, the prophet of the new religion, dragged into the limelight the first Marx, admittedly ambiguous, but nevertheless real.

So in the rare periods of hope, philosophers were able to cite high philosophical culture, including Marx's works, to affirm that human beings are not 'cogs' in a machine, their essence is not a mere reflection of given social relations, an individual is not simply a Punch figure, a puppet obediently making a fool of himself and other puppets. On the contrary, human beings are subjects who, through the exercise of their wills, construct, reconstruct and transform those same 'social relations' which make them who they are. And the theoretical basis of such an understanding of human beings – including Marxist versions – was energetically discussed, especially among philosophers and scientists. The ideologists grumbled away behind the scenes of these discussions, but contented themselves with circulating scathing appellations which, in the heat of debate, were sometimes used by serious scholars. If one philosopher accused another of 'epistemologizing' some issue, or of being (horror of horrors) an 'abstract humanist', the ideologists would pick up these terms and drop them into various party pronouncements, thereby establishing new forms of philosophical heresy. Nonetheless, if the party ideologists noticed, for example, that philosophers were not taking seriously 'the class war of ideas', or seemed no longer to believe that, as Lenin put it, 'the struggle between "materialists" and "idealists" is as real today as two thousand years ago', then their anger grew more menacing and they moved to destroy the proponents of such ideas.

Thus it transpired that when critical discussion was possible, its focus often fell on our status as beings whose nature is constituted by society. For example, a wide-ranging nature–nurture debate sprang up in the 1960s and 1970s, and the pages of our 'thick journals' abounded with contributions by biologists, medics, physiologists, psychologists, educationalists and, of course, philosophers. Opinions were divided about whether the most significant determining factor in individual development was our biological inheritance, with its obscure origins buried somewhere in the beginnings of the evolution of living forms, or the environment, our social surroundings, upbringing – the by now clichéd 'ensemble of social relations'.

Both sides in the debate had their positive aspects. Both sought, in different ways, to emphasize the idea of human individuality. The 'nativists' can be seen as asserting that our biological endowment constitutes a source of each person's uniqueness in the face of standardizing social forces, while the 'nurturists' can be presented as stressing the plasticity of human development, the infinity of human potential in the right social setting.

However, as the debate played out, these positive dimensions were greatly compromised. The nativists, with their utopian confidence in science and technology, would usually gesture in the direction of a future science which would reveal the genetic code underlying the realization of the intellectual and physical capacities of any individual. With this came the suggestion that such a science would permit far-sighted administrators to fashion people in the interests of state and society. In contrast, the nurturists quoted Marx all out in an effort to 'prove' that the collective wisdom of the community, subordinated to the highest interests of society, was responsible for the character, temperament, talents, and all other qualities of particular individuals. And here once again, the suggestion emerged that a proper understanding of the processes which form human beings would enable the 'production' of people to serve the interests of state and society. (It is worth remembering that, in the *German Ideology* [1845–6], Marx and Engels insisted that so-called 'social needs', 'state interests', and so on, are nothing but the self-seeking interests of that particular group of people who, given the distribution of social forces, are able to pass their interests off as the general interests of all people.)

It seems that this nature–nurture debate presents two contrary views of human beings, of consciousness, will and the nature of personhood. In their deep logic, however, the two views are as one. According to both, a person realizes his or her singular individuality through a form of determination 'external' to him or her. What is the difference between a biological programme and a social programme? The main thing is that here the individual endures rather than causes. These views may aim to assert our individuality, but from both positions free will turns out to be an illusion, perhaps even a harmful one.

But such nature–nurture debates are not the whole story. It is crucial that a significant blow against Bolshevik ideology was struck by those philosophers who rediscovered the first Marx for themselves and for all of us. These thinkers worked largely in the theory of knowledge and were able to find a way to express a view of personhood which did not pitch social influences and human freedom against one another. The primary subject of these philosophers' studies was *human beings*, their place in the world, the world of their real, spiritual-practical life. Their focus was the uniqueness of each person, of his or her *self-consciousness*, formed in voluntary (aim-oriented) activity which alters the circumstances of life and thereby alters itself. They understood thought not as a spontaneous product of the physiology of each isolated body or brain, but as the outcome of social interaction or, better, as the content of the activity of social interaction. Precisely the *content* of this activity – its subject-matter, its ways and means – is moulded into stable *universal forms* of people's turning-towards-each-other (and towards themselves). The aim-oriented transformations of these forms reveal to people the *universality* of their being, and their objective possibilities.

How wonderful were the passionate works that appeared after the war, devoted to excavating from the mummified texts of Marx ideas from the culture of European rationalism. The Hegelian logic they found in Marx – the logic of the self-development of the organic system of human social being – was sharply opposed to the ruling ideology, which had subordinated itself to the empirical logic of scientific discourse. One need only remember the administration's devotion at this time to Pavlov. In that context, all one could discuss were the conditional and unconditional reflexes which supposedly underlay and determined all functions of the organism, including those of the so-called 'second signal system' (speech, language). These empty Pavlovian ideas formed the basis of vulgar, mechanistic theories of personhood, consciousness and cognition, which were ideal for representing human beings as malleable, wholly subordinate to social influences that ultimately could be controlled by the state. Pavlov's prestige lent a veneer of scientific respectability to these blatantly ideological conceptions. In almost every publication we read claims like: 'Pavlovian scientific materialism is the foundation and the confirmation of the truth of dialectical and historical materialism, the scientific proof of the final and total victory over idealism!'

What pompous banalities spewed forth from those who sought to 'extract philosophy from physiology'! For example, it was proposed that the mental is part of the 'reflex arc'. The peripheral input branch is, they said, purely physiological, an exclusively material process. In contrast, the output (affective) branch is already enriched by a mental component, because the central (unifying) part of the reflex arc is at the same time a mental act. This is because, when the signal from the outside is 'brought together' with the signal of muscle tissue control, an awareness of the external world necessarily arises. Variations on this nonsensical theme were accompanied by abundant quotations from Engels's *Dialectics of Nature* (1873–83) and from Lenin's works. One can say without fear of exaggeration that at this time to be a Soviet Marxist was to be an unthinking apologist for physiological mechanism. From that position the aim was to 'unmask' Hegelians and 'epistemologizers'.

From such a mechanistic perspective the following were anathema: Einstein's theory of relativity (of course its dismissal was only partial and temporary, because the military could not afford to ignore fundamental ideas of contemporary physics), genetics, cybernetics, the theory of chemical resonances, and indeed all and everything in science that was necessarily beyond the grasp of mechanistically minded scholars and ideologists. In the articles, books and brochures with which the reading public was flooded, the mechanists made bloodcurdling threats to every new 'class enemy' cowering behind the cover of science. This climate was particularly dangerous for anyone who turned to the works of the early Marx. For in the categories of 'objectification', 'reification' and 'de-reification', 'alienation', 'sublation' and so on (categories not developed by Lenin and never mentioned by Stalin), a far more complex picture is painted of the objective processes which were set in motion by human beings at the dawn of their becoming and which are realized to this day in every human life. On this view, the embodied *homo sapiens* can exist physically only if he sees his reflection in the subjective perception of other people, who relate to the individual as one who perceives the *meaning* of their turning-towards-him-as-themselves. Precisely in this way the individual becomes a subject of his will – the subject of a volitional relation to himself, to his body, his states and feelings, his needs and capacities acquired in activity with other people. Among these needs and capacities are the need for interaction and the capacity for articulate speech; these are fundamental – from them, the entire system of mental functioning is generated and on them the hierarchy of all other human needs and capabilities is built.

In order to threaten those interested in the young Marx, the legend that Marx's works could be divided into two discrete periods was set in motion. On this view, the late Marx was an authority, an unqualified genius (though admittedly he was difficult to read). In contrast, the early Marx was said to be consistently guilty of Hegelian scholasticism; he had not yet made any great discoveries and could not be considered a dialectical and historical materialist (moreover, he was even harder to read!). However, the party ideologues also counselled a cautious approach to the mature Marx: one had to be wary of his frequent lapses into Hegelianism. The then editor-in-chief of one of the central publishing houses once told me a secret: the publishers had a special censor – the censor for quotations. If a manuscript in preparation for publication was found to contain too many quotations from Marx and too few from Lenin, the latest resolutions of the CPUSSR and the speeches of the General Secretary, then the manuscript would be dropped from the plan of production. We even managed to treat Marx as a dissident!

Thus, when despite all this insanity the works of Evald Ilyenkov appeared on the scene – one of the first significant contributions to Soviet philosophy of the post-war period – it immediately became clear to the thinking reader that Marxism was something other than he or she had been led to believe. This was not the *Short Course* with its 'philosophical' fourth chapter, allegedly written by Stalin himself (*History*, 1938). Marxism was not about 'cogs', but about the individuality of human personhood, formed in spiritual labour in communion with others. Moreover, it became clear that even Marx's critique of political economy, his *Capital*, with all its specificity (devoted as it was to a particular historical time and place and analysing primarily material production and, more generally, the reproduction of the material conditions of our lives) is actually a critique of the limitations of empirical generalization, and empirical theorizing in general. This was the subject of Ilyenkov's first major work, *The Dialectics of the Abstract and the Concrete in Marx's 'Capital'* (1960).

This book, and Ilyenkov's significant early article on the problem of the ideal (1962), stimulated much work on the social character of the individual, of consciousness and all the specifically human needs and capacities. There emerged a strong tendency in Soviet philosophy, critical of biological determinism, and urging a deeply humanistic (and hence objectively anti-Bolshevik) understanding of human spirituality and the externalization in culture of the universal forms of human Being. The fact that this humanism was opposed as much to one-dimensional nurturism as to innatist ideas is important. Though in his more strident writings Ilyenkov might appear to be straightforwardly in the nurturist camp, in fact the situation is more complex, for his message is not that individuals are determined by society, but that they determine themselves in an essentially social medium. In trying to articulate this view, Evald Ilyenkov once again discovered Marx for thinking Russia.[3]

Ilyenkov was a crucial figure; but he was not, of course, the only voice. Much could be said about many philosophers who began their careers by making contact with the 'hidden Marx' and who were able to read him for his own sake and in the context of the philosophical culture in which his works were written. For such thinkers as Merab Mamardashvili, Eric Soloviev, Boris Grushin and Georgii Shchedrovitsky, Marx was no idol, but one among many philosophical authorities whose works had special significance in our quest to understand ourselves, our history and our place in nature. For them, Marx's works represented not a set of answers already given, but a source of research problems and novel insights for their development and solution. Marx was a stimulus to creativity, not a means to silence thought. This is evident, for example, in Mamardashvili's remarkable analysis of Marx's conception of consciousness (Mamardashvili, 1968, 1990). It is hard to overestimate the influence of the first Marx in the renewal of Soviet thought after Stalin. Even our renowned dissident, Alexander Zinoviev, started out from Marx (his candidate's thesis was on the logic of *Capital*). And Gorbachev admitted that as a student he found friends among those philosophers who were rediscovering Marx; so the re-emergence of the first Marx had much to do with the decline of the third.

It is important to appreciate the complexity of this situation if one is to evaluate current attitudes to Marx in post-Soviet Russia. Marx is now indiscriminately, and hysterically, condemned for the Bolshevik coup of 1917, for collectivization, for Stalinist repression: indeed, for the whole tragedy of the Soviet empire. 'The Achilles' heel of Marxism', 'To get to the bottom of this once and for all', 'Marx's mistake' – articles with such titles appear one after the other, without end. It is interesting, of course, that most of these pieces are written by people who have seen the light so recently that they have not been able to change their style: they now attack Marx with the zeal they formerly reserved for the anti-Marxists. Almost all those who would overthrow the idol were formerly united by the ruling mythology of the addressee of their invective: they celebrated (albeit sometimes reluctantly) Stalinist Marxism-Leninism and its chief saint: Karl Marx. And they read Marx now (if they read Marx at all) in the way they did before: as a source of quotations to which they can point. An excellent example of this approach is to be found in recent writings by Alexander Yakovlev, a leading democrat and one of the founders of perestroika. For him, it is Marx pure and simple who is to blame for Soviet communism (Yakovlev, 1993).

Other voices are sometimes heard urging a more careful and considered appreciation of exactly how Marx figures in Soviet history (see, for example, Kantor, 1993).[4] But it is hard to stop the flow of ideological denunciations, if only for a minute, so that a more subtle and reasoned approach might emerge. Well, God be with them, the 'overthrowers'; they could not read Marx properly in the past and it is too late to learn now. Ideologues remain ideologues; they live, act and proclaim in the same 'objective forms of thought' that were forged by decades of 'the moral-political unity of all peoples' in the name of which Soviet ideology was disseminated.

It is a shame that people who vehemently denounce one idol so often search for a new one. Russia's special historical mission, Russian orthodoxy, the philosophies of Berdyaev and Florensky, are among the candidates to fill the vacuum the third Marx has left. In this climate, it is most important that we should find, not a new god, but a new path to *culture*, including the culture of intellectual labour, the culture of philosophy. Then Russia will understand that Marx – the first Marx – is not dead. He lives just as Plato, Aristotle, Descartes, Husserl and Freud continue to live. They and numerous others are our contemporaries; they are involved today just as intimately in the construction and solution of problems as they were in their own time. Their lives have not finished and will not finish so long as there are human beings striving to understand themselves in the world and the world within themselves. Marx, with his vision of human beings as social agents, constituted by the history they themselves create, is, and will continue to be, a significant figure in the culture of philosophical reflection.

Notes

Translated by David Bakhurst. Thanks are due to Marina Vitkin for invaluable help with the translation.

1. Sergei Nechaev (1847–82) was the founder of 'The People's Vengeance', a secret revolutionary organization committed to brutal methods to further the revolution. Nechaev's *Revolutionary Catechism* rejects all existing morality, identifying the good as that which furthers the revolution and the bad as that which inhibits it. Nechaev stands as a symbol for the most voluntarist and ruthless species of Russian revolutionary thought and action. He and his followers are among Dostoevsky's targets in the novel *The Devils* (1871). D.B.

2. The Russian term is *vintik* ('screw'). D.B.

3. I say 'once again' because Marx's idea of the historical development of the human essence was properly appreciated by certain Russian philosophers in the 1920s, particularly those of Abram Deborin's school. However, the 'Deborinites' were routed by Stalin in 1930 and in the clannish struggle of the pre-war period the humanistic interpretation of the materialist understanding of history was submerged (see Bakhurst, 1991: ch. 2, for a treatment of the Deborinites in the context of Ilyenkov's work).

4. Some of the many Russian debates about the 'death of Marxism' are reproduced in *Voprosy filosofii*, 10 (1990) and Gusejnov and Tolstykh (1990, 1993).

References

Bakhurst, David (1991) *Consciousness and Revolution in Soviet Philosophy*. Cambridge: Cambridge University Press.

Dostoevsky, Fyodor (1871) *The Devils*, trans. David Magarshack. Harmondsworth: Penguin, 1971.

Dostoevsky, Fyodor (1880) *The Brothers Karamazov*, trans. Richard Peaver and Larissa Volokhansky. London: Vintage, 1990.

Engels, Friedrich (1873–83) *Dialectics of Nature*, trans. Clemens Dutt. Moscow: Progress, 1976.

Gusejnov, A. A. and Tolstykh, V. I. (eds) (1990) *Osvobozhdenie dukha* (*The Liberation of the Spirit*). Moscow: Politizdat.

Gusejnov, A. A. and Tolstykh, V. I. (eds) (1993) *Studies in East European Thought*, 45. Special Issue, *Marxism and the Socialist Idea in Russia Today*.

History of the Communist Party of the Soviet Union (Bolshevik). Short Course (1938), ed. Commission of the Central Committee of the CPUSSR (B). Moscow: Foreign Language Publishing House.

Ilyenkov, E. V. (1960) *The Dialectics of the Abstract and the Concrete in Marx's 'Capital'*, trans. Sergei Syrovatkin. Moscow: Progress, 1962.

Ilyenkov, E. V. (1962) 'Ideal'noe'. *Filosofskaya entsiklopediya*, vol. 2. Moscow: Sovetskaya entsiklopediya.

Kantor, K. M. (1993) 'A quick and unjust trial', in Gusejnov and Tolstykh (1993).

Mamardashvili, Merab (1968) 'Analiz soznaniya v rabotakh Marksa' ('The analysis of consciousness in Marx's works'), *Voprosy filosofii*, 6, 1968. Reprinted in Mamardashvili (1990) and translated in *Studies in Soviet Thought*, 32 (1986).

Mamardashvili, Merab (1990) *Kak ya ponimayu filosofiyu* (*How I Understand Philosophy*). Moscow: Progress.

Marx, Karl (1844) *Economic and Philosophic Manuscripts of 1844*. Moscow: Progress, 1977.

Marx, Karl (1845) 'Theses on Feuerbach', in Marx and Engels (1968).

Marx, Karl and Friedrich Engels (1845–6) *The German Ideology*, ed. C. J. Arthur. London: Lawrence & Wishart, 1970.

Marx, Karl and Friedrich Engels (1848) *The Communist Manifesto*, in Marx and Engels (1968).

Marx, Karl and Engels, Friedrich (1968) *Selected Works in One Volume*. London: Lawrence & Wishart.

Mikhailov, F. T. (1990) Contribution to the Symposium, 'Is Marxism Dead?', *Voprosy filosofii*, (10).

Yakovlev, Alexander (1993) *The Fate of Marxism in Russia*, trans. Catherine A. Fitzpatrick. New Haven, CT: Yale University Press.

6

Death in Utopia: Marxism and the Mortal Self

Christine Sypnowich

To what extent should politics aspire to transform the human condition? It might be thought that in an ideal society, limitations of the self would be overcome, and selfishness, ignorance and infirmity eradicated. Indeed, in utopian literature the idea of transcending human finitude is often expressed as the abolition of death itself: our participation in a perfect polity should never cease or diminish. Thus in fantasies ranging from Sir Thomas More's *Utopia* (1516) to Aldous Huxley's *Brave New World* (1932) or James Hilton's Shangri-La of *Lost Horizon* (1933), human beings either live forever or have the ravages of old age forestalled. And dreams of overcoming mortality are not confined to fiction; the project of modernity, whereby in the spirit of human improvement reason penetrates and subdues the mysteries of the universe, gave rise to speculation about the abolition or indefinite postponement of death from such thinkers as Descartes and Condorcet.[1]

It is often argued that Soviet ideology was akin to a secular religion, and that the Bolsheviks saw their revolution in apocalyptic terms, rupturing all links with the past to form a new Jerusalem (see e.g. Berdyaev, 1966). But some commentators have gone further and noted that the theme of abolishing death also featured, sometimes officially, as an important part of the self-definition of the Soviet era (Wiles, 1965; Freeborn, 1982: 239–58; Bethea, 1989: ch. 3; Masing-Delic, 1992). According to these studies, Soviet literature, science and culture are all affected by the ideal of immortality. The significance of this finding for politics, and in particular for the Marxist ideal of emancipation, has yet to be investigated. In this chapter I examine the role played by the aspiration to overcome the finitude of the self both in Marxism, and in its historical offspring in the 'Great Utopia' of post-1917 Russia.[2] I will argue that this aspiration is implicit in the communist ideal itself, and explicit in the Promethean themes of Marxist theory and Bolshevik culture. In the wake of the demise of 'actually existing socialism', this inquiry may shed light on how utopia has failed us, and how we might better conceive of emancipation.

Marxism and mortality

To portray Marxism as a species of immortalizing utopianism is by no
means uncontroversial. Marx and Engels heaped scorn on 'utopian
socialism' for attempting to convert the bourgeoisie by moral suasion, and
for drawing up blueprints of ideal societies in the absence of an analysis of
historical circumstances. In contrast, they claimed to offer a 'scientific'
theory which eschews idealism in all senses of the word (Marx and Engels,
1848; Engels, 1890). Moreover, the atheistic and materialistic outlook
of Marx and his followers is an inauspicious context for notions of
everlasting life. Marxism seems the most anti-utopian of utopianisms,
unencumbered by communist centenarians or red fountains of youth. Thus
commentators concur that Marxism's contribution to the idea of
immortality in the Soviet tradition is not straightforward. Masing-Delic,
for example, stresses that the hostility of classical Marxism to religious
notions of salvation and omnipotence meant that only in the 'loopholes' of
the doctrine could an immortalizing creed be found (1992: 10). And Peter
Wiles maintains that Soviet ideas were prompted, not by Marx, but by a
distorted, Soviet form of Marxism (1965: I, 129–31).

Nevertheless, Marxism is certainly utopian insofar as its aim is not the
mere improvement of society but the attainment of a radically new, ideal
society. Moreover, I will show that Marx's thought contains themes which,
if they do not amount to a doctrine of immortality, certainly are capable
of inspiring such doctrines.

One important factor is that Marx's philosophical anthropology
suggests the idea of achieving permanence through activity. We are natural
beings who labour in order to exist, and as such, whether we are alienated
or fulfilled stems from the nature of productive relations. Marx departs
from rationalist understandings of the human essence as lying in our
unique capacity to think and reason; what makes us different from the
other species is labour. Human labour requires foresight and design: it is
'what distinguishes the worst of architects from the best of bees' (Marx,
1867: 344). This renders it an intellectual activity, albeit a practical one at
the same time. We constitute ourselves in labour, not just because we
provide food for ourselves and thus reproduce the conditions of our
existence. Labour is a means of developing our capacities and enriching
our lives. And there is a sense in which the idea of a self-constituting self
carries with it the promise of liberation from nature. While Marx's
emphasis on labour reminds us, *contra* Descartes, that we are biological
beings, it also underscores, against cruder materialisms, that we are not
merely biological beings; we do not live and die by instinct, accepting the
deliverances of bounty or drought. We act on nature and form and shape
it according to our will. The role of design in labour endows our method
of self-sustenance with a special temporality compared to that of animals:
we plan our creations before we make them, and leave them behind once
we die. The permanence of our production is essential to Marx's idea of

objectification, in which we stamp nature with our personalities, objectify ourselves in the physical world in the form of the things we make and the designs we employ. In so doing, we leave monuments to ourselves, testimonies to our existence. Labour therefore has a commemorative aspect.

Our control over nature and our natural being is of a piece with Feuerbach's demystification of religion: God does not make us, we make God. This reversal serves not just to dethrone God, but to deify human beings. But human beings can take the place of God only if they act in concert: labour is distinguished by its social character. Even the solitary labourer relies on a craft, a technology, which is inevitably a social inheritance, an objectification of the labour of others. And our ability to constitute our identities in labour derives from our nature as social beings, where, in interacting with others, we each forge our particular identity. As Marx puts it in the sixth of the 'Theses on Feuerbach': 'the human essence . . . is the ensemble of the social relations' (1845: 145). This focus on the social has a normative dimension; the good life is one where our social nature is allowed to flourish. Marx criticizes capitalism for its hostility to community, its inability to foster concern for our fellows. And it is by means of community in the form of the collective action of the working class that capitalism is overthrown. Communism restores to human beings control over their work by means of a recovery of social control over production. It is 'only in community' that each individual has 'the means of cultivating his gifts in all directions; only in the community, therefore, is personal freedom possible' (Marx and Engels, 1845–6: 197).

While Marx insists that under communism the social allows people to express their individuality, to enjoy personal freedom, there is also a sense in which the particular individual life is obscured by the wider social entity. Here there is another respect in which individual finitude is eclipsed. We are not just individual beings but 'species beings', not empirically given persons, but world historical individuals whose mission is to emancipate humankind (Marx and Engels, 1845–6: 161–2). The meaning of a particular, corporeal individual's life is supplied by a larger, more significant project of redemption. Here, particular deaths must be countenanced, since for Marx and Engels there is no question that communism is likely to require violence: 'The Communists . . . openly declare that their ends can be attained only by the forcible overthrow of all existing social relations' (Marx and Engels, 1848: 500). Individuals are subsumed by and live in and through the wider social organism, which by their particular deaths achieves a harmonious permanence. It is as if, like the surgeon's knife, the proletariat's ruthless but well-aimed assault saves the body politic as a whole by sacrificing the lives of individuals.

Finally, there is a sense in which the transcendence of death figures in the communist ideal. Communism ends the cleavage between the particular and the universal interest, where the free development of each will be the condition for the free development of all (Marx and Engels, 1845–6: 160). As the means for mediating disputes and confirming the power of the dominant class, politics and law will disappear. In *State and Revolution* Lenin amplifies this theme, arguing that in the absence of class divisions, individuals will become so accustomed to think of the commonweal that they will abide by the rules of social life instinctively, without regulation (Lenin, 1917: ch. 2; see Polan, 1984 and Sypnowich, 1990: ch. 1).

So while history is the history of class struggles, struggles of all kinds cease with the rise to power of the proletariat and the achievement of that class's goals. This is because the proletariat is unique among all oppressed classes in that in pursuing its emancipation it pursues the emancipation of all; its struggle to be the dominant class results in the abolition of all classes, and the superfluity of all struggles. Communism alone can leave behind 'all the muck of ages' (Marx and Engels, 1845–6: 193); it is 'the riddle of history solved and knows itself to be this solution' (Marx, 1844: 84). Thus we see a utopia in the true sense of a society beyond finitude and limitation, which rids humanity of all social problems, ignorance, dissension and unease. Want and need disappear, not just because communism's superior economic system ushers in new conditions of abundance and creates the resources for egalitarian distribution, but because communism's superior social relations solve all problems of communication and co-operation. Communism promises to be a transparent society, premised on, as A. J. Polan puts it, 'the dissolution of all institutions that effected separations and differences between people, that allowed corners to remain dark and private, and that assumed the continued existence of different and distinct practices' (1984: 28–9).

The image of a communist utopia, in its fixity, its lack of dynamism or struggle, suggests the conquest of human beings' mortal condition. In this imaginative space where all desires are sated, all impulses for change quelled, and all our relations harmonious and trouble-free, time seems to stand still. Thus Polan concludes that communism ultimately promises to put an end to 'the fundamental anguish of being' and indeed to 'time itself' (Polan, 1984: 206). It is, we might say, a finite infinity, where history has reached its final destination at a point where all is possible.

In sum, there is within the Marxist critique of capitalism and the call for communism an aspiration to overcome finitude. First, the commemorative dimension of labour, in which the subject masters nature and imprints upon it a testimony to human existence; second, the representation of discrete and diverse individuals as parties to a species being which subsumes them; and finally, the idea of an idyllic society which has conquered scarcity and selfishness, marking the end of history – all suggest the possibility of surmounting our limitations as mortal beings. For all Marx's contempt for utopianism, his own thought betrays a yearning for a temporal salvation. Marx can scoff, 'everything that exists has this much worth, that it will perish' (Marx, 1852: 599), because he has in mind a realm which redeems the demise of what has gone before it. We shall see how the Bolsheviks attempted to realize this project of destruction and redemption and, in so doing, expanded the Promethean themes of Marx.

Bolshevik culture and communist man

The Bolshevik attitude to death has a complex set of origins. One important, if unlikely, influence on the Bolsheviks was the conception of resurrection developed by the nineteenth-century thinker, Nikolai Fyodorov. Fyodorov held that the problem of the human condition lay in the sacrifice of one generation for another; until we can bring our ancestors back to life we are condemned to a human existence of strife and conflict. For Fyodorov, this was not a theological matter of retrieving lost souls. The reconstruction of the flesh was a scientific possibility which would, once perfected, enable the true brotherhood of the human race (extracts from Fyodorov are translated in Edie et al., 1965: 16–61).

The bizarre vision of this modest library clerk was astonishingly influential. The principle that resurrection could be achieved with the scantest of ingredients gave rise to a host of even wilder versions throughout the Soviet era, including the idea that a sample of handwriting was all that was needed to remake a dead person (Kline, 1968: 165). The poet Vladimir Mayakovsky was inspired by his reading of Fyodorov. Moreover, it could be argued that there was an explicit attempt to put Fyodorov's ideas into practice with the embalming of Lenin. Certainly Fyodorov is credited with having inspired the political leaders and scientists involved in the project (Tumarkin, 1983: 181 and Stites, 1989: 120).

Fyodorov's project gave rise not just to fanciful ideas about resurrection but also to a second, more familiar conception of immortality: everlasting life – that, as Mayakovsky put it, 'one day there will be no death' (Young, 1979: 192–3). This was an inherent part of the 'Godbuilding' movement in pre-revolutionary Russia, a trend which both rivalled and influenced Marxist and socialist circles (see Read, 1979: ch. 3). Taking up Feuerbach's lead, the Godbuilders held that human beings should recognize the eternal within themselves, so that they may find universal salvation and secular immortality. One famous Godbuilder was Maxim Gorky, who believed that instead of exceptional individuals or an inaccessible God, the divine could be found among the Russian people, where 'little men' might achieve 'great deeds' (Clark, 1978; Hare, 1962: 79). In his novel *A Confession*, a lame girl has her power to walk restored to her as a result of the intervention of, not God, but the human community. The narrator ends proclaiming, 'Thou art my God, O sovereign people. . . . And the world shall have no other gods but thee, for thou art the only god that works miracles' (Gorky, 1910: 318–20).

The Godbuilding movement was the object of derision among Marxists such as Plekhanov and Lenin, for whom the distinction between traditional religion and this new, humanist version was moot (see Read, 1979: ch. 3; Hare, 1962: 80). Moreover, Godbuilding was a special cause of resentment insofar as it appealed to intellectuals who might otherwise have been drawn to the Bolshevik cause. Nevertheless, while the idea of human beings achieving divinity on earth was hardly Marxist, Marxist Prometheanism certainly complemented, and helped shape, the ideas of the Godbuilders. That nature can be transformed by human labour, human possibilities subsumed under the meta-individual 'species being', and an ideal society established which transcends the finitude of the past, were certainly congruent with the aspirations of Godbuilding. In turn, the influence of the Godbuilders on the Bolsheviks should not be underestimated. The notion of 'Godmanhood' blended easily with many Bolshevik ideas of fashioning a new being fit to dwell in the earthly utopia under construction in Soviet Russia (Stites, 1989: ch. 5). If the socialist community, equipped with sophisticated means of production and solidaristic social relations, would abolish scarcity, could not other forms of finitude also be surmounted?

After the revolution, literature abounded with examples of the 'new Soviet man', a retooled human product who is humane and altruistic, industrious and efficient, with a quicker pulse and a keener intellect than his inferior, pre-revolutionary ancestors (Clark, 1978). The *proletkult* movement of Alexander Bogdanov and Anatoly Lunacharsky, the Minister of Enlightenment after the revolution, was in keeping with this ideal of human transformation. Its studios and workers' clubs were laboratories for the education of citizens of the new utopia. It was hoped that workers would create a proletarian culture with which to criticize past culture and inaugurate new aesthetic forms stressing creative labour, co-operation and community (Sochor, 1988: ch. 6; Fitzpatrick, 1970: ch. 5; see also McClelland, 1985).

The idea of refashioning society and its members was reinforced by a modernist aesthetic. Among the constructivists, the machine and the mechanical became a metaphor for the ideal of a fabricated new person in a world entirely within human control. Society's workings were also to be transparent, self-regulating and efficient, in line with the thesis that public authority, state and law would wither away in a flourishing communist society. As Zamyatin parodies in his anti-utopian novel, *We* (1920–1), many artists took up the line, exemplifying perfection and infinity, as a symbol for the promise of the new age. Some artists were so taken with the idea of their work as 'projects for a new universe' that their constructivism prescribed a new vocation, as artist-constructor, or indeed artist-engineer, and many came to prefer the tasks of the drafting table to that of the easel (Gassner, 1992: 305). There was a burgeoning of activity in the applied arts: teapots with patterns of cogs and wheels, dress fabric printed with a skyscraper motif – there seemed to be no limit to the fevered imagination of the constructivist utopians (Bowlt, 1985).

This brave new world bred a nihilistic attitude to the past. Anti-intellectualism was a legitimate posture in the new workers' state. Indeed, philosophy itself became the target of 'liquidationist' views, as some Bolsheviks proclaimed that the only knowledge required by communism could be found in science (Bakhurst, 1991a: 27–31). For many revolutionaries, what had gone before was to be rooted out and removed, as though a reminder of a now defunct human frailty (Stites, 1985). Other dispensable relics of the past included monuments, churches, and even theatres and museums. This attitude of contempt for previous culture was a feature of the futurist aesthetic, to which Mayakovsky was an important contributor (see Jangfeldt, 1977: 57–60). In the end, cooler heads prevailed and while certain monuments were removed and private treasures appropriated by state museums, outright destruction was halted by the Bolshevik leaders. Nonetheless, the idea that the future was to be utterly unlike the past, that human beings could become completely other than what they were, was a heady theme of the revolutionaries. Mayakovsky proclaimed that 'a new eternity' was in the making. Another poet, Alexander Blok, similarly declared the purpose of the revolution to be 'to *remake* everything. To organize things so that everything should be new, so that our false, filthy, boring, hideous life should become a just, pure, merry and beautiful life' (quoted in Stites, 1989: 38).

The theme of immortality was explicit in much Bolshevik science fiction (Stites, 1989: ch. 8). Bogdanov's 1908 novel, *Red Star*, tells the story of a utopia on Mars, organized on fraternal and egalitarian principles, united by a single language (picking up on a theme of the Esperantists, who were very popular in Russia at the time). Even our biological limitations are transcended: sexual differences are muted, and life expectancy is extended by the 'comradely exchange of life' – mutual blood transfusions (with which Bogdanov himself later experimented at the cost of his life). At the same time, the mortality of particular individuals is superseded by the life of the community to which individuals are inextricably bound, developing some of the communitarian themes of Marx. Monuments to the dead are disallowed as individuals are not to be singled out for their contributions: 'the whole lives in each and every one of us, in each tiny cell of the great organism, and each of us lives through the whole' (Bogdanov, 1908: 80).

Here emerges a third, more metaphorical conception of immortality which draws on Marx's idea of objectification: the commemoration of the dead by means of great deeds, of which the socialist community is the consummation. Mayakovsky voiced this in poems such as 'To Comrade Nette – Steamer and Man' in which Soviet citizens die only 'to become immortal, cast in steamers, verse and other things that last' (Mayakovsky, 1972: 69–71; see Masing-Delic, 1992: 13). The reference to verse suggests Mayakovsky had himself in mind, and indeed the immortality of the poet is the subject of another, powerful poem, 'Aloud and Straight'. There the memorials of 'marble's frozen slime' are contrasted with Mayakovsky's verse which 'like any rank and file' will live on in the 'common monument' of socialism (Mayakovsky, 1972: 261–7). Indeed, the trite claims of biographers to the immortality of their subjects takes a new cast in the lyrical biography of the poet by Mayakovsky's contemporary, Viktor Shklovsky. Shklovsky concludes that on the death of Mayakovsky, 'the list of pains, sorrows and hurts was finished' but 'the poet' had remained (Shklovsky, 1972: 203).

The painter Kazimir Malevich, creator of the famous black square, took the view that artists had a duty to immortalize, not themselves, but the revolution in their works. After Lenin's death, Malevich sought a full-scale religious cult of Lenin, in which every home had a miniature of the Kremlin mausoleum as a sacred artifact (Stites, 1989: 120). In contrast, Malevich considered the idea of genius in art to be antithetical to the collectivism of the revolution. Artists should be anonymous: just as religious fanatics destroyed themselves before God in the past, the artist should seek to obliterate him- or herself before the community (Shatskikh, 1992: 56).

Bolshevik rituals surrounding actual deaths suggest a similar ambivalence about immortality, as Richard Stites's research demonstrates. Is 'communist man' a revolutionary hero to be revered by his fellows or an anonymous member of the collective whose particular life is transcended by the whole? In the immediate post-revolutionary period, funerals were uneasy combinations of party speeches and rites of piety, giving way to modest affairs devoid of ceremony. The Bolsheviks were torn between downplaying the role of individual death in the face of the ongoing life of the community, or celebrating the dead for their contributions to the common good. At the same time, their egalitarian and atheistic principles dictated a standardized, non-religious mode of mourning. Thus by the mid-1920s there emerged on the one hand the 'clean, rational and economical' administration of death by means of crematoria, even proposals for a 'crematorium-columbarium' in which mourners would advance the cause of sound health. On the other hand, there was a call for secular red funerals complete with original music and choreographed tableaux (Stites, 1989: 112–14).[3]

In sum, the Bolshevik utopia involved three conceptions of immortality: resurrection, the abolition of death, and the commemoration of the dead in the great works of socialism. We shall see how all three came together in the most fantastic attempt to deny human finitude.

Lenin's tomb

The Lenin Museum is now closed, the buildings of the Kremlin stripped of reminders of Russia's Bolshevik past, and the General Secretary of the Communist Party has long been evicted from his splendid office within; but at the time of writing, in Red Square, there still sits the embalmed corpse of Vladimir Ilyich Ulyanov. That Lenin should 'live forever' was the cry of grief-stricken mourners, Bolshevik polemicists and political opportunists alike immediately upon the Bolshevik leader's death in 1924. That Lenin was prevented from taking his leave offers the most revealing piece of evidence about the role of death and immortality in the Marxist tradition.[4]

The preservation of Lenin was begun as an effort to stave off decay until burial so that thousands of mourners could pay their respects. But the cult of Lenin, brewing since the attempt on his life in 1918, was such by the time of his death that the idea of maintaining his corpse for eternal gatherings of the faithful seemed inevitable. In her study of bodysnatching in Britain, Ruth Richardson discusses traditional beliefs about the power of the corpse. Occupying a period between death and burial, it was thought to be neither alive nor fully dead, with a sentience and spiritual power that made it an object of fear and reverence; the dead might be slighted if the corpse was not properly respected (Richardson, 1987: 15–24). Our study concerns a different context, but it seems probable that beliefs of this kind were prominent in Russia. Traditions among Russian peasants suggest that the dead were not just respected, but cared for: for example, the corpse was assigned a special place in the icon corner of the house until burial, then dressed in fine clothes and placed in the coffin with food for the journey to come (Matossian, 1968: 29–30). In Lenin's case, such considerations would have been magnified. There were those, such as the commissar in charge of the preservation of the body, Leonid Krasin, who even nursed Fyodorovian hopes that Lenin might one day be resurrected. Moreover, there would have been a shared interest in having Lenin as a symbolic guardian of communism, keeping leaders, subjects, rivals – potential foes of all kinds – in line.

The enterprise involved a top-secret formula for the elixir, repeatedly refined until the 1950s, when the final compound was reached. Lunacharsky presided over the project of housing Lenin, which involved a massive mausoleum, constructed after a grand contest for the best design. Maintenance of the corpse required a team of scientists and guardians, some of whom to this day have this as their sole vocation (Tumarkin, 1983: ch. 6; *Globe and Mail*, 1991). The project was successful, not just in the sense that Lenin's corpse was preserved. Popular culture also bore witness to Lenin's 'life after apparent death'. Tales from Soviet folklore such as 'Clever Lenin' have Lenin pretending to be dead, then visiting various sites of socialist construction incognito to reassure himself that all is proceeding well without him. In children's literature, nursery pictures and decorations, Lenin also figured as a kind of Soviet Saint Nicholas, who visits children to inspire them to attain socialist virtues (Tumarkin, 1983: chs 6–7).

That Lenin's body had to be preserved for the sake of the Bolshevik project indicates that the immortalizing utopia was in decay after all. The paradox of the venture was that while the idea of preserving Lenin's body was inspired by reverence for Lenin, it could only be achieved by interfering with, indeed desecrating, his corpse. The decision to embalm rather than bury Lenin thus underscores not just the prominence of the ideal of communist immortality, but anxiety about its continued power.

It was not just Lenin that was embalmed, but socialism itself. For Stalin, revolutionary utopianism no longer had a place in the ideal society. And insofar as Stalin aspired to absolute control over every aspect of society, there was no room for experimentation or the avant-garde. Because the aesthetics of Bolshevism, for all its immortalizing themes, involved the random and the uncontrolled – in short, human possibility and human frailty – it ultimately posed a threat to the Stalinist ideology of the Shangri-La *accompli*. By the 1930s the ideal of immortality had become a state orthodoxy with which to repress idealism and iconoclasm. The Promethean theme lived on, as Stalin embarked on ambitious economic strategies, cultural policies, technological projects and, with the onset of the Second World War, daunting military campaigns. And the idea of abolishing death came to be a legitimate object of scientific inquiry throughout the Stalin era and after. In the 1960s, many scientists took the conquest of space to be a model for the conquest of human finitude on earth and Fyodorovianism flourished as an enterprise of serious laboratory research. Extraordinary efforts to refashion and subjugate nature, from plans to redirect rivers to dangerous nuclear power projects, can be seen as expressions of the urge to master human finitude that continued long after the Bolsheviks. But the original utopianizing spirit of artists and intellectuals had become enshrined in official culture at the expense of the vitality of the spirit itself (see Sochor, 1988: 216; Wood, 1992).

The move to socialist realism provides an interesting illustration of Stalin's attempt at fixing cultural activity and monumentalizing immortality. Realism was an established aesthetic long before the revolution, and it continued to thrive spontaneously after 1917, alongside more formalist modes. But in 1928–31 there occurred a 'cultural revolution' in which realism was embraced as a rigid prototype for socialist culture.

Why realism? Formalist genres aroused suspicion; abstraction was deemed either too sophisticated for ordinary people to understand, or insofar as it was comprehensible, too anarchistic and decadent in its implications. Indeed, futurism, for all its antipathy to bourgeois culture, was deemed of questionable class pedigree by proletarian-minded critics before the rise of Stalin. According to Stites, the low-brow realist culture under Stalin was far more to the taste of the masses than the utopian culture of the Bolsheviks, which was intimidatingly cerebral, however anti-intellectual its posture (Stites, 1992: 204–9). Realism meant, however, not the creative form in the hands of a Tolstoy or a Dostoevsky. Socialist realism meant, as the *Great Soviet Encylopaedia* describes it: 'depicting reality in its revolutionary development' (Markov and Timofeev, 1976: 244–6).

But as Régine Robin points out, the imaginary is inherently antici-
patory; it unfolds a future and fashions new interpretations of the past
(Robin, 1992: 69). Under the new genre, in contrast, the future was to be
dictated, rendered transparent, its social relations homogeneous. The
heroes of socialist realism could not be troubled in any existential sense;
their fate was positive and certain (Robin, 1992: 235). The past, on the
other hand, for all the reverence for its literary traditions, was forbidden
territory, since it threatened to call the present to account.

Put baldly, the Stalinist project of socialist realism sought, like utopian
ideals of immortality before it, to defeat time itself, to conquer finitude.
Robin thus calls socialist realism an impossible aesthetic, for ridding art of
the indeterminate robs it of precisely that which is essential to its status as
art. As an ideology, too, socialist realism was self-defeating; the truth, the
articulation of the real, was not after all permitted. An instrumental
conception of literature in an increasingly brutal context meant that
verisimilitude was in fact far too dangerous to be truly undertaken.
Socialist realism was thus, paradoxically, a form which concealed.

What had to be concealed was the failure to realize even the most
remote, metaphorical understanding of the socialist idea of immortality.
For example, the conquest of finitude in the form of co-operatively
organized, creative labour in which the worker bequeathes a product that
bears his or her personality was in fact never possible after the October
revolution. Labour was organized either along quasi-market lines under
the New Economic Policy or by centralized state authority, its purpose
dictated by a productivist obsession and the severe shortages and
irrationalities imposed by conditions of war and famine.

As for everyday conditions, they were far from the ideal of *Red Star*.
Even during peacetime Soviet policy betrayed a disregard for the living
body. This is not just because the imperatives of the arms race meant that
the society established in the name of a heaven on earth found itself
devoted to the continuing improvement of the means of death. Living
conditions were a source of great disappointment to those visionaries who
foresaw a society where the socialist deployment of modern techniques
would mean a standard of living so high that even mortality would be put
into question. The average Soviet citizen lived in a small, uncomfortable
and poorly maintained flat, sharing with (at least) an extended family.
Food, while affordable during the Soviet era, was usually in short supply.
Health care was often of a low standard, and disregard for bodily health
was manifest in the numerous environmental hazards with which people
lived. Soviet science, while boasting notable achievements in state-oriented
research, has done comparatively little to ease the life of the ordinary
person (see Bakhurst, 1991b: 215–16).

And, far from discovering the elixir of life, the Bolsheviks seemed
condemned to take life. Not only was life stifled in a context of repression;
actual deaths, including those of the most creative visionaries, must be
reckoned in our assessment of the death of utopia, as Roman Jakobson

makes clear in his famous essay, 'On a generation that squandered its poets' (Jakobson, 1973: 11). In the purges, Stalin killed in order to preserve a lifeless socialism. One of the subtleties of Stalinism, however, was that many voluntarily participated in their own demise. This is most evident in the show trials, where Old Bolsheviks confessed to conspiring against the revolution and chose personal death for the sake of communism. Sloterdijk calls this a 'doubling of murder by the judiciary with suicide' which takes place within a

> schizophrenic structure, where the ego that kills can no longer be distinguished from the ego that is killed. Only one thing is certain: in the end corpses of intelligent human beings are lying on the ground, strangled, shot, beaten. (Sloterdijk, 1987: 96–7)

Mayakovsky himself, who had prophesied that one day 'there will be no death', took his own life. By 1930 his aspiration for an abstract aesthetic, a new relation between creator and creation, was doomed. It is said that a crass candy wrapper produced by the state sweet factory is what prompted Mayakovksy to give up all hope for Bolshevik art. Mayakovsky's suicide did not end his participation in a betrayed utopia: he was canonized poet of the revolution by Stalin, and his futurist commitments and independent, critical outlook whitewashed with claims about his 'profound faith in the victory of communism' (Goncharov, 1976: 616–17). Boris Pasternak, hardly a supporter of the Bolsheviks at any point, remarked that this was Mayakovsky's second death, but in this case, one for which Mayakovsky was not responsible (Blake, 1975: 9–50).

This picture of the decay of the Bolsheviks' quest for utopia risks implying a rigid distinction between the Bolshevik ideal and its manipulation under Stalin. Certainly this was the official word in post-Stalinist assessments of that era ('Communist Party', 1976: 288). But the visionaries and fantasists of 1917 bear a significant responsibility for later events. Mayakovsky, after all, was one of the authors of the cult of Lenin. In his poem 'Komsomolskaya', he proclaims:

Lenin and Death –
these words are enemies.
Lenin and Life –
are comrades . . . (quoted in Tumarkin, 1983: 166)

In light of this public celebration of Lenin, Mayakovsky's editorial for the journal *LEF*, 'Don't traffic in Lenin', which denounced Lenin memorabilia for sullying the memory of the great Bolshevik leader (Tumarkin, 1983: 235), seems to rely on an overly subtle distinction between legitimate, artistic expressions of reverence for Lenin and vulgar cults. In the wake of the disappointing actualization of Lenin's vision in *State and Revolution*, the reification and 'kitschification' of ideals became inevitable. In an effort to hide or efface the increasingly degraded mortal self of everyday life, the idea of immortality by virtue of one's membership in a utopian community had to be propped up with tangible images of immortal selfhood, be it

Lenin's tomb, the splendid mausoleum-like Moscow Metro, the anonymous workers, farmers and soldiers celebrated in statues, the dead heroes
commemorated by place names, or the great halls and chambers where
public life was carried out.

Finitude and politics

We have seen how the hope for immortality, intrinsic to the idea of
socialist utopia, was part of its undoing. It remains for the philosophical
underpinnings of this hope to be critically assessed. In Fyodorovian ideas
of resurrection there is a conceptual problem about personhood (notwithstanding questions of practical feasibility!). What is involved in
bringing a person 'back to life'? Not simply the recreation of a human
body, for the idea that a body double – another *me* – could come into
existence at some later date does not so much allay morbid fears as
accentuate them, arousing unease, alienation, indeed downright jealousy
(see Williams, 1973 and Dennett, 1981 on personal identity). One is
reminded of Gogol's fanciful story of the nose who leaves its owner's face
to live an independent life, even having the effrontery to masquerade
around town as a citizen of higher rank than its former owner (Gogol,
1836). Fyodorov's insistence on a communitarian framework, where self-
realization is achieved through the restoration of the lives of others, leaves
unresolved the question of whether self and others can even be demarcated
in his resurrected universe.

An untenable conception of the self, albeit a more sophisticated one,
underlies the more metaphorical treatments of immortality. The ideal of a
community where finitude is to be overcome suggests that the self is an
object of perfectionism. On this view, not just physical and intellectual
capacities but the very identity of the person are infinitely expandable, and
so the differences between persons can be muted: in short, individuality is
something to be eliminated in the post-mortal utopia. Individuality after
all refers to the myriad ways – from petty vices to marvellous talents – in
which one finite self differs from another. That the self is an individual,
with individual tastes, interests and perspectives, means that it is bound to
be at odds with others. This is not to invoke the view, traditional since
Hobbes, which finds in us an innate selfishness and propensity to war;
rather it is to note that it is our inherent capacity for *self-ness*, for
uniqueness, which gives rise to the complexities of human interaction
requiring social mediation, that is, politics.

Marx of course insisted that communism would enable individuality to
flourish, but he had a curiously apolitical understanding of what this
meant, since there are to be no serious differences between persons under
communism. Our disagreements, our capacity for change (whether to
revise our views or take on new projects), our expressions of doubt and
misgiving are conceived as problems to be defeated, instead of inevitable

features of the human condition. Such a view takes utopia to be a kind of moribund state, without vitality or change. This is encapsulated in the utopian novel itself, which as a genre is notorious for its lack of narrative dynamic: in utopia, nothing happens; politics is superfluous (Bethea, 1989: 147–8). As the Bolshevik experiment attests, the conquest of time proves impossible and politics inevitably re-emerges, enlisted to prop up the dream of immortality. But still severed from the classical conception of politics as the pursuit of the good life, politics takes the most brutal form. The result is a society which is anathema to the original utopian ideals of equal and comradely individuals transparently communicating their needs and wants. The mortal body, far from granted eternal life, is mortified.

To acknowledge the reality of individuality is not to suggest that politics becomes stymied in the recognition of difference. In my view, the contemporary interest in difference (see, for example, Laclau and Mouffe, 1985; Young, 1990) also betrays a certain urge to transcend finitude. In fixing, not on the remedy of injustice that accrues from difference, but on the recognition of difference itself, identity politics suggests that the finitude of the self can be overcome, that social diversity is somehow to be dealt with or resolved. Thus the politics of multiculturalism in the liberal West and the assertion of 'ethno-anarchism' (G. M. Tamas's useful phrase) in Eastern Europe seek to find unitary spaces for diverse cultural identities. Paradoxically, these invocations of difference risk essentialism, where we reify a certain identity and proclaim its immutable nature, eclipsing the differences within the identity itself, and ignoring the damage done to the new 'others' defined in opposition to the reclaimed identity. As I have argued elsewhere (1993), the result is an endless cycle of accusations and inclusions as we intone ever longer moralistic lists of identities in a futile attempt to dam the floods of interminable difference.

The irony of difference is thus its complicity with the idea of homogeneity after all. A focus on difference ultimately seeks either to unite the different in a 'we' which is a source of social unity, as in the multiculturalism debates, or to exclude the different for the sake of social unity, as in post-Soviet nationalism. The recognition of difference might appear to suggest an acquiescence in human limitation, in which we recognize that we are all defined by different, perhaps incommensurable, cultural identities. But in much of this work there is a hope that if we could only hear other voices aright, dialogue would then be possible and differences could be surmounted, transcended or eclipsed. Advocates of difference find it hard to let identity be.

A similar example of this politics of bad faith in the face of human finitude is the extent to which contemporary Russians – with the support of Western leaders – persist in trying to control the past. With the rejection of communism has come an attempt to rewrite Soviet history, again to rename streets and towns, to obliterate the immediate past for the sake of some prior, supposedly pristine history. For both reformers and nationalists, this has involved censorship of the press, the blocking of opposition; in effect, another cycle of repression, another futile attempt to deny that the self is a creature of time, conditioned by the past and with obligations to the future. We should be wary of assuming that contemporary politics is devoid of that potent urge to defy finitude which typified the Soviet era; we cannot release ourselves from the burdens of personhood.

Conclusion: beyond utopia

It is time, many Russians now say, to give Lenin a decent burial. In this spirit of reconciling ourselves to the fact of our mortality, it remains to consider how we can conceive of our mortal existence in a way that makes for a better approach to politics. Mere resignation in the face of our finitude is a tempting response. We might admire, for example, the medieval view of death as a public act, which bade farewell to the worldly community and marked the much-heralded entry into the community of God (Ariès, 1974). But maturity about our finitude was obtained at the cost of a disregard for the public domain of the living: politics was understood fatalistically, the province of superiors whose rule was beyond most mortals' ken or control. Political theory has been poorly served by this resigned view of death (see Sypnowich, 1991).

We moderns have erred in assuming that the only alternative to Christian fatalism about mortality is Promethean arrogance.[5] Another option may lie in confrontation with finitude, an attempt to render death meaningful by means of a contribution to the social. This is, of course, one strand of the Marxist and Bolshevik view of immortality, which as we saw has its dangers. In particular, the idea of activity which commemorates the actor suggests that the reality of individual death is somehow effaced by personal contributions to the public. Such utopianism can result in a contempt for the living. But the idea of commemoration can be conceived in a way which offers the possibility of a politics that takes the improvement of social conditions, the betterment of the milieu of the mortal, labouring self, as its aim. If the idea of labour which transforms the world and honours the memory of its author takes as its starting point the finitude of human existence, it is possible to forge a politics that aims to improve the conditions of life without transforming the nature of life itself. There are three aspects to this, as follows.

First, when we admit that human beings are not after all gods, but flawed, mortal creatures, we are in a better position to strive for social change which makes the most of our capacities and possibilities. It is, after all, a society fit for such beings which is the true utopia (if I may continue to use the term). Second, while the Soviet obsession with monuments obscured the reality of mortality, there does exist a dialectical relationship between the public monument to longevity and the improvement of conditions for the corporeal, finite self. And it should be achievements on behalf of mortal bodies that serve as the monuments for generations to come. This would mean that the finite self, far from a repressed ghost, is in fact a guide to politics, providing a sense of the obligation between generations. As Richard Wollheim notes, mortality provides the ground for our choices; a deathless life would be meaningless, morally empty (Wollheim, 1984: 265–80). The idea of a memory which outlives our own existence is a kind of conscience under which we form our actions.

Thus, recognizing our short time on earth, our obligation to those who come after us affords us the humility and modesty necessary for political projects. We will not achieve utopia, but the utopian urge, constantly to improve and remake our world, can be harnessed to give our mortal existence meaning and fulfilment. Today's Russia is characterized by a marked indifference to the public realm, as Russians abandon the civic culture of monuments, patriotic duty and sacrifice of self for the common good. A drive for mere self-preservation, a relentless pursuit of self-interest or, as Hobbes put it, 'commodious living' is the preoccupation of individuals in the graveyard of Soviet communism. The opulent public buildings of the Soviet era are neglected, but some individuals ape their pretensions as they exploit opportunities afforded by the introduction of the market in the context of unequal access to modes of enrichment. Instead of utopian immortality, the aggrandizement of corporeal existence is now the explicit and unabashed creed of the new entrepreneurs in post-communist Russia. So long as the dream of socialist utopia fails in the hands of those who get rich on its defeat, it is not surprising that the popular imagination concludes that getting rich is all there is left to pursue. This is also a kind of denial of death, but one of private bad faith, the sense of immortality of the immature person, which conceives the pursuit of life in its sensual forms as the only thing that matters. It lacks the sinister politics of the grand designs of immortality, but it too fails to look to politics as a collective endeavour for confronting the realities of the self.

I have argued that the theme of immortality is inherent in utopia, and in particular in the Bolshevik utopian ideal. The struggle against finitude cannot be dismissed simply as quackery in the domain of science; it was also an all too real cultural phenomenon with roots in the Marxist tradition. Marx's view of labour, his theory of history, his ideal of communism, cannot therefore stand as pristine philosophical counters to Soviet history. The struggle against finitude was the impetus for a marvellous visionary project, but it gave socialism an impossible task which spawned an authoritarian response, and ultimately, a cynicism about politics. Moreover, the aspiration to transcend finitude continues to haunt contemporary political projects in Eastern Europe and the West. Instead of conceiving of mortality as an obstacle to full human flourishing, I have proposed that we acknowledge our mortality as the basis for a utopian urge which recognizes its status as a perennially unmet aspiration. This utopian urge serves as an impetus for the pursuit of emancipatory projects which would give our lives meaning and purpose while fulfilling our obligations to those who come after us. It would also provide a more balanced outlook on the past, as something from which we can learn, not by simple reversal, but by a frank reckoning with its legacy for the present. Only then can we hope to achieve a politics worthy of the mortal self.

Notes

A version of this paper was presented at the political philosophy seminar series of the University of Toronto in February 1994; I am grateful to David Dyzenhaus, Danny Goldstick, Mark Kingwell and other participants for stimulating and helpful comments.

1. Bernard Williams relates that as a young man Descartes believed that medical science, based on physics, would be able to slow down ageing (see Williams, 1978: 258). Condorcet, in true Enlightenment spirit, proposed that human beings' perfectibility was infinite and everlasting life a possibility. He harboured fears, however, about the prospect of overpopulation (Condorcet, 1795). Malthus seizes upon these in his *Essay on the Principle of Population* (1806: Vol. 2, bk. 3, ch. 1).

2. 'The Great Utopia' was the name of a 1992 exhibition of Russian and Soviet avant-garde art from 1915 to 1932, organized by the Guggenheim Museum of New York, the Tretyakov Gallery of Moscow, the Russian Museum of St Petersburg and the Russian Ministry of Culture. An impressive book of essays was produced for the exhibition (Guggenheim Museum, 1992), to which reference is made in the course of this chapter.

3. Neither enjoyed much popularity in practice; Stites notes that peasants were indifferent to, or disliked, these new modes of marking death, while some communists distrusted ritual, 'no matter how Bolshevized'.

4. This section relies heavily on Nina Tumarkin's illuminating study (1983).

5. In Mary Shelley's *Frankenstein*, for example, a revolt against mortality is effected by blaspheming against the Christian understanding of immortality in the making of a new being out of human remains.

References

Ariès, Phillippe (1974) *Western Attitudes Toward Death*, trans. Patricia M. Ranum. Baltimore: Johns Hopkins University Press.

Bakhurst, David (1991a) *Consciousness and Revolution in Soviet Philosophy*. Cambridge: Cambridge University Press.

Bakhurst, David (1991b) 'Political emancipation and the domination of nature: the rise and fall of Soviet Prometheanism', *International Studies in the Philosophy of Science*, 5(3).

Berdyaev, Nicolas (1966) *The Russian Revolution*. Ann Arbor: University of Michigan Press.

Bethea, David M. (1989) *The Shape of Apocalypse in Modern Russian Fiction*. Princeton, NJ: Princeton University Press.

Blake, Patricia (1975) 'The two deaths of Vladimir Mayakovsky', Introduction to Vladimir Mayakovsky, *The Bedbug and Selected Poetry*. Bloomington: Indiana University Press.

Bogdanov, Alexander (1908), *Red Star*, ed. Loren Graham and Richard Stites, trans. Charles Rougle. Bloomington: Indiana University Press, 1984.

Bowlt, John E. (1985) 'Constructivism and early Soviet fashion design', in Gleason et al. (1985).

Clark, Katerina (1978) 'Little heroes and big deeds: literature responds to the first Five-Year

Plan', in S. Fitzpatrick (ed.), *Cultural Revolution in Russia, 1928–31.* Bloomington: Indiana University Press.

'Communist Party of the Soviet Union' (1976), *Great Soviet Encyclopaedia*, 3rd edn, Vol. 12. London: Collier Macmillan.

Condorcet, Marquis de (1795) *Sketch for a Historical Picture of the Progress of the Human Mind*, trans. J. Barraclough, intro. S. Hampshire. New York: Noonday, 1955.

Dennett, Daniel (1981) 'Where am I?', in *Brainstorms: Philosophical Essays on Mind and Psychology.* Brighton: Harvester.

Edie, James, Scanlon, James and Zeldin, Mary-Barbara (eds) (1965) *Russian Philosophy*, Vol. 3. Chicago: Quadrangle Books.

Engels, Friedrich (1890) 'Socialism: utopian and scientific', in Marx and Engels (1978).

Fitzpatrick, Sheila (1970) *The Commissariat of Enlightenment: Soviet Organisation of Education and the Arts under Lunacharsky, October 1917–21.* Cambridge: Cambridge University Press.

Freeborn, Richard (1982) *The Russian Revolutionary Novel: Turgenev to Pasternak.* Cambridge: Cambridge University Press.

Gassner, Hubertus (1992) 'The constructivists: modernism on the way to modernization', in Guggenheim Museum (1992).

Gleason, Abbott, Kenez, Peter and Stites, Richard (eds) (1985) *Bolshevik Culture.* Bloomington: Indiana University Press.

Globe and Mail (1991) 'The keeper of the corpse in Red Square', (repr. from *Der Spiegel*), Toronto, 21 September.

Gogol, Nikolai (1836) 'The Nose', in *Diary of a Madman and Other Stories*, trans. A. McAndrew. New York: Signet, 1961.

Goncharov, B. P. (1976) 'Vladimir Vladimirovich Mayakovsky', *Great Soviet Encyclopaedia*, 3rd edn, Vol. 15. London: Collier Macmillan.

Gorky, Maxim (1910) *A Confession*, trans. William Frederick Harvey. London: Everett.

Guggenheim Museum (1992) *The Great Utopia.* New York: Rizzoli International Publications.

Hare, Richard (1962) *Maxim Gorky: Romantic Realist and Conservative Revolutionary.* London: Oxford University Press.

Jakobson, Roman (1973) 'On a generation that squandered its poets', in E. J. Brown (ed.), *Major Soviet Writers: Essays in Criticism.* Oxford: Oxford University Press.

Jangfeldt, Bengt (1977) *Majakovskij and Futurism: 1917–21.* Stockholm: Hylaea Prints.

Kline, George (1968) *Religious and Anti-Religious Thought in Russia.* Chicago and London: University of Chicago Press.

Laclau, E. and Mouffe, C. (1985) *Hegemony and Socialist Strategy: Towards a Radical Democratic Politics.* London: Verso.

Lenin, V. I. (1917) *State and Revolution*, in *Selected Works in Three Volumes*, Vol. 2. London: Lawrence & Wishart.

McClelland, James C. (1985) 'The utopian and the heroic: divergent paths to the communist educational ideal', in Gleason et al. (1985).

Malthus, T. R. (1806) *An Essay on the Principle of Population.* London: J. Johnson.

Markov, D. F. and Timofeev, L. I. (1976) 'Socialist realism', in *Great Soviet Encyclopaedia*, 3rd edn, Vol. 24. London: Collier Macmillan.

Marx, Karl (1844) 'Economic and Philosophic Manuscripts' in Marx and Engels (1978).

Marx, Karl (1845) 'Theses on Feuerbach', in Marx and Engels (1978).

Marx, Karl (1852) 'The Eighteenth Brumaire of Louis Bonaparte', in Marx and Engels (1978).

Marx, Karl (1867) *Capital*, Vol. 1, abridged in Marx and Engels (1978).

Marx, Karl and Engels, Friedrich (1845–6) *The German Ideology*, in Marx and Engels (1978).

Marx, Karl and Engels, Friedrich (1848) *Manifesto of the Communist Party*, in Marx and Engels (1978).

Marx, Karl and Engels, Friedrich (1978) *The Marx–Engels Reader*, ed. Robert C. Tucker. New York: W. W. Norton.

Masing-Delic, Irene (1992) *Abolishing Death: A Salvation Myth of Russian Twentieth-Century Literature*. Stanford, CA: Stanford University Press.

Matossian, Mary (1968) 'The peasant way of life', in Wayne S. Vucinich (ed.), *The Peasant in Nineteenth Century Russia*. Stanford, CA: Stanford University Press.

Mayakovsky, Vladimir (1972) *Poems*. Moscow: Progress.

Polan, A. J. (1984) *Lenin and the End of Politics*. London: Methuen.

Read, Christopher (1979) *Religion, Revolution and the Russian Intelligentsia, 1900–1912*. London: Macmillan.

Richardson, Ruth (1987) *Death, Dissection and the Destitute*. London: Routledge & Kegan Paul.

Robin, Régine (1992) *Socialist Realism: An Impossible Aesthetic*, trans. Catherine Porter. Stanford, CA: Stanford University Press.

Shatskikh, Aleksandra (1992) 'Unovis: epicenter of a new world' in Guggenheim Museum (1992).

Shklovsky, Viktor (1972) *Mayakovsky and his Circle*, trans. and ed. Lily Feiler. New York: Dodd, Mead.

Sloterdijk, Peter (1987) *Critique of Cynical Reason*, trans. Michael Eldred. Minneapolis: Minnesota University Press.

Sochor, Zenovia A. (1988) *Revolution and Culture: The Bogdanov–Lenin Controversy*. Ithaca and London: Cornell University Press.

Stites, Richard (1985) 'Iconoclastic currents in the Russian revolution: destroying and preserving the past', in Gleason et al. (1985).

Stites, Richard (1989) *Revolutionary Dreams: Utopian Vision and Experimental Life in the Russian Revolution*. Oxford: Oxford University Press.

Stites, Richard (1992) *Russian Popular Culture: Entertainment and Society since 1900*. Cambridge: Cambridge University Press.

Sypnowich, Christine (1990) *The Concept of Socialist Law*. Oxford: Clarendon Press.

Sypnowich, Christine (1991) 'Fear of death: mortality and modernity in political philosophy', *Queen's Quarterly*, 98(3).

Sypnowich, Christine (1993) 'Some disquiet about "difference"', *Praxis International*, 13(2).

Tumarkin, Nina (1983) *Lenin Lives! The Lenin Cult in Soviet Russia*. Cambridge, MA: Harvard University Press.

Wiles, Peter (1965) 'On physical immortality', pts 1 and 2, *Survey*, 56, 57.

Williams, Bernard (1973) 'The self and the future', *Problems of the Self*. Cambridge: Cambridge University Press.

Williams, Bernard (1978) *Descartes: The Project of Pure Enquiry*. Harmondsworth: Penguin.

Wollheim, Richard (1984) *The Thread of Life*. Cambridge, MA: Harvard University Press.

Wood, Paul (1992) 'The politics of the avant-garde', in Guggenheim Museum (1992).

Young, George M. (1979) *Nicolai F. Fedorov: An Introduction*. Belmont, MA: Nordland Publishing.

Young, Iris Marion (1990) *Justice and the Politics of Difference*. Princeton, NJ: Princeton University Press.

7

The Social Self in Political Theory: The Communitarian Critique of the Liberal Subject

Stephen Mulhall and Adam Swift

If politics is about anything, it is about how societies govern themselves – how communities establish and exercise power over the individuals who make them up. The theme of this collection, then, is not merely tangential to, nor merely one amongst many of, the concerns of political theory. The question of how to conceive the relation between self and society constitutes the very centre of that discipline.

It may, however, be unduly optimistic to think of this matter in terms of a single answer to a single question. For there are at least two distinct ways in which one might be concerned with the relation between society and the individual. On the one hand, there are explicitly normative questions. We may, for example, wish to determine what moral obligations, if any, bind an individual member of society to other members, or whether she can live a worthwhile and fulfilling life without participating in society – or at least in some supra-individual or communal institutions. On the other hand, there is a 'genetic' question which at its simplest runs as follows: should we understand society as the product of individuals, or individuals as the product of society? Here, the issue is whether it is sensible to regard society as the outcome of decisions made by *ex hypothesi* pre-social individuals, or whether we should rather acknowledge the extent to which societies precede, form and constitute the individuals who together compose society itself.[1]

That these questions can be distinguished does not imply that they are readily separable, nor is it at all easy to specify the precise way in which they are related. It has, for example, seemed plausible to some theorists that rejecting the (sociologically and philosophically naive) understanding of society as the outcome of an agreement between individuals entails rejecting moral individualism of the sort that is associated with much liberal thinking. But is it really the case that recognizing the genetic priority of society over the individual makes any given moral or political claim (e.g. concerning individual rights, or duties to the community) more or less plausible? Can factual or conceptual premises really lead so directly and so unproblematically to evaluative conclusions?

As this collection makes clear, the claim that the self should be understood to be 'socially constituted' is making a difference to a great many
academic disciplines. Undoubtedly, some of the excitement generated by
that claim has been due to the belief that it provides the basis for
substantive moral and political conclusions, perhaps conclusions of a kind
critical of prevailing norms and ideologies. In this chapter we discuss a
contemporary debate within political theory that has brought such issues
to the fore: the communitarian critique of liberalism, which objects to
liberalism's failure to acknowledge the socialness of the self, a failure that
some have taken to warrant the rejection of liberalism as a substantive
moral and political doctrine.

Our discussion will be structured as follows. First, we shall examine the
communitarian critique as it applies to the most influential statement of
contemporary liberalism, John Rawls's theory of justice as fairness. We
will suggest how Rawls might defend himself, thus indicating that at least
certain varieties of liberalism need not be vulnerable to the charge of
denying the socialness of the self. Second, we shall outline Charles Taylor's
communitarian attack on the libertarianism propounded by Robert
Nozick. Here we shall argue that the Nozickian variant of rights-based
political theorizing is indeed guilty of myopia with respect to the socialness
of the self, but that the consequences of this are less fundamental than
might be thought. Finally, we shall discuss the communitarian critique of
the methodology, as opposed to the substance, of liberal political
theorizing. Here the focus is upon the alleged tendency of liberal theorists
to deny or repress their own socialness – their own cultural situatedness as
representatives of a political tradition with a specific history. We shall
conclude with an attempt to establish the true significance of this charge.

The two faces of the social contract

Almost from its inception, liberalism has been accused of operating with a
conception of the self that is 'atomistic', one that denies or overlooks the
importance of human society to the development and flourishing of the
individual. The classical liberal emphasis upon society's obligation to
respect and defend the rights of its individual members has led many to
suspect that a liberal polity cannot help but ignore or repress the value of
community. And the traditional foundation for individual rights, a picture
of individuals emerging from a state of nature to found society by means
of a social contract, has reinforced the idea that the autonomy liberalism
attributes to human beings presupposes a conception of persons as
essentially pre-social. Nonetheless, this charge of 'atomism' has proved
notoriously difficult to press home in a way that elicits widespread
conviction. Its centrality to the communitarian critique of liberalism was
welcome in seeming to promise a precise and sophisticated formulation –
if not a definitive resolution – of the issue.

The writers who were gathered under the communitarian banner exhibited a wide range of interests and opinions, but their rejection of atomism and their suspicion of its foundational importance to liberalism formed one of their most basic common features. Michael Sandel (1982) referred to the liberal conception of the person as 'antecedently individuated', the boundaries of its identity fixed prior to experience and immune to revision. Alasdair MacIntyre (1981, 1988, 1990) talked of an 'emotivist self', essentially unencumbered by the social roles or evaluative perspectives it adopts. Charles Taylor (1985, 1989) referred simply to an 'atomist conception of the self' which denied the 'social conditions for the full development of our human capacities'. And Michael Walzer (1981, 1983, 1987, 1994) saw this tendency to abstract the self from its social contexts as flowing into an excessively abstract methodology in political theory. It is therefore hardly surprising that these writers were thought to manifest a deep family resemblance.

Another similarity was evident in their most common choice of target, Rawls's *A Theory of Justice* (1971). A brief presentation of his key idea makes it easy to see why. For Rawls, the proper way to think about justice is to imagine what distributive principles would be agreed to by people in an 'original position' behind a 'veil of ignorance', deprived of all knowledge of their particular circumstances – their social position, their natural endowments, and their conceptions of the good. The intuition captured here is that which links fairness to ignorance. If I do not know which of the five pieces of cake that I am cutting I am going to end up with, then it makes sense for me to cut them fairly; similarly, if people do not know how the social arrangements upon which they are deciding will affect them personally, then it will make sense for them to choose fair ones.

Given these constraints and the degree of uncertainty they generate, Rawls argues that people in the original position would choose certain specific principles of justice, and a clear system of priority among them. But since, as he emphasizes, the original position is constructed precisely so as to deliver conclusions of this sort, it is clear that the weight of the theory rests upon the coherence and attractiveness of that construction. Critical attention has therefore tended to focus upon the substantive claims that are embodied in the veil of ignorance and, in the case of Rawls's communitarian critics, upon the conception of the person that they seem to presuppose. For who are these shadowy people that populate the original position? Could one sensibly imagine subjects who lack all self-knowledge, all awareness of their circumstances, attributes and conceptions of the good, and yet regard them as able to make choices concerning principles of justice? Could one sensibly imagine them as subjects at all? In short, it seemed that Rawls, by placing the device of a hypothetical contract between individuals deprived of their social and cultural particularity at the centre of his theory, was susceptible to the same objection that confronts all who understand society as the outcome of a contract: the objection that this is to take seriously what can only be a

myth – the myth of the pre-social or asocial individual. The original
position was thus understood as making explicit what those suspicious of
liberalism's individualistic tendencies had always alleged – that liberals fail
to acknowledge the socialness of the self.

Indeed, adherence to the contract metaphor seems to amount to a
failure to acknowledge the socialness of the self in each of the two senses
we distinguished earlier. First, by conceiving society as something that
individuals agree to create, it appears to neglect the point that people
necessarily derive their self-understandings, identities and conceptions of
the good from a social matrix, and so that society precedes (because it
constitutes) the individual. Whether we understand this as an empirical
claim about socialization and psychological development or as a conceptual point about the impossibility of thought or moral life outside a
social setting, the contract model seems not so much to neglect it as to
deny it. It therefore gets the relevant genetic priority the wrong way round.
Second, and more substantively, the contract metaphor seems to imply
that liberalism regards society as essentially a co-operative venture for the
pursuit of individual advantage, an association formed by individuals
whose essential interests and identities are defined without reference to the
community of which they are members. Rawls's assumption that the
parties to his hypothetical contract are mutually disinterested and
motivated only by a concern to maximize the satisfaction of their goals in
conditions of uncertainty seems to neglect conceptions of the good and
self-understandings that are communal in content. It appears to ignore the
possibility that relations with others are intrinsically valuable over and
above any instrumental worth they might possess as part of the pursuit of
one's personal goods.

Or so the communitarians argued. But even before Rawls himself began
to contribute directly to the debate, there was evidence enough in the text
of *A Theory of Justice* to cast doubt on both of these communitarian
claims. First, it was clear that the original position was a device of
representation, a means of modelling a substantive moral understanding of
people's interests and capacities. For Rawls justifies the epistemic
constraints of the original position on the grounds that they model the
sense in which it is appropriate, when thinking about justice, to regard
people as free and equal. By depriving the choosers of all knowledge of
their social position, income and talents, he effectively nullifies the
inequalities that result from the distribution of natural and social
advantage, rendering all equal. Since people are not responsible for being
born into one family rather than another, or for being talented or
untalented, a theory of justice should take no account of such differences.
And, by depriving the choosers of any knowledge of their conceptions of
the good, Rawls claims to be representing the sense in which it is appropriate to regard ourselves as free. For on his view, what is of fundamental
importance is not the particular conceptions of the good that individuals
have chosen, but their capacity to frame, revise and rationally pursue such

conceptions. What matters, from the point of view of justice, is people's freedom to make their own choices, not whatever it is that they choose.

Rawls therefore holds that the capacity to reflect upon and revise one's particular attachments is of great moral significance. He also presupposes that it is possible for people to refrain from invoking certain facts about themselves in certain argumentative contexts. But he is not committed to the incoherent idea that people can mentally detach themselves from all their values at the same time, or to denying that such ends and commitments are often (or even always) derived from the societies into which we are born and raised. In short, the original position models a normative claim about the relative importance of certain human capacities and characteristics in the form of a self-denying epistemic ordinance. It neither expresses nor presupposes any sociological or philosophical claim about the origins of human ends and self-understandings or the feasibility of some sort of psychological dismemberment.

Moreover, the substantive moral values that Rawls's theory embodies, although individualistic in a certain sense, are not such as to accord no place to shared goals or conceptions of value that are communal in content. For although his conception of society as a fair system of social co-operation between free and equal persons does place emphasis upon essentially individual capacities and upon the establishment and maintenance of individual rights, it does not reduce social relations to instruments of purely individual advantage. Explicitly rejecting such an understanding of his contract doctrine, Rawls insists that human beings have shared final ends and value their common institutions and activities as goods in themselves. And just as science, art, families and friendships are examples of what he calls, following Humboldt, 'social union', so a society well ordered by the principles of justice as fairness can itself be regarded as a social union of social unions. The successful carrying out of just institutions is the shared final end of all the members of society, and these institutional forms are prized as good in themselves. A liberal society will, of course, be good for the individuals within it, since it will provide an arena within which their most fundamental capacities will be respected and will flourish. But this is a genuinely social good, only realizable through joint activity based on a shared final end.

It seems, then, that even if the contract metaphor can be used so as to deny the socialness of the self in both the genetic and the normative senses of that phrase, it need not have this role in contemporary liberalism. This conclusion is supported by Rawls's more recent writings (1993), where he argues that those who accuse him of denying the socialness of the self have misinterpreted both the substance and the method of his theory. Justice as fairness, Rawls now claims, is a purely political conception of justice. By this he means that its scope is restricted to the basic structure of constitutional democratic regimes (applying only to their most fundamental social, political and economic institutions, and not, for example, to churches, universities and hospitals); that it does not depend upon the truth of any particular comprehensive philosophical, religious or moral doctrines about human well-being; and that it is formulated only in terms of certain fundamental ideas that are implicit in the public political culture of democratic societies.

This understanding of the theory of justice as fairness raises a host of questions, not least that of its relation to the theory's original presentation in *A Theory of Justice*; and Rawls himself has admitted that certain aspects of that presentation were seriously misleading. But what matters for our purposes is whether or not this purely political reading of the original position and its veil of ignorance provides any further reason for believing that liberalism can retain the contract metaphor without thereby committing itself to an asocial view of the self. For on this interpretation, Rawls can continue to claim that the original position is intended to model a substantive normative vision of society as a fair scheme of co-operation between people conceived as free and equal. But he is also free to emphasize that this is a view of persons as citizens (i.e. one that applies only to their role as members of the political community and not to their non-political lives), and that it is derived solely from ideas that are available in the public political culture of Western democracies – ideas that are common to people who may nonetheless have very different comprehensive conceptions of human well-being.

Rawls's reason for seeking and promoting a conception of justice that is political in this last sense is that he wants it to be publicly justifiable to all members of a pluralist society. He is well aware that a diversity of comprehensive moral, philosophical and religious doctrines have flourished in Western democratic societies, and that as a result, the citizens of these societies affirm a plurality of conflicting, and indeed incommensurable, conceptions of the meaning, purpose and value of human life. In such circumstances, any conception of justice that presupposed the truth of one particular comprehensive doctrine would necessarily conflict with some other, precluding the possibility of agreement between citizens committed to these alternative views. If, however, a conception of justice can be developed that draws only upon ideas that are implicit in the public political culture and so implicitly shared by all, whatever their comprehensive doctrines, it can form the basis of a conception of politics that can be justified to and affirmed by all citizens, regardless of their other commitments.

This notion of public justifiability, of the value of a society that can be justified to all of its members, is central to Rawls's thinking about the status of his own theory because it follows directly from its substance. Rawls is committed to liberalism in politics, and so to a conception of citizens as free and equal. Political power, however, is coercive; so its exercise must, if it is to be legitimate, respect the freedom and equality of all citizens, which is possible only if it is publicly justifiable to all of them. In other words, the goal of public justifiability presupposes a distinctively liberal understanding of the nature of politics and the proper relation between the individual and society.

This point is relevant to our concerns because the methodological restrictions imposed by the goal of public justifiability reinforce Rawls's claim that he is fully aware of the socialness of the self. First, Rawls must avoid relying upon any controversial philosophical, metaphysical or sociological doctrines – and the idea that the individual precedes society, or that individuals can detach themselves from all of their values at once, would certainly count as controversial. Second, his insistence that his conception of the person as citizen is constructed from resources that are available in the public political culture implicitly acknowledges that the ends, commitments and values that go to make up our self-understandings have a social origin. Third, it is precisely because Rawls recognizes the important influence of the social matrix on individuals' self-understandings that he requires a fully public justification of his conception of justice; only then can the influence of the social be compatible with the individual freedom that liberalism aims to respect.

The purely political nature of Rawls's liberalism thus reinforces his claim to be fully cognizant of the socialness of the self understood in a genetic sense. But it also provides him with a further response to those communitarians who advance a normative version of that thesis. We saw earlier that some of them criticized his conception of society as instrumental, calling for a stronger conception of the intrinsic worth of common goals. In reply, we suggested that these critics failed to appreciate the sense in which Rawls's view of a well-ordered society regulated by his conception of justice would invoke and embody genuinely communal goods. Now we can see that, for Rawls, those communal goods must be understood as such in a very specific sense – on pain of failing to respect the limits of the purely political. For we might gloss the idea of the intrinsic worth of participation in political community in two very different ways. One would centre on the fact that the preservation of democratic liberties requires the active participation of citizens possessed of those virtues (e.g. tolerance, mutual trust) needed to maintain a constitutional regime. With such a view Rawlsian liberalism is entirely compatible, since political participation of this sort is crucial to the long-term viability of any society that embodies an understanding of justice as fairness, and can be justified solely by reference to ideas about citizenship that are available in the public political culture.

However, the good of political community could also be understood in ways which depend on the idea, advanced by Aristotle amongst others, that political activity is the privileged locus of the good life for human beings, that participation in the political life of one's society is an indispensable part of human flourishing. With this view Rawlsian liberalism would be in direct and explicit conflict, because such an understanding of politics invokes a comprehensive conception of the good. Its vision of citizenship derives from a wider vision of human well-being with which many citizens will inevitably disagree, and so violates the requirement of public justifiability. Any political action taken on its authority would amount to employing the coercive powers of the state in ways that fail to respect the freedom and equality of all citizens. In short, insofar as Rawls's communitarian critics took him to have failed to consider such substantive conceptions of the intrinsic worth of political community, they entirely misunderstood his position. He did not overlook such possibilities, but rather rejected them as a threat to the rights of citizens in a context of moral and political pluralism. If to do this is to propound a normative commitment to the asocialness of the self, then the Rawlsian liberal would happily plead guilty to the charge.

The presuppositions of libertarian individualism

So far, we have offered an array of reasons for thinking that modern liberal attempts to articulate an understanding of politics on the model of a social contract need not entail any commitment to a belief in the asocialness of the self, whether understood in a genetic sense or in any normative sense short of a neo-Aristotelian, civic humanist vision of political community. However, the distinction between the genetic and the normative has not in fact been very carefully observed by the participants in this debate. Some communitarians tended to run the two levels together, assuming that to establish the philosophical or sociological priority of society over the self was enough to undermine any assignment of normative priority to the self over society. As we have suggested, the use of the contract metaphor in the liberal tradition encourages this confusion. In apparently embodying both a philosophical or sociological stance about the relation between self and society *and* a substantive or moral one, it encourages the belief that an attack on one amounts to an attack on the other. But this in turn raises the more general question of whether there is any necessary connection between genetic and moral questions in this area. Would establishing the sociological or philosophical truth about the relation between individual and society limit the normative options open to us in political theory? Does, for example, the tenability of a substantive commitment to the priority of individual rights hang (even in part) on denying that society is prior to the individual in a genetic sense?

Our examination of Rawls's version of liberalism suggests a negative conclusion. But matters may look different if we focus on more extreme versions of individualism in politics – ones we might categorize as libertarian rather than liberal; and in this context an influential case has been made by Charles Taylor for believing that claims about the genetic priority of society over the individual can subvert the self-understandings of certain political theorists. Taylor's target is that class of theorists – among which he includes Locke and one of his most provocative modern-day descendants, Robert Nozick (1974) – who make individual rights a fundamental principle in politics, but who deny the same status to a principle of belonging or obligation. Individual rights are unconditionally binding on all of us, but any obligation to support, obey or sustain society is conditional or derivative, dependent upon our consent or our calculation of our individual advantage. Taylor argues that, given the truth of certain sociological and philosophical claims about the priority of society over the individual, this position is internally inconsistent.

Taylor begins by asking why such theorists ascribe rights to human beings: what is the point or purpose of so doing? His answer is that they do so because they regard human beings as possessed of certain potentialities or capacities that are valuable, and so worthy of respect, and it is the nature of these capacities that determines the shape of the proposed schedule of rights. The idea that all human beings have the right to life, freedom, the profession of convictions, and so on, reflects a belief that the capacities involved in the exercise of such rights (the capacities for rationality, self-determination, the free development of one's mind and character) are of special significance; without them, the specifically human potential of the human animal would be crippled or remain dormant.

If, however, we acknowledge the intrinsic worth of these capacities, then we are committed not only to acknowledging people's rights to them (and so to the negative injunction that we avoid interfering with or suppressing them) but also to furthering and fostering them. For if the capacities are good in themselves, then their development and realization (both in others and in ourselves) are also good, and so the task of aiding their development (at least in certain circumstances, and insofar as we can) is something in which we ought to engage.

In the case of libertarian thinkers, the capacity that is given supreme importance is autonomy – the freedom to choose one's own mode of life. If, then, it could be shown that this capacity, together with any others with which it is connected, could only be developed in society, or in a society of a particular kind, an assertion of the primacy of rights could not be combined with the assignment of a secondary or derivative status to the principle of obligation or belonging. For if, as Taylor believes, the capacity to develop independent moral convictions is impossible outside a political culture sustained by institutions of political participation and guarantees of personal independence, then any failure to sustain those institutions would undermine the very capacities whose preservation is the implicit goal of our commitment to a schedule of rights. The moral conviction that grounds our ascription of rights also commits us to whatever actions are necessary to sustain a society that protects rights. The two commitments or obligations are equally unconditional, and stand or fall together.

Taylor considers two ways of avoiding the conclusions of this argument. One is for the rights theorist to reduce the schedule of rights by pruning the list of human capacities that she considers to be worthy of respect. Thus, instead of citing human capacities for autonomous moral thought, she might talk solely of sentience. Since the capacity to feel pleasure or pain is widely thought to be part of the endowment of any living creature, and not to be such as to require development or realization, its creation and preservation will not presuppose any particular social context. Such a move would certainly be consistent, but the cost of making it would be high. For the schedule of rights that respect for such a capacity would support would be minimal indeed: it would include only the right to life, to desire-fulfilment and to freedom from pain – any other rights would be means to these ends. We would therefore have no reason for thinking that non-human animal life-forms were of any less value or significance than human ones; and we would have no grounds for objecting to a practice of transforming autonomous human agents into child-like lotus-eaters by means of drugs or, Nozick's own example, the use of 'experience-machines'. What this picture leaves out is precisely freedom in the sense of autonomy, the precondition for self-development and self-realization.

Alternatively, the theorist asserting the primacy of rights could contest the thesis about the essential socialness of the self with which Taylor forges the connection between rights-ascription and the obligation to play one's part in sustaining the relevant social practices. She might, for example, argue (very implausibly) that the capacity for autonomy and self-realization could emerge and be maintained in the complete absence of any and all social structures – the wolf-child option. Or she could claim that the only social context necessary for individual self-development is the family, and not the wider political and social community. Taylor rejects such a view, insisting that both a certain type of political community (with constitutional government, democratic voting practices and methods of representation) and a web of economic and cultural institutions (such as a culture of trade union activity, wage bargaining and business contracts, unarranged marriages, artistic and philosophical representations of the significance of individual autonomy) are required for the full development and maintenance of the relevant human capacities. But the outcome of this disagreement is irrelevant to our concerns: the fact that the argument concerns the degree of importance to be assigned to the social matrix, and that both sides recognize the pertinence of its outcome to their normative dispute, indicates that genetic questions about the socialness of the self do have implications for normative questions about the relation between individual and society. The moral issue of whether we are obliged to sustain particular social practices depends on the genetic issue of the extent to which they are necessary preconditions for our becoming fully human selves.

It is, however, equally important to appreciate that this conclusion need not unduly ruffle the feathers of those concerned to defend the autonomy of the evaluative sphere. For what Taylor's argument shows is that, given the truth of certain hypotheses about the acquisition and development of human capacities, those committed to a certain conception of human worth are compelled to accept certain other obligations. But this is a point about the logical consequences of an initial value-commitment: it demonstrates that even an extreme version of political individualism involves certain communal obligations, but it neither justifies nor condemns that individualism. To be sure, Nozick's belief that we have an absolute right to do as we wish with our property is shown to be inconsistent with the very moral claim that motivates his libertarian emphasis on individual freedom of choice, so that a genetic contention certainly serves to undermine a substantive political-theoretical conclusion. But the very fact that Taylor's argument exposes an inconsistency rather than questions an evaluative premise indicates that we have here no bridging of the supposed chasm between evaluative and non-evaluative matters.

Taylor himself cannot be said to confuse genetic and normative matters: his argument does not point out the social origin of certain human capacities in order to demonstrate their value. His aim is rather to show that no one who values those capacities can disown an obligation to sustain their social preconditions. Pointing out the social origin of highly valued individual capacities certainly demonstrates that that high valuation should extend to include the relevant social matrices: we cannot consistently will the end and not will the means necessary to it. But this merely highlights the communitarian implications of individualism rather than identifying any reason to reject individualism per se. The libertarian is left facing a choice; she is not told which choice to make.

A similar conclusion must also be drawn with respect to a related mode of argument that is often associated (however erroneously) with Taylor and with communitarians more generally. This argument depends upon the claim that the particular ends, goals and values that individuals hold, as well as their conception of themselves (whether as individuals possessed of a certain identity or as creatures possessed of a self and so capable of developing such an individual identity), have an essentially social origin. The argument runs as follows. Liberalism presupposes a conception of human beings as possessing certain fundamental capacities, primarily the ability freely to develop, pursue and revise both their conception of human well-being and their specific identity as persons. This essentially individualistic conception, however, is itself derived from society: people do not come into the world already possessed of this self-understanding, and they will not come to acquire it or to develop the capacities it presupposes (and so to live their lives in the manner it demands) in the absence of certain very complex and pervasive social institutions and practices. But then the individualistic content of this conception of the person flatly contradicts the circumstances of its realization. It imputes a degree of autonomy to the individual as against society which could not even be conceived, let alone pursued, except in a very specific social context; its very existence therefore depends upon something that it attempts to deny or reject. The inevitable conclusion would then seem to be that it is this conception of the person that must be rejected.

In the light of our discussion, we can easily see where such an argument breaks down. First, to affirm the fundamental importance of individual rights is not to reject the importance of social arrangements necessary for their achievement and protection. A normative commitment to

individualism not only need not deny the socialness of the self in a genetic
sense, it can happily be combined with its acknowledgement – as Rawls
combines his individualism with a commitment to the necessity and value
of membership of a political community structured in accordance with his
principles of justice. For, second, even if an individualistic conception of
the person has a social origin and requires certain social conditions if it is
to be developed and enacted, all that follows is that those committed to
that conception must also commit themselves to certain sorts of social
participation. It does not entail that this conception of the person is any
more or less valuable and appropriate than we originally thought. As we
saw with the debate between Taylor and Nozick, there may be something
contradictory about an individualist ideal that regards the obligation to
sustain the social matrix as a secondary or derivative obligation. But there
is nothing contradictory about a society that is structured in such a way as
to encourage the development and flourishing of an individualist ideal, and
so nothing contradictory in supporters of such an ideal encouraging
themselves and others to participate in its establishment and maintenance.

The social self of the political theorist

So far we have been exploring the consequences of accepting that the self
is socially constructed for those versions of political theory that place
individual rights at the centre of political concern. The focus has been
upon what impact, if any, this assumption has upon the liberal vision of
individual and society. However, acknowledging that the self is socially
constructed inevitably affects more than the conception of the self
advanced by a given theorist in, as it were, the substance of her theory; it
must also affect her understanding of her own position as a theorist – her
self-understanding. When all is said and done, theorists are selves, too.
And if selves are socially constructed, then the question of a theorist's own
relation to her society and to the political traditions of which she stands as
a contemporary intellectual representative might also take on a new aspect
and a new pertinence.

The inevitable reflexivity of the issue of the socially constructed self was
clearly manifest in the development of the communitarian critique of
liberalism. We have seen that the question of how this issue might alter the
liberal conception of self and society was thoroughly canvassed by communitarians, but the question of how it might alter the liberal theorist's
self-conception was no less central. Michael Walzer, for example, took
issue with Rawls on both levels: he offered a very different theory of justice
(one based on a notion of complex equality) as an alternative to Rawls's
conception of justice as fairness, and he also questioned the philosophical
and normative coherence of what he took to be the methodology manifest
in *A Theory of Justice*.

Walzer's target is the abstractness of Rawls's approach. The original position was constructed on the assumption that a just distribution of social resources would be the one chosen by ideally rational people knowing nothing of their own situation and barred from making particularist claims. In order to ensure impartiality, Rawls claims that the social resources of which justice demands a principled distribution are 'primary goods' – things it is supposed a person wants whatever else she wants, things of which one will want more rather than less regardless of the particular life-plan one wishes to follow. To meet these criteria, primary goods must be defined in a very general and abstract way – as rights and liberties, opportunities and powers, income and wealth – rather than more specifically defined social resources whose worth will differ according to the purposes for which they might be employed. Walzer's claim is that such a disattention to the particularity of social goods is conceptually and normatively incoherent.

It is conceptually incoherent, Walzer argues, because it fails to recognize that the significance of a given social good derives from the community whose good it is. Its meaning is not given by nature but by essentially social processes of conception and creation, and so will differ between societies. Even bread can signify not only sustenance, but also the Sabbath, the body of Christ, the means of hospitality; which meaning predominates on a given occasion is dependent on the particular culture concerned. Moreover, the social meaning of the good in part determines its right distribution. Walzer claims, for example, that the meaning of health care in our society connects it with the treatment of illness and restoration of health, from which it follows that it should be distributed to people only insofar as they are ill and not insofar as they are able to afford it. The principles for distributing social goods cannot be determined independently of a grasp of their precise social meaning and so of their particular cultural context. In other words, the abstractness of Rawls's primary goods ensures that any principles derived from them will not be usefully applicable to the concrete cases that interest us. But if attention is paid to the particularity of the goods concerned, then distributive principles will emerge from their social meanings, and the principles derived from consideration of hypothetical primary goods will be entirely superfluous.

Walzer's normative argument against abstraction is that any political philosophy that seeks detachment from the particular society of which the philosopher is a member will fail to accord proper weight to the opinions of the philosopher's fellow citizens; it will, in short, be undemocratic. The theorist aims for truth, for a blueprint or principle which has a superior status to the mere opinion of his fellow citizens. Democracy, however, is not about truth but about making decisions that embody the will of the citizenry – citizens have the right to make their own laws even if they make them wrongly. Only if the philosopher's blueprint is offered to the citizenry as one more opinion, for which democratic support is solicited, can it avoid the trap of valuing reason above the general will. Only thus can it respect the particular traditions, culture and practices of the society to which it applies, and hence the particular understandings of the philosopher's fellow citizens. What Rawlsian abstraction lacks, in Walzer's view, is a proper respect for people as culture-producing creatures, beings who make and inhabit meaningful worlds. We do them justice by respecting, not overriding, their creations in all their particularity.

Walzer thus offers a specific interpretation of the idea that the social-situatedness of the theorist places constraints on her methodological strategies. Only by restricting herself to interpreting the social meanings of specific goods in the culture of which she is a member can she hope to construct a theory that has enough content to be useful and that is couched in terms that respect the capacity of her fellow citizens to make and inhabit meaningful worlds. This methodological point may contradict the assumptions of some liberal theorists, but whether it undermines an essential aspect of liberal political theorizing is more doubtful; certainly it fails to count as a critique of Rawls. As we have seen, in his recent writings Rawls expresses a commitment to a purely political liberalism in which his theory of justice figures as the intellectual expression of the public political culture of constitutional democracies and as applicable only to the political sphere of such democracies. In other words, Rawls's theory is now presented as culture- (and sphere-) specific in a way remarkably similar to that advocated by Walzer. Moreover, Rawls's reason for these restrictions is normative – the idea of public justifiability expresses Rawls's belief that the exercise of coercive state power should respect the freedom and equality of all citizens. Against this background, the construction of primary goods can be seen as Rawls's interpretation of prevailing social meanings. His claim is that our conception of people as citizens implicitly demands that in our treatment of them we abstract from their particular conceptions of the good – respecting rather their capacity to frame, revise, and pursue such conceptions – and the notion of primary goods is designed to embody this normative commitment. In this respect, the abstractness of Rawls's primary goods is a function of his desire to respect prevailing social meanings: it is not an abstraction from cultural particularity but rather a result of attending to the specifically liberal culture of which we are a part.

It seems then that liberal individualism is not necessarily vulnerable to the methodological critique that flows from Walzer's understanding of the socialness of the political theorist. However, another communitarian writer, whose substantive commitments tend towards the neo-Aristotelian, has offered a significantly different interpretation of the socialness of the theorist – and one that he believes also engenders a specific critique of liberalism.

Alasdair MacIntyre argues that, just as any individual is capable of acquiring the conceptual resources necessary for moral agency only from participation in essentially communal practices and institutions, so any individual theorist must recognize that the possibility of engaging in her very specific sort of intellectual enterprise depends upon participation in what he calls a tradition. A tradition is constituted by a set of practices and is a mode of understanding their importance and worth; it is the medium by which such practices are shaped and transmitted across generations. Traditions may be aesthetic (e.g. literature or painting), economic (e.g. crafts, professions or trade unions) or even simply geographically based, but their most evident manifestation is in political, moral and religious form. They all provide a communal matrix within which an argument about their purpose (their contribution to human well-being) and the best way of achieving it, as well as about their changing understanding of how such arguments can best be conducted, is developed and sustained. Only traditions can provide an individual (and so a theorist) with the resources needed for making rational decisions about how to pursue the good, for it is in terms of a specific tradition's best understanding of itself that she evaluates and criticizes her efforts to live the good life. Part of developing a conception of the good life for human beings is developing a conception of how one might evaluate and criticize one's attempts to enact and extend that conception. And just as the former is open to revision and redefinition, so the standards by which such revisions are justified and rendered intelligible are themselves open to reshaping.

MacIntyre's argument for the socialness of the self embeds the theorist in a communal matrix in a way that differs from Walzer's in at least two respects. First, the relevant structure is a tradition rather than a political community or a society – the former may cut across either or both of the latter. Second, that structure provides not only a specific way of conceptualizing social resources and visions of the good but also a specific conception of how to go about evaluating them. For MacIntyre, the view that there is an ahistorical, eternally applicable mode of practical reasoning to which all rational individuals must commit themselves is no more intelligible than the idea that there is an abstract, universally applicable notion of a social good. It follows that the work of any political theorist is essentially tradition-bound: both its conception of politics and its conception of how one ought to engage in theorizing about politics are relative to a historically and culturally specific communal matrix.

In MacIntyre's view, acknowledging this truth has unenviable consequences for liberal political theorists, for it means acknowledging that their work is the contemporary expression of a tradition with a peculiar history. On MacIntyre's account, liberal political theory originally formed part of a historical project designed to develop a morality that transcended tradition. The aim was to found a social order in which individuals could emancipate themselves from the contingency and particularity of traditions by appealing to genuinely universal, tradition-independent norms: to provide a political, legal and economic framework in which assent to a set of rationally justifiable principles would enable those who espouse widely differing conceptions of the good to live peaceably together. However, in the process of attempting to realize this project, liberal thought and practice generated a highly specific conception of moral and political life, and of the appropriate standards with which to evaluate and criticize that conception. In particular, it developed a distinctively procedural conception of a just social and political order, within which moral beliefs are treated as expressions of purely private and personal preference and the good life for human beings is understood to be one in which a variety of goods is pursued but no overarching good supplies any overall unity to life. This conception of the just society is embodied, debated and carried forward by a set of texts and in social, legal and cultural institutions. In short, what began as an attempt to transcend tradition ended with the creation and perpetuation of a new one.

This sounds like another attempt to accuse individualism of advocating principles that are inconsistent with the social presuppositions of its continued existence – only this time the problem arises not from the liberal theorist's emphasis on the independence of the individual from society, but from her understanding of herself as enunciating a tradition-independent vision of politics and society. But is this attempt any more successful than the earlier one? After all, as our examination of Rawls's political liberalism should have made clear, contemporary liberal theorists would hardly be surprised to be told that the continued sustenance of a specific social and political order was their overriding aim. What their liberalism seeks to transcend is not tradition but the particular comprehensive conceptions of the good espoused by citizens in pluralistic societies. Its goal is neutrality of a particular sort. Liberals cannot avoid discriminating between liberal political orders and other forms of politics; nor can their doctrine be expected to be neutral in its effects on the ways of life favoured by citizens. But they do espouse neutrality of justification, which forbids them from invoking comprehensive conceptions of the good in defence of state policy and actions. If the tradition that liberal theorists represent embodies only this sort of neutrality, then their espousal of it does not seem to stand in any real contradiction with that dependence on tradition of which MacIntyre is so keen to remind them.

Even if this defence is accepted, however, we should acknowledge several grains of truth in MacIntyre's accusations. First, granting that contemporary liberal theorists have always known that they are beginning from liberal starting points, that fact may not have been so evident to many in contemporary society for whom the primary appeal of liberalism may well consist precisely in its claimed neutrality between competing conceptions of the good. It may not be inconsistent for liberalism to acknowledge the true extent of its neutrality and toleration, but such an acknowledgement might well alter our views about its attractiveness as an ideology. Second, we should recall that Rawls's political liberalism is able to maintain its claim to neutrality because it distinguishes between a purely political liberalism (upon which it can legitimately draw because its elements are generally available in the public political culture) and a comprehensive liberalism (which it must eschew on the grounds that it would not be accepted by many citizens). This distinction is, in effect, a methodological version of the split between public and private spheres in society that forms one of the substantive linchpins of liberal thought. By emphasizing the tradition-dependence of liberal theorizing, MacIntyre underlines the fact that both distinctions are tradition-specific. And just as the distinction between public and private realms is rejected by many comprehensive conceptions of human well-being (by neo-Aristotelians and by many religious traditions, for example), so Rawls's political/comprehensive distinction may itself be a matter of real controversy. MacIntyre's argument against Rawls thus points to this distinction's reliance on specifically liberal conceptions of practical reasoning and of human life more generally; it claims that the very distinction between purely political theories and comprehensive moral doctrines is itself a part of a comprehensive liberal conception of the good. If that claim could be substantiated, then we would have grounds for saying that the tradition-dependence of liberal political theorists points to a contradiction within their theory itself; even the claim to a limited form of neutrality between conceptions of the good would be impossible to sustain.

On the reading just presented, MacIntyre's charge against those who advocate individual autonomy in politics is not that there is some inherent logical or practical contradiction between being necessarily tradition-dependent as a theorist and advancing an individualist political vision. Rather, it suggests that the tradition-dependence of liberal theorizing highlights in a particularly revealing way two points about the content of such theorizing: its exaggerated claims to neutrality, and (most importantly) its exaggerated emphasis on autonomy. If one of the most fundamental facts about people who propound a theory that gives absolute priority to individual autonomy is that they are not and cannot be autonomous of a communal matrix of inquiry, then perhaps we should question their substantive claim that the most fundamental fact about people is their autonomy. We might, indeed, insist upon the limited extent to which even the autonomous individual can transcend her social context.

Of course, emphasizing the non-autonomous status of the defenders of autonomy with a view to questioning the absolute priority of the value of autonomy is not to generate a knock-down normative case from a philosophical premise. It is rather an ad hominem argument designed to induce in liberal political theorists a sense of existential paradox: their individualistic beliefs do not correspond to the real circumstances of their lives. And the normative point is not that autonomy is valueless, but rather that its worth must be understood against this backdrop of individual dependence upon and respect for structures and resources external to the individual – a backdrop against which autonomy takes its place as one good among many rather than as something to which unquestionable and absolute priority must be assigned. Even if, in the end, this argument fails to convince, it is at least not obviously incoherent. We must accept, therefore, that a philosophical claim about the socialness of the self can have an impact on our assessment of the significance liberals attribute to autonomy.

These considerations also bring home to the professional intellectual an important point about the way in which we understand individual autonomy. For just as the contemporary liberal theorist has to regard herself as the inheritor of, and to some extent constrained by, a particular tradition of social and political thought, so the social actor, however capable of framing, revising and pursuing ends for herself she may be, necessarily operates in a manner that is limited by the particular ends and self-understandings she affirms at any given time, and by her culture-dependent conception of their significance. If the communitarians are wrong to suggest that liberals must think us able to detach ourselves from all our particular ends and values simultaneously, they are surely right to insist on two things. First, that it is only by taking some commitments as given that we can have any basis for evaluating those ends regarded as up for revision at any particular time; and second, that the ends and commitments we have must in some sense be given to us by our society. The liberal emphasis on our capacity to change our minds must be supplemented by an appreciation that, in the absence of grounds upon which to justify it, any such change can be wholly arbitrary, and that those grounds are inevitably given by the social matrix. The autonomous individual no less than the political theorist necessarily works with the conceptual resources made available to her by her society.

This is not, of course, to say that the individual is unable to criticize, reflect upon, and even reject the values that pervade the culture in whose terms she comes to conceive herself and her ends. The impossibility of autonomy as complete transcendence of commitment and context does not consign the individual to slavish internalization of the norms that prevail in her society. Here, again, we may draw a parallel between the theorist and the actor, for it is equally important to note that Walzer's and MacIntyre's methodological prescriptions have been interpreted as implying the impossibility of a genuinely critical political theory. This is because the emphasis they both place upon the theorist's relation to her social context has been thought to raise the methodological spectre of relativism and the normative spectre of conservatism. If all that political theorists can do is interpret the prevalent social meanings of goods, or provide new interpretations of one, essentially tradition-bound understanding of social justice, then it will be impossible to construct theories that might seriously challenge the status quo in their own culture or be used legitimately to criticize other cultures. From this perspective, it seems, judgements of justice are inescapably relative to a given culture, and are not likely to stray far from that culture's prevailing understanding of justice. In that case, the critical momentum of the idea of justice disappears, and the practice of political theory changes very substantially as a result.

This is a deep and difficult issue that we cannot pursue here. Suffice to note that both MacIntyre and Walzer deny that any such conclusions should be drawn from their work. Each defends a conception of the theorist's relation to her milieu that is sufficiently nuanced to allow for potentially radical disagreement with prevailing conceptions of justice, and to permit legitimate criticisms of other cultures and their practices. If their accounts are correct, we need not conclude that acknowledging the socialness of the self even at the level of the theorist's self-understanding would affect the conduct of political theory in a fundamentally undesirable way. It will not, however, leave that conduct entirely unaffected, for it might significantly alter our conception of how the activities of the political theorist, and the academic institutions in which those activities are pursued, relate to the political community in which they are embedded. And granting the socialness of the self in the substance of one's political theory will surely be no less significant a change. It may not force us to abandon individualism for neo-Aristotelianism. But it may require us to admit the inconsistency in valuing the individual's right to autonomy whilst not accepting the obligation to sustain the kind of society that makes autonomy possible, or to recognize that liberals share a vision of the intrinsic good of political community. Acknowledging the socialness of the self may profoundly change the way we define and defend liberal individualism.

Note

1. We should note that assigning priority to society over the individual in this second, genetic sense can itself be defended in two different ways. The first relies upon empirical evidence and arguments. Familiar processes of socialization make it banal to observe that human beings derive their self-understandings (and much more) from the social contexts into which they happen to be born and, more interestingly perhaps, the deliverances of developmental psychology suggest that it is implausible that human beings could develop their full potential in the absence of social structures and interaction with others. The second approach, however, would rely upon conceptual analyses of the kind familiar in philosophy. We may, for example, argue that no creature could count as a human being if it lacked certain rational capacities, and then attempt to demonstrate that nothing would be identifiable as a manifestation of rationality outside certain complex communal contexts. (See the introduction to this volume: pp. 5–6). Often, of course, these two different types of consideration are run together (sometimes confusingly so) in one chain of argument, as when someone draws upon psychological studies to claim that language acquisition is a precondition of individual development, and then uses the private language argument to demonstrate that language is an inherently social phenomenon. For our purposes, the implications of assigning genetic priority to society over the individuals who make it up are more pertinent than the consequences of offering a conceptual as opposed to an empirical justification of that assignment. So we will do no more than note this further complexity, and emphasize at the outset that our decision to label these issues as 'genetic' is intended solely to stress their non-normative nature. It does not indicate any desire to deny or downgrade the importance of non-empirical considerations in any full exploration of the matter.

References

MacIntyre, A. (1981) *After Virtue*. London: Duckworth.

MacIntyre, A. (1988) *Whose Justice? Which Rationality?* London: Duckworth.

MacIntyre, A. (1990) *Three Rival Versions of Moral Enquiry*. London: Duckworth.

Nozick, R. (1974) *Anarchy, State and Utopia*. Oxford: Blackwell.

Rawls, J. (1971) *A Theory of Justice*. Cambridge, MA: Harvard University Press.

Rawls, J. (1993) *Political Liberalism*. New York: Columbia University Press.

Sandel, M. (1982) *Liberalism and the Limits of Justice*. Cambridge: Cambridge University Press.

Taylor, C. (1985) *Philosophical Papers* (Vol. 1: *Human Agency and Language*; Vol. 2: *Philosophy and the Human Sciences*). Cambridge: Cambridge University Press.

Taylor, C. (1989) *Sources of the Self*. Cambridge: Cambridge University Press.

Walzer, M. (1981) 'Philosophy and democracy', *Political Theory*, 9(3).

Walzer, M. (1983) *Spheres of Justice*. New York: Basic Books.

Walzer, M. (1987) *Interpretation and Social Criticism*. Cambridge, MA: Harvard University Press.

Walzer, M. (1994) *Thick and Thin: Moral Argument at Home and Abroad*. Notre Dame, IN: University of Notre Dame Press.

8

The Gendered Self

Diana Coole

The question of the self has always been central to feminism since in society we are never simply selves, but gendered selves. The status and consequences of this gendering lie at the heart of feminist inquiry. For political theorists more generally, problems of the self have also recently been the focus of attention, stimulated by debates between liberals and communitarians and by postmodern concerns with deconstructing subjectivity. While my focus in this chapter is on the gendered self, my wider aim is to see how feminist theories are related to these other discourses.

The social self

Approaches to the self which interest political theorists can be located on a continuum ranging from the liberal-individualist, through the dialectical-communitarian, to the poststructuralist-postmodern.

At the *liberal-individualist* pole are positions usually associated with capitalist modernity and the Enlightenment, although a number of distinct variants should be recognized. First there is the *methodological individualism* associated with classical liberalism (Hobbes, Locke, Bentham), where society is never more than an aggregate of its individual constituents and human nature is universal and static. Rational self-interest, exchange relations and contracts, together with the coercive power of the state, hold competitive individuals together in a precarious state of peace. Co-existence is seen to inhibit liberty rather than enriching persons, while co-operation never transcends the individual (or familial) interests that motivate it. Second, there is the *epistemological* emphasis on individual autonomy associated with Descartes, Kant and the Enlightenment, where a universal reason inherent in each individual grounds knowledge and morality. Although individuals on this account are not immune to the effects of the natural and social worlds, they are capable of transcending them in order to reason in an impartial and formally universal way. Finally, there is the *ethical individualism* associated with nineteenth-century liberals like John Stuart Mill, which emphasizes individuality in the sense of developing one's personality and capacities. Although individuals remain the focus of analysis, and there is a residual hostility towards society and state as threatening liberty, there is some movement towards a more social conception of participants. Their talents cannot develop in isolation but require stimulus from a vibrant culture, itself dependent upon the openness, and even eccentricity, of individuals.

Despite variations within these positions, they all have an individualist foundation: the social threatens freedom or reason while the powers of rational, autonomous individuals are a means of controlling the external domain. Typically, they invoke an essential self, unencumbered and decontextualized: values and identities comprise an outer circle of options amenable to rational choice, but the inner self sustains an integrity independent of its shifting identifications or the specifics of its embodiment. Such an account is also attributed to contemporary liberals like Rawls (by e.g. Sandel, 1982), although its roots lie in older notions of the soul.

Moving further along the continuum, we arrive at *dialectical-communitarian* conceptions of the self. Here the notion of a social self finds more straightforward articulation. Although these conceptions gesture towards an opposition between society and self, they ultimately reconcile them, for they suggest a dialectical relationship whereby interpersonal exchanges restructure the personal while personal evolution in turn influences the social. In general, exponents of this view also subscribe to a belief in a core self which is free and autonomous, but they further insist upon the profound influence of the social in shaping that subjectivity over time (see Kymlicka, 1988: 192). This self is as much a product of modernity as the atomistic and competitive qualities dialectical-communitarians denounce (see e.g. Habermas, 1987; Taylor, 1989; Benhabib, 1992). It is irrevocably situated and its identity inseparable from its values and beliefs, which in turn arise less from acts of pure choice than from shared cultural horizons and habitual practices.

Certain tensions nevertheless haunt this dialectical resolution. To what extent are individuals caught within horizons that remain immune to conscious retrieval and rational criticism? Controversies about agency versus structure (or culture) rage within this position, with exponents shifting between an emphasis on autonomy on the one hand and social determination on the other. For while communitarians fear an assertive individualism that corrodes communities and shared values (a particular concern among recent communitarians), they are also eager to strengthen the critical powers of autonomous selves against potentially damaging encroachments by the social order, which they associate with ideology, bureaucracy and a social pathology of conformity (a particular concern among neo-Marxists). Thus dialectical-communitarians tend to see the effects of the social as ambiguous: as both enriching and inhibiting, liberating and oppressive. From this perspective, modernity itself is dialectical, engendering both the emancipatory powers of the self and the social forces that crush it. Like liberal-individualism, dialectical-communitarianism has strong normative dimensions, with exponents often adding to their descriptions of the social self an ethical commitment to more sociable, communal subjects.

Finally, at the other end of the spectrum, there are *poststructuralist-postmodern* positions.[1] Again, these harbour much diversity. A psycho-analytically informed wing associated with Lacan declares the stable, self-identical self to be fundamentally illusory. Similarly for Foucault, power does not oppress pre-existing subjects but constructs them, such that their sense of self is only a product of modern discourses and disciplinary techniques. Individual differences are produced by ranking and classifying persons according to current norms; subjectivity is an effect of replicating those norms under conditions of surveillance and discipline. Foucault insists that the modern self is produced by a discourse of confession, wherein we are induced to articulate what seem to be deep truths of the inner self. That self, however, is created rather than revealed in this process. Thus, the individual

> is not to be conceived as a sort of elementary nucleus, a primitive atom, a multiple and inert material on which power comes to fasten or against which it happens to strike, and in so doing subdues or crushes individuals. In fact, it is already one of the prime effects of power that certain bodies, certain gestures, certain discourses, certain desires, can be identified and constituted as individuals. (Foucault, 1980: 98; see also 1981: 58–70)

Our modern sense of autonomy, in short, is the result not of liberation but of power.

These views should not be confused with more extreme versions of the dialectical approach, such as those neo-Marxist positions which argue that modern societies have become so ideologically closed and totally administered that the self has effectively disappeared. The latter criticisms are still motivated by nostalgia for the critical subject of an earlier modernity. Where communitarians conceptualize the social as a dialogical community modelled on conversation and aiming to enhance communi-cation (e.g. Taylor's 'webs of interlocution' [1989: 39]), postmodernists discern only a cacophony of voices caught in competing language games that are riddled with power. Subjects emerge only as the nexus point of criss-crossing threads of meaning, or as an effect of the microcircuits of power. Thus Lyotard writes:

> a *self* does not amount to much, but no self is an island; each exists in a fabric of relations that is now more complex and mobile than ever before . . . a person is always located at 'nodal points' of specific communication circuits, however tiny these may be. Or better: one is always located at a post through which various kinds of message pass. (1984: 15)

Subjectivity so produced is highly unstable. In opposition to modern ideals of a coherent and transparent self, the postmodern self is fluid and heterogeneous, decentred and dispersed across multiple identities. In contrast to the unifying, homogenizing discipline of modern normalcy, postmodern fragmentation is often presented as liberating, euphoric, schizophrenic (see, e.g., Jameson, 1991: 29).

This completes my introduction of the three approaches to the self dominant within political theory. I have located them on a continuum which traces the extent of the social's influence on the self. Thus for liberal-individualists, the social has no necessary role in constituting selves and is more likely to inhibit them. For exponents of the dialectical-communitarian position, there is an irreducible reciprocity between society and self. For postmodernists, there is no essential core self, it is the social (qua discourse) that produces the self as an effect of power.

It is in light of these three positions that I will address the question of the self's gendering. Before doing so, however, it will be helpful to look more closely at the terminology deployed. So far I have used the terms individual, subject and self fairly interchangeably and this is indeed how they often appear in the relevant literature. Yet some distinction is surely required. 'Individuals' are typically found within liberal discourses, especially among methodological individualists. In their classical formulation they are seen from the outside, as isolated, embodied units, even machines (Hobbes), possessors of certain human powers and interests but fundamentally separate from one another and standing in opposition to society.[2] Their subjectivity follows from a common human nature.

An explicit preoccupation with subjectivity arises in the eighteenth century. Ethical, political and aesthetic theories focus on the 'inside' of individuals conceived as possessors of inner depths. These are, as Macpherson (1977) puts it, developmental rather than possessive individuals, for whom an opposition between inside and outside is complemented by a distinction between a higher and lower self. Rousseau, Kant and later Mill all associate moral and intellectual activities with the control of a lower, appetitive self associated with desire and the body. The 'subject' is thus defined in opposition to objects, which include nature and society as well as the body and its passions. Subjectivity means separation from the object realm, yet paradoxically the subject who dominates objects must also exercise control over itself in order to banish its own contingency: the self becomes radically self-reflexive, an object for itself. This recognition that human beings are both objects of knowledge *and* subjects who know provided the impetus for the dialectical perspective that acknowledges the costs of modernity and its project of subjectivity.

With this there emerges a distinction between 'self' and subject. Once the self became an object of knowledge, a plethora of public discourses arose, aiming to inform it of its true nature and to prescribe criteria of normality and authenticity. Such discourses, from ethics to psychoanalysis, speak from a third-person position of detachment, such that the self becomes the subject of objective theories operative in the social realm. The self, on the other hand, is their alleged referent, a mystery which each bears within itself and which such discourses attempt to disclose. It is that inner core, a disposition of 'me-ness', an identity and first-person intuition, that reflection strives to recover.

On this view, the subject is irremediably social insofar as it is articulated through public languages. But what of the self? Here we confront, both conceptually and politically, the problem of the precise relationship between subject and self. How far do the effects of the social and its discourses reach? Does the self express itself through them? Can it exist at all outside them? From this perspective, it is the self that is properly the target of ethical concern, but any discussion must nevertheless rely on theories of subjectivity. Such theories might be perceived as emancipatory if they help enlighten the self about its true needs and motivations (thus, for example, psychoanalysis might be seen as therapeutic insofar as it stabilizes the self through self-knowledge), but they can never fully capture a self that is of an other order. Moreover, there is always the danger that discourses of subjectivity manipulate, or even construct, the self of which they speak (thus, for Foucault, psychoanalysis does not free or enlighten the self, but produces and normalizes it).

This fear is especially pronounced among romantics and feminists concerned that the self is misrecognized in objective accounts of subjectivity, so that an expressive or feminine self finds itself silenced. For them, the question is whether a more authentic self might express or create itself through aesthetic (or other non-cognitive) practices that bypass rational theories of the subject and the norms inherent in them. Indeed, for feminists such questions are especially crucial because the dominant discourses of subjectivity have been advanced by men using male norms, while the very language in which subjectivity and selfhood express themselves can be seen as phallocentric (Kristeva, 1986; Irigaray, 1985).

Postmodernists, on the other hand, avoid such concerns by collapsing the tripartite distinction between individual, subject and self into a single category of subjectivity. Eliminate discourses of subjectivity, and the illusion of an inner, autonomous self, like the quest for individuality, disappears. Selves, in other words, are but special effects, and the question of power arises at the level where they are discursively constructed rather than at the point where the integrity of the self might be threatened.

Gender and the self

Although all three positions sketched above seem indifferent to considerations of gender, and will therefore be faulted from a feminist perspective, they can nevertheless be developed to provide an explanatory framework for understanding gender and a political practice for challenging its oppressive consequences. This is because gender raises problems intimately connected to those posed by the individual, subject or self. Thus feminists ask whether gender reveals a truth about our inner selves and identities or whether it is only relentlessly reproduced through social practices and rituals that sustain sexual hierarchy. Does gender enrich or impoverish us? How far, in any case, is it amenable to political change or personal choice?

Historically, feminism emerged within liberalism and operated specifically within liberal horizons of ethical individualism. For both Wollstonecraft and Mill, human nature was essentially gender-neutral and rational while femininity was an artificial and degrading set of characteristics imposed on women by patriarchal culture and its practices. Sexual emancipation was accordingly associated with women's accession to the higher form of subjectivity already achieved by (bourgeois) men, facilitated by equal rights and opportunities. Subsequent feminists have argued, however, that the model of subjectivity equated with this autonomous civic self was not gender-neutral but constituted by idealized norms of masculinity, predicated on an exclusion and denial of everything designated feminine. On this view, the problem is not only one of women's inequality but of a gender bias increasingly seen as fundamental to Western culture, which splits mind and body and then grants the former – equated with the masculine – control over the latter – equated with the feminine. Women are thus associated with an irrational, lower self, requiring mastery. Such criticisms may be readily extended to Enlightenment accounts of autonomous, disembodied subjects.

This broad cultural critique of ethical individualism and epistemological rationalism has been supplemented by an equally far-reaching attack on methodological individualism. Like the communitarians, some feminists have disputed its universalist account of human nature and relationships, finding it morally and existentially impoverishing as well as methodologically inaccurate. Such feminists have urged a reappraisal of femininity as a source of sociable and associative ideals. Methodologically, they have disdained the formal, rationalistic accounts of human nature utilized by liberal-individualists, adapting instead sociological and psychological theories about the actual development of human subjects within society. In this context, socialization theories have been used extensively to explain the nature and origin of gender.

'Socialization' is a term often used synonymously with 'internalization', to suggest a process whereby rules external to the self enter into it, largely in the form of implicit norms and habits. This opposition between 'inner' and 'outer' is central to the understanding of subjectivity in socialization theories.[3] For such theories, a central question is how thoroughly the self is structured by socialization. This is especially important for the politics of gender. For unlike education, socialization suggests forces operative below the level of consciousness whose retrieval for rational scrutiny remains difficult, if not impossible. According to the tripartite distinction drawn above, socialization theories suggest sexed individuals, gendered subjects and ungendered (or androgynous) selves. The first is a pre-social given, the last an a priori assumption. Change must therefore occur at the second level, where socialization intervenes. Thus the type of gendered selves formed, the norms they take for granted, the sexual division of labour and the context of socialization, all become crucial for feminist politics. Indeed, virtually all shades of feminism shared this social constructionist approach until around 1980, even if Marxist feminists placed more emphasis on extra-familial experiences and the functional requirements of the economy in the reproduction of roles and their players.

In *Sexual Politics*, a classic example of socialization theory, Kate Millett explained sexual domination as the result of patriarchal ideology operating via 'internal colonization', 'interiorization' and 'conditioning'. Although both sexes are socialized into the requisite temperament, role and status, this does not emerge in men's consciousness as a problem, since their acquisitions are almost always advantageous and the whole process sustains their power.

For Millett, the most significant aspect of socialization is the development of 'temperament', which 'involves the formation of human personality along stereotyped lines of sex category ("masculine" and "feminine")' supplemented by sex role, an 'elaborate code of conduct, gesture and attitude for each sex' (1977: 26). Thus mind (temperament) and body (behaviour), inner and outer, coincide. Sex and gender, however, may in principle be related only arbitrarily, for sexual behaviour is 'almost entirely the product of learning' from the social environment, where we are socialized into (male) aggressiveness or (female) passivity. Patriarchal ideology thus seems to operate on two related levels. It socializes naturally androgynous selves into gendered individuals, where 'each personality becomes little more, and often less than half, of its human potential', and it produces an unquestioning acceptance of the myriad privileges and degradations that structure everyday life under patriarchy, thereby shaping 'character structure' and a 'habit of mind'; in short, a 'way of life'.

Feminists have subsequently criticized this approach for assuming essentially passive subjects who have a startlingly uniform set of characteristics and values imposed upon them. Millett sees no *active* dialectic between society and self, no diversity in the identities produced. Gender is imposed on sex with an extraordinary degree of success. For Millett, patriarchy rests on tacit consent rather than coercion, so 'perfect is its system of socialization, so complete the general assent to its values' (1977: 43). It is thus difficult to see how nonconformity might arise. Millett's tone contrasts sharply with the insistence of later feminists that gender does *not* align readily with sex, and that their correspondence, demanded by patriarchal cultures, is a site of misery, struggle and misrecognition (Rose, 1983: 9).

There is a certain irony in Millett's work. Although it was associated with the first flourishing of radical feminism, Millett retained the liberal-individualist conclusion that gender is a patriarchal imposition on an original self which she idealizes as genuinely human and authentic. She perceived femininity as a contingent, social construction, an impoverished identity to be resisted by strategies typically associated with ethical individualism: consciousness-raising, self-criticism, critical explication. Yet as her critics discern, she also subscribed to a determinist account whereby the social, in the form of patriarchy, so reconstructs each self that it is difficult to see how its impoverishment might be recognized or its authenticity restored.

More recent work on socialization has moved away from the liberal-individualist paradigm. Gender-neutral or androgynous selves are no longer idealized, for it is argued that gender is rooted so early and so profoundly within personality that prior to its acquisition there is no self at all. In addition, femininity is no longer seen as an impoverished identity but is praised for its sociable rather than individualistic qualities.

Important here is the use made by feminists of object-relations theory, which emphasizes the social aspect of the self insofar as it focuses on the development of selves through their relations (of separation and intimacy) with others (their 'objects'). However, this is not the conversational, dialectical sociability of communitarians, since the foundations of the gendered self are laid during the first, pre-Oedipal and pre-verbal year of life. There is thus little scope for autonomous participation in self-formation; if change is to occur, it will be by altering the conditions of socialization. Object-relations theory thus implies a politics not of the self, but of the family.

Originally object-relations theory associated maturity with separation and autonomy, but feminists detected in this a specifically masculinist bias and urged a focus on the differential evolution of feminine selves. This development owes much to the work of Nancy Chodorow (1978). Chodorow explains the emergence of distinct feminine and masculine personalities not as a result of internalizing different values, but as a function of the asymmetrical family: women, who universally mother, elicit contrasting responses from daughters and sons. Thus in consequence of the profound identification between mother and daughter, girls remain longer in the primary relational mode, developing fluid and permeable ego boundaries. Boys, on the other hand, separate from their mothers earlier and develop a self in opposition to the feminine with more rigid ego boundaries but a weak and defensive gender identity. As a result, boys are drawn to a value system and subject-orientation centred on autonomy and detachment. In other words, males are socialized to become the sort of selves that liberal-individualists describe as natural, while empathy, compassion and co-operativeness appear in girls because feminine selves are constituted through relatedness, connectedness and intimacy. Female selves have a stronger proclivity for experiencing the needs and feelings of others as their own; they feel more continuous with nature and more embedded in social contexts. While Millett associated gender difference with masculine activity versus feminine passivity, object-relations theory equates it with separation versus attachment. The implication follows that if we take communitarian values seriously, we should adjust our child-rearing practices to produce more feminine selves (notably through more shared parenting).

The ethical significance of this approach has been extensively explored by feminists, building on research by Carol Gilligan. Gilligan's psychological studies of moral development revealed 'two distinct ways of speaking about moral problems, two modes of describing the relationship between self and other' (Gilligan, 1982: 1).[4] Typically, male responses were liberal and individualistic, prescribing abstract and formal solutions to moral problems. Female moral responses, in contrast, overlapped with those espoused by communitarians, evincing 'a more contextual mode of judgment' (p. 22) predicated on a distinct conception of the self as embedded in a tissue of relationships requiring connectedness and care for others.

In this account of the feminine self, there is an internal relationship between the conditions of that self's production, its feminine characteristics and its normative commitments. The specificity of girls' socialization lies in their special closeness to the primary carer; the distinctness of the feminine personality lies in its capacity for empathetic connectedness; the particularity of a 'different' (feminine) moral voice resides in its predilection for caring. It is therefore no coincidence that a politics of community and an ethic of care should have attracted similar criticisms.

An ethic of care may threaten self-loss and self-sacrifice, just as the appeal to community suggests a dangerous collapse of boundaries between self and others. Too much care and community also pose a threat to otherness and difference, by absorbing them into the orbit of the self in its desire for closeness and mutual understanding (e.g. Young, 1990: 123), a threat analogous to that posed by the all-powerful mother. Politically too, feminists are aware that consensus and community have often meant marginalization of the feminine *as* the other. Thus the stronger the emphasis on the social, caring self, the more concerns about individuality (*qua* difference) return to haunt us. And the more theories of sexual identity emphasize the social character of the feminine self, the more they are criticized for the uniformity they imply. Recent efforts by democratic theorists to describe a dialogical community which combines openness with identity and pays attention to both 'general and concrete others' (Benhabib, 1992) are thus inflected through feminist arguments and anxieties concerning masculine and feminine voices (White, 1991).

We have seen how feminists turned to empirical accounts of socialization in order to understand gender as an aspect of individual development (influenced especially by *mothering*) within a patriarchal context. Compared with the extremely generalized and unsubstantiated accounts of human nature and the self advanced in much political theory, feminists' interdisciplinary approach to subjectivity, incorporating both moral and psychological studies of development, is instructive. It is nevertheless apparent that such studies soon lead us back to more general political and ethical questions about selfhood in its various modes and capacities. For if gendered selfhood is socially engendered, differently gendered selves might also sustain alternative kinds of society. It is also evident that questions of gender and selfhood are neither purely empirical nor purely theoretical.

It may yet be, however, that the very idea of a self to be uncovered is a mistake, since postmodernists suggest that the self is but a fabrication of discourse. It is to the postmodern account of the gendered subject, the third position on our continuum, that I now turn.

Postmodernists take up the idea that the gender of the self does not coincide with biological individuality. As we saw, the earlier social-constructionists made a distinction between sex and gender, an important move in denaturalizing and thus contesting sexual difference. Sex was presented as biological and gender as cultural, hence mutable. Although a few feminists tried to tackle the biological side of the equation (such as Firestone's proposal [1971] that reproductive technologies replace women as childbearers), a more popular move was to diminish its importance, treating fixed anatomical difference as virtually insignificant in light of its cultural mediations. For postmodernists, however, the problem lies in the psychic and cultural closures that are inscribed within the duality of the sex-gender system as such. Politically their strategy is to subvert the poverty of its either/or; to reinscribe gender and culture while trans-forming gendered subjectivity. For is not the existence of only two genders already an unwarranted assumption derived from dualistic and heterosexist ways of thinking? Why should two sexes be mapped on to only two cultural identities? Can we even be categorical in identifying two sexes? We might instead describe a continuum or matrix of differences which cultural dualism has forced into an oppositional and exclusionary dichotomy where 'diverse sexual differences are overdetermined in order to produce a systematic effect of sexual division' (McNay, 1992: 22). In other words, sexual difference might be an effect of gender rather than its cause.

This suggests that the sex/gender distinction itself is suspect and in unwitting collusion with a masculine hierarchy, where (feminine) body-nature is to be suppressed and transformed by (masculine) mind-culture. As Judith Butler puts it: 'This production of sex *as* the prediscursive ought to be understood as the effect of the apparatus of cultural construction designated by *gender*' (1990: 7). The effect of such arguments is to reconnect sex and gender. The body is a bearer of codes and not a biological given, and gender is no longer an arbitrary imposition on sex, but co-produced with it. Gender seems somehow to elaborate sex via shared social fantasies and practices, but the politically important conse-quence is that the entire system might be regendered (not degendered), in particular by subverting the dualism of gender itself.[5]

These arguments against sex/gender or masculine/feminine oppositions follow the general anti-binary approach of postmodernism and can be variously advanced using post-Lacanian psychoanalysis, Derridean deconstruction or Foucauldian genealogy. Whether a pre-Oedipal register of signification, a metaphor for what lies beyond the oppositional structure of metaphysics, or that which is constructed as the rational subject's Other, the feminine now suggests certain structures of meaning that are fluid and heterogeneous, subversive of the dualities of gender or the monolithic, unified self. If the feminine is affirmed here, it is because it disrupts the dichotomy of gender and not because it is itself an authentic identity. Indeed, on this view the feminine may have no particular relationship to women insofar as either sex might invoke this register of the pre-gendered, pre-self.[6] If those attuned to the feminine are sympathetic to co-existence, it is not because they are more caring or empathetic, but because they are open to otherness and difference, to the uncanny dimensions of the self and the non-rational dimensions of meaning (Kristeva, 1991). To be open to the feminine in oneself is to be in-process; to recognize that one is conscious and unconscious, incomplete, heterogeneous, radically unknowable and gender-complex.

Thus the feminine/masculine opposition shifts again: from passive/ aggressive and attachment/separation, to openness/closure. But now, feminine openness suggests the dispersal of gender duality itself. Sexual difference is inscribed across culture and the self such that the two are indissoluble. The paradigm favoured by modernist theories of subjectivity, where a (gender-)neutral account would reveal the truth about the sexual characteristics of the self, is precluded by the postmodern insistence that language constructs the reality of which it speaks.

Although postmodern accounts defy stable selfhood or sexual identity, their exponents generally insist upon the impossibility of instantiating an alternative sexual, or counter-symbolic, order of the feminine (the Other). There is scope only for transgressions; for an invocation of radical alterity invoked through aesthetic strategies. Psychoanalytically inspired post-modernists such as Julia Kristeva nevertheless insist that only those who are firmly positioned as subjects within the symbolic, within the Law, can summon the feminine without risking psychosis, a terrifying loss of selfhood not to be confused with liberation. This position is distinct from more cultural postmodernisms which have often emphasized not only the instability of the self, but also the ecstasy of its fragmentation.

Foucault has been important to feminists because his work focuses on the material construction of bodies via various disciplinary practices, rather than the psychological dimensions of the inner subject. For Foucault, the gendered body is a site of resistance as well as a target of power. Several feminists have applied the genealogical approach of Foucault's middle period to explain the constitution of female flesh via, for example, regimes of diet, exercise and fashion. This work, however, has tended to treat Foucault as merely extending socialization models, whereby the disciplining of the body supplements the colonizing of the mind, casting the body in an essentially passive role. Such approaches suffer from the same flaws as socialization theories; disciplinary power again seems too successful, too paralysing, to accommodate political contestation. More recent feminist work, and especially that which draws on Foucault's later thought, has restored a more active and resistant role to the body, where sexual difference and desire also emerge as discursive, rather than natural, regulators.

Judith Butler, for example, insists that there is no interior to the body's surfaces; bodily behaviour does not express some inner self. Gender is not an identity, but a fabrication or performance, sustained by corporeal signs and rituals: 'The various acts of gender create the idea of gender, and without those acts, there would be no gender at all' (Butler, 1990: 140). A 'tacit collective agreement' emerges with the repetition of performances to reproduce binary sex-gender. Sedimented over time, these repeated surface stylizations are so credible as to appear natural, maintaining the myth of a gendered core. Butler nevertheless insists that politics is possible because patterns can be reconfigured. Subversive strategies consist in a resistance to, or parody of, gender rituals. She cites the dissonant performance of cross-dressing as a particularly effective tactic: 'In imitating gender, drag implicitly reveals the imitative structure of gender itself – as well as its contingency' (1990: 137). The politically important consequence of such aesthetic transgressions is that the entire system might be regendered, in particular by multiplying the dualism of gender itself and subverting its apparent naturalness.

From a liberal or communitarian perspective, this position remains vulnerable to criticisms widely levelled at Foucault: there is no agent or motivation for staging resistance. However, Butler's response is to insist that the discursive production of subjects need not mean their determination. Rather, agency itself becomes the site of contestation. Indeed, if postmodernists are right in presenting subjectivity as a product of modern discourses or performances, then the success of these discourses lies precisely in the fact that we are constructed to feel relatively autonomous (a requirement of self-discipline), contesting the power that constrains even as it incites us.[7]

In his later work, Foucault suggested that subjectivity might even be an effect of self-creation, where the power exercised is of the self over itself. In a crucial passage he says:

> I do indeed believe that there is no sovereign, founding subject, a universal form of subject to be found everywhere. . . I believe, on the contrary, that the subject is constituted through practices of subjection, or, in a more autonomous way, through practices of liberation, of liberty, as in antiquity, on the basis, of course, of a number of rules, styles, inventions to be found in the cultural environment. (1988: 50)

Clearly much hangs on this 'or'. Historical considerations are crucial here. The particular aesthetic practices of self-creation he describes – an 'elaboration of one's own life as a personal work of art' (1988: 49) – were practised by the Greeks and could not be repeated in modern contexts. Yet Foucault suggests that self-creation is again a possibility as Christian morality declines and questions of sexuality and subjectivity come to the fore, due in part to the dissonance wrought by the women's movement and the subversions achieved by postmodernism.[8] There is scope to 'choose', or at least improvise on, a gendered style of existence, although within the constraints of the particular bric-à-brac and fragments we inherit. The aim must be to resist power (discipline, normalization) and to engender a coherent, but flexible and open, self. It is not then a question of *discovering* an authentic inner core, but of *self-invention*.

Although feminists like Butler have seized on this idea of gender restylization, it is precisely this project of self-creation which has provoked accusations that Foucault in fact reverted to the worst excesses of the liberal model: his aesthetic selves are accused of being individualistic, atomized, isolated, decontextualized, materially privileged, self-indulgent, apolitical, irresponsible, unethical and asocial (Dews, 1989: 40; Flax, 1990: 217; McNay, 1992: 10). The charge is levelled from a more dialectical perspective which emphasizes the significance of intersubjectivity and context.

It might seem, then, that our continuum is actually a circle, which only returns us to the empty, abstract and sexually unspecific, liberal-individualist self. However, one should not underestimate the role of either the unconscious and linguistic intransigence of sexual difference, from a psychoanalytic perspective, or the sheer weight of sedimented rituals in the literally more superficial corporeal inscriptions of gender described by Foucauldians. Indeed, Foucault's position in his later works can be interpreted as more akin to the dialectical-communitarian one: the self is capable of a certain freedom in relation to itself although limited by cultural constraints. It is precisely because modernity constructs subjectivity and certain ideals of selfhood, which are ultimately destabilizing, that regenerative strategies and a politics of the self are possible. Power and resistance – the discourses of subjective production *and* the aesthetic reinvention of selfhood – are two sides of one coin.

Moreover, although Foucault and Butler prescribe a personal politics, its strategies are surely collective to the extent that each recreation of subjectivity further weakens prevailing norms (although of course it only generates new ones, of which postmodern exhortations to multiplicity might be an example). Admittedly, there are echoes of a Millian voluntaristic individualism, with its eccentricity and experiments in living, but accusations of atomization seem wide of the mark given Foucault's hostility to the prescriptive subjectivity found in Mill and in liberalism generally. Moreover, Foucault (and Butler) must surely contest any claim that gender can be rationally and intersubjectively renegotiated within a dialogical community, since gender is a script played out in a non-rational domain. Strategies are thus open to the self which suggest an efficacious politics for feminism avoiding both the paralysis of communitarianism (or indeed of psychoanalysis in many of its guises) and the rationalism or naive voluntarism of liberal-individualism. But they are postmodern performative and aesthetic strategies quite different from those more traditionally employed in emancipatory politics.

Conclusion

I do not want to conclude by privileging any one account of the gendered self, since it seems apparent that questions of the self and its gendering are not of the sort that can be resolved by appeal to either empirical or introspective evidence, or rational deduction. The way we regard selfhood, and indeed ourselves, cannot be extricated from our cultural horizons with their particular political projects and discourses of subjectivity. This may rule out liberal-individualist claims regarding a universal human nature or essential self. But questions of whether there is a core self, and of the origins of gender, remain irresolvable and are probably misconceived tasks set within a particular discursive configuration with a penchant for grand narratives or universals. Regardless of the truth about selfhood, the point is surely that in modernity we are incited or socialized to act and think as relatively autonomous selves. In other words, if the self is an effect, it is not an illusion; if it is constituted by social and discursive powers, its freedom and autonomy (or sociability and relatedness) are an integral component and goal of its modern construction, whether that construction is associated with liberation or power. For feminists the question is only how far these processes are differentiated by gender.

Politically, the important thing is not somehow to 'get it right' by discovering the truth about the self in order to make the correct emancipatory response, but to recognize that there is quite legitimately a plurality of discourses on subjectivity, each bearing within it a politics that is discursively comprehensible and strategically appropriate. In terms of the distinctions introduced above, we might draw the following conclusions. Since discourses about *individuals* concern socially and economically positioned bodies, with their labour, sexuality and integrity, a politics of equality and rights – that is, struggles over economy and citizenship – seems apposite here. But discourses of *subjectivity* operate on a more unambiguously discursive level, where gender is prescribed and reproduced, such that practices of socialization, performance, language, normalization and identity are rightly contested, yielding a cultural and deconstructive politics. Because any politics of the *self* would necessarily resort to explication via discourses of subjectivity, it becomes inextricable from this politics of subjectivity; at best one might anticipate an ethics or aesthetics of the self, with political implications.

In light of this, feminist concerns with the gendered self appear deeply problematic, precisely because there is a tension – a discursive hiatus – between feminism's theoretical accounts of gender and its political commitments. Thus in trying to understand the durability of sexual difference and patriarchy, feminists have located gender ever more fundamentally and integrally within the self. Since however they renounce essentialism as politically conservative and paralysing, the deeper gender goes, the more its contingency must be asserted. Yet at the same time, that contingency must be portrayed as profoundly inertial and weighty, otherwise a naively voluntaristic politics ensues and patriarchy suddenly seems improbably flimsy. All the positions sketched above court this danger, whether it is via a liberal faith in self-education and willpower, a communitarian commitment to rational, intersubjective negotiation, or a postmodernist fantasy of self-reinvention. It seems, then, that a politics of gender is either too hard or too easy; the requirements of critique and of political change are always pulling against one another.

At the same time, feminists have been torn between deconstructing gender dualism and endorsing its multiplicity, on the one hand, and retaining notions of gendered identity and difference in order to ground a women's politics, on the other. Moreover, while feminist politics seems to require some notion of rational and autonomous agency, feminist theory has been busy demolishing it. Feminists have been unable to decide whether gender difference is impoverishing or enriching and whether a feminine identity, or subject-orientation, is a sign of oppression or liberation. Again, these questions seem to me to be fundamentally undecidable and relative to the context of inquiry. Where I find feminism to be exemplary is not in discovering the truth about the self and its gendering where others failed, but in its openness to an interdisciplinary approach which recognizes an internal relationship between theories of subjectivity, norms of selfhood and practices of individuals, thereby yielding a complex politics with multiple strategies.

Notes

1. The precise relation between poststructuralism and postmodernism is a complex matter. 'Poststructuralism' refers to a broad school of criticism which emerged in response to French structuralism in the 1960s and is associated with Derrida, Lacan, Deleuze, the later Barthes, Foucault, Kristeva and Baudrillard. Like their structuralist predecessors, poststructuralists treat all cultural phenomena as 'systems of signification', the meaning of which derives from the interrelations of their parts rather than a relation to an independent 'reality'. However, poststructuralists attack structuralist pretensions to objective analysis, 'deconstructing' the 'binary oppositions' at structuralism's heart and deploring the 'logocentrism' of Western culture. They celebrate the indeterminacy or plurality of meanings. 'Postmodernism' has been used to refer to the fractured and ironic cultural mood of late capitalist societies. However, the term now often denotes an intellectual posture that reflects loss of confidence in the ideas and 'grand narratives' that characterized 'the modern era' since the mid-seventeenth century: the project of finding foundations for human knowledge, the ideals of reason and scientific objectivity, the hope of founding a rational political order, the notion of an integral self, and so on. Thus conceived, 'postmodernism' embraces many poststructuralist ideas about language and culture. For simplicity's sake, in the rest of this chapter I use only the term 'postmodernism' deployed in this latter, general sense. Readers should be aware, however, of the complexities at issue.

2. The cultural variability of conceptions of individuation – the boundaries which define

the individual – is a fascinating issue. Liberal conceptions seem especially austere in comparison with, for example, Athenian, medieval or Hindu alternatives (see Parekh, 1992: 161).

3. I was struck by the frequency with which Carol Gilligan, in a public lecture at the London School of Economics in October 1993, invoked this opposition between inner and outer, insisting that the 'voice' of her *In a Different Voice* (1982) was literal not metaphorical, the medium by which the inner (self) was rendered outer.

4. Gilligan emphasizes, however, that her 'different voice' is not necessarily a female one. But like Chodorow, on whose work she drew, she found the correlation to be pervasive because of the universality of patriarchal conditions.

5. This is broadly the solution suggested by Plumwood (1989); see also Gatens 1991.

6. Some feminists, such as Irigaray (1985) and Braidotti (1991), have been hostile to this severance and seek to reassociate women and the feminine via the morphology of women's bodies and their particular libidinal economy. They insist that this remains a non-essentialist strategy, insofar as a feminine identity is one which remains to be created and is heterogeneous, fluid, etc.

7. Foucault writes: 'He who is subjected to a field of visibility, and who knows it, assumes responsibility for the constraints of power; he makes them play spontaneously upon himself; he inscribes in himself the power relation in which he spontaneously plays both roles; he becomes the principle of his own subjection' (1977: 22–3).

8. Kristeva makes a similar argument; she contends that fundamental questions about ethics, subjectivity and the symbolic are being reopened in the West due to a variety of factors which include feminist interrogations (Kristeva, 1981: 166, 167; see also passages reprinted in Moi, 1987a: 115 and 1987b: 31, 275, 295–7).

References

Benhabib, S. (1992) *Situating the Self*. Cambridge: Polity Press.

Braidotti, R. (1991) *Patterns of Dissonance*. Cambridge: Polity Press.

Butler, J. (1990) *Gender Trouble. Feminism and the Subversion of Identity*. London and New York: Routledge.

Chodorow, N. (1978) *The Reproduction of Mothering*. Berkeley: University of California Press.

Dews, P. (1989) 'The return of the subject in the late Foucault', *Radical Philosophy*, 51(1).

Firestone, S. (1971) *The Dialectic of Sex*. London: Paladin.

Flax, J. (1990) *Thinking Fragments. Psychoanalysis, Feminism and Postmodernism in the Contemporary West*. Berkeley: University of California Press.

Foucault, M. (1977) *Discipline and Punish*. Harmondsworth: Penguin.

Foucault, M. (1980) *Power/Knowledge. Selected Interviews and Other Writings 1972–77*, ed. C. Gordon. New York: Pantheon Books.

Foucault, M. (1981) *The History of Sexuality*. Harmondsworth: Penguin.

Foucault, M. (1988) *Michel Foucault. Politics, Philosophy, Culture. Interviews and other Writings, 1977–1984*, ed. L. Kritzman. New York and London: Routledge.

Gatens, M. (1991) *Feminism and Philosophy: Perspectives on Difference and Equality*. Cambridge: Polity Press.

Gilligan, C. (1982) *In a Different Voice*. Cambridge, MA: Harvard University Press.

Habermas, J. (1987) *The Philosophical Discourse of Modernity*. Cambridge: Polity Press.

Irigaray, L. (1985) *This Sex which is not One*. Ithaca, NY: Cornell University Press.

Jameson, F. (1991) *Postmodernism, Or, The Cultural Logic of Late Capitalism*. London: Verso.

Kristeva, J. (1981) 'Interview – 1974. Julia Kristeva and *Psychanalyse et Politique*', *m/f*, 5 & 6.

Kristeva, J. (1986) 'Stabat Mater', in Moi (1987b).

Kristeva, J. (1991) *Strangers to Ourselves*. Hemel Hempstead: Wheatsheaf-Harvester.

Kymlicka, W. (1988) 'Liberalism and communitarianism', *Philosophy and Public Affairs*, 18(2).

Lyotard, J.-F. (1984) *The Postmodern Condition*. Manchester: Manchester University Press.

McNay, L. (1992) *Foucault and Feminism*. Cambridge: Polity Press.

Macpherson, C. B. (1977) *Democratic Theory: Essays in Retrieval*. Oxford: Oxford University Press.

Millett, K. (1977) *Sexual Politics*. London: Virago.

Moi, T. (ed.) (1987a) *French Feminist Thought. A Reader*. Oxford: Blackwell.

Moi, T. (ed.) (1987b) *The Kristeva Reader*. Oxford: Blackwell.

Parekh, B. (1992) 'The cultural particularity of liberal democracy', *Political Studies*, 40 (special edition on D. Held (ed.) *Prospects for Democracy*).

Plumwood, V. (1989) 'Do we need a sex/gender distinction?', *Radical Philosophy*, 51(1).

Rose, J. (1983) 'Feminism and its discontents', *Feminist Review*, 14.

Sandel, M. (1982) *Liberalism and the Limits of Justice*. Cambridge: Cambridge University Press.

Taylor, C. (1989) *Sources of the Self. The Making of the Modern Identity*. Cambridge: Cambridge University Press.

White, S. (1991) *Political Theory and Postmodernism*. Cambridge: Cambridge University Press.

Young, I. M. (1990) *Justice and the Politics of Difference*. Princeton, NJ: Princeton University Press.

9

Becoming Women/Women Becoming: Film and the Social Construction of Gender

Helene Keyssar

> What are little boys made of?
> Slugs and snails and puppy dog tails,
> That's what little boys are made of.
>
> What are little girls made of?
> Sugar and spice and all things nice,
> That's what little girls are made of.

I was about five when I learnt these lines – my first conscious lesson in sex, gender and difference. I vividly remember taunting my younger brother with them. The nursery rhyme's explicit message is that girls and boys are by nature, or essentially, different: girls are universally sweet and boys universally horrid. Of course, we are not born knowing the differences the rhyme suggests. We learn the discourse of difference from diverse media and from the values and practices of those around us. Children soon learn not only that there are differences in anatomy but that these differences are meaningful. What these meanings do to people in the late twentieth century, and how they might be transformed, are the concerns of this chapter.

In recent years it has become common practice in academia to refer to certain anatomical/biological differences under the title 'sex' and to use the term 'gender' to designate the social behaviours and attributes that distinguish girls from boys, women from men.[1] These categories, however, have vague boundaries: as Michel Foucault points out in the case of Herculine Barbin (1980), anatomy does not always settle matters of sex identity, and gender is by definition uncertain because of its sociohistorical mutability. Furthermore, the relation between gender and biological sex is a source of great controversy. Are boys and girls made as certain types of people in the womb or in the world? Is it genes that determine whether we are male or female, and culture that makes us man or woman, as the use of the terms sex and gender imply? If we give the same treatment to boys and girls will we eliminate, or at least minimize, the differences between them? An anti-essentialist position often underlies these questions: if we can isolate the source or cause of gender differences, perhaps we can alter the understandings that contribute to the oppression of women and the tyranny of patriarchy for both men and women.

Like other instances of the nature–nurture debate, these questions about the origin and limits of gender identity are as familiar as they are frustrating.[2] Much feminist theory takes one or the other pole in a binary opposition between biological and social explanations of gendered behaviour. Yet the hesitations in even the most strident arguments are as notable as the arguments themselves. Famously, Carol Gilligan has argued that men and women have 'different voices', but, like the psychologist Nancy Chodorow who influenced Gilligan's work, she aspires to a more androgynous world (Gilligan, 1982). At times both thinkers sound as if they are making essentialist arguments; yet they in fact disclaim essentialism, insisting that sex-roles can be changed. There is thus a sense in which their work resembles that of writers like Judith Butler who finds gender to be socially constructed and lauds androgyny as a domain for the proliferation of alternative gender positions (Butler, 1987).

The necessary relation of the physical to the symbolic that defines the psychoanalytic branch of feminism further exacerbates tensions between essentialism and constructivism. After all, concepts like Freud's idea of penis envy invoke a physical organ as well as a symbolic one, and the significance of the division of labour in reproduction remains largely unexplored. Questions such as these may be potential sources of insight as much as they are problems for feminist thought. As an illustration, consider a recent exchange between British sociologist Nicky Hart and American historian Elizabeth Fox-Genovese. In a rare Marxist-essentialist article, Hart argues that crucial biological differences have not been given appropriate social value:

> [The] representation of childbirth as a labour of love – spiritual, sensuous and life-affirming – must be anathema to those convinced of the lack of essential difference between the sexes. This is why, with the exception of writers like Adrienne Rich, feminists are rather tight-lipped regarding natural childbirth, a decidedly female movement intent on challenging the forces of formal rationality, bureaucracy, and the medicalized commodity of the creation of life. (Hart, 1992: 74–5)

Hart rejects social constructivism on the grounds that it belittles the female role in procreation which, she argues, is vital to women's identity and sense of self-worth and to the development of a flourishing society. She sees mothers as exploited labourers; the root of gender inequality, she argues, lies in the undervaluing of procreation and mothering. For Hart, reproduction and mothering are potential sources of power for women.

In a response to Hart, Fox-Genovese agrees with the importance of biological difference in the construction of the self but rejects the focus on procreation. Fox-Genovese detects in Hart's views an over-confidence in the power of the individual and suggests that this distorts issues in the equality/difference debate that, as she puts it, 'runs like a fault line through the centre of academic feminism' (Fox-Genovese, 1992: 2). 'How,'

Fox-Genovese asks, 'can a humane society protect women's difference as women without curtailing their access, as individuals, to equality?' Only by grasping that the recognition of difference 'does not dictate the social consequences of difference,' she answers. Instead of Hart's solution of universal payment for labour in procreation and mothering, Fox-Genovese proposes that women's equality is a 'derivative' of true community and collective social life (Fox-Genovese, 1991: 244).

Not unlike the ancient (male) Greeks, Fox-Genovese envisions an egalitarian society in which a new and non-nostalgic spirit of community is the context for an equality that manifests itself as likeness despite obvious differences between individuals. (Fox-Genovese would not, of course, exclude whole categories of persons – slaves, women, foreigners – as did the Greeks.) She imagines a state in which individual rights are subordinate to social order and in which relationships of rivalry presuppose relations of equality. Within that framework, she struggles with the meaning and import of difference, insisting at one point that 'difference lies at the core of our humanity', and at another that difference of a sexual sort 'has few necessary consequences for political and economic roles in a world of adult women and men' (1991: 247). For her, essential sex attributes exist but are made more or less meaningful by social constructions.

I cite these writings because they show the difficulty in attempting to resolve gender issues within the essentialist–constructivist dichotomy. While I resist the essentialist claims that underlie Hart's arguments, the events which she gathers under the essentialist banner – menstruation, pregnancy, childbirth, breastfeeding and menopause – are precisely those that make me hesitate to adopt a rigid social constructivist position. At the same time, Fox-Genovese's attempt to preserve difference within the walls of community leaves unclear the relations between biology and difference on the one hand, and the role of difference within social constructivism on the other. If a woman undergoes a total hysterectomy and a double mastectomy, do we doubt that she remains a woman? And whose judgement decides the question? Faced with experiences that are undeniably gendered, neither essentialism nor constructivism suffices as explanation, and the binary oppositions that structure these queries are unhelpful.

What is at stake here? The debate between essentialists and constructivists continues because of its motivation: the desire for, or opposition to, social change. Notably, there is no one-to-one correlation here: some essentialists, like Hart, seek change as much as their constructivist opponents. It is interesting that, imagining the future, both essentialists and social constructivists – and indeed most feminist theorists – have a difficult time representing the present. Perhaps this is why so many feminist critics are drawn to film as a text through which to read society: the events of film do not threaten us because they have already occurred; we can leave the cinema, and the film, behind. Yet, while what we view is a record, it is not just that. Like the theatre of many other cultures, and especially that of ancient Greece, one of film's tasks is to address the most complex and unresolved issues of the present. Indeed it is because film is photographic, and thus a medium of recording, that it urges us to behold the ordinary alongside the miraculous. And because it is film and not daily life, the world is changed only by means of changing the way we see it.

These are reasons – the call, simultaneously, to the ordinary and the magical, to the view of the world changing (or, as I shall go on to say, *becoming*) – why many feminists choose to write about film. Film, of course, can legitimize gender roles, and much feminist writing is pre-occupied with the medium's sexism. However, film can also undermine the binary, rigid view of gender. Close to the traditions of theatre of many cultures, but with the resources of sophisticated technologies, film persistently undermines our confidence in our understanding of men as men and women as women. Greta Garbo, Marlene Dietrich and Marilyn Monroe top a long list of women in film who have presented themselves as men. Sometimes this is a matter simply of theatricality or character, sometimes it is a matter of disguise, and occasionally it involves a char-acter's desire to be other. Always, however, the instances of cross-dressing and blurred or altered gender in the movies are a reminder of the possibility that, and indeed the facility with which, men and women on screen, at least, can become other. In film, we find compelling evidence of Jacques Derrida's hypothesis that 'the sex of the addresser wants its determination by or from the other . . . nor is this decided once and for all. It may go one way one time and another way another time' (Derrida, 1984: 52).

That film delights in the possibilities of polysexuality is apparent throughout the history of the medium. Several commercial films made in the 1970s and 1980s have attempted to take on gender differences and gender ambiguity not simply as givens or contexts for comedy. However, with a few exceptions – for example, Robert Altman's *Come Back to the 5 & Dime, Jimmy Dean, Jimmy Dean* (1982), Claudia Weill's *Girlfriends* (1978), Ridley Scott's *Thelma & Louise* (1991), Arthur Hiller's *Outrageous Fortune* (1987) – most of them reduce gender issues to familiar male and female attributes and are no less dominated by conventional male roles than films that appear to have no explicit interest in gender as an issue (Keyssar, 1991). Indeed, a number of post-1960s films put forward strong, complex women characters, played by appropriately powerful actresses, but in most instances the reliance on genre conventions serves the interests of a cultural backlash against feminism. *Tootsie* (1982) uses the star power of Dustin Hoffman to tell a tale of a man who pretends to be a woman. While the movie initially seems to be a humorous salute to the difficulty of women's lives, its message is ultimately that a man does a better job of being a woman than any woman in the world of the film (see Waller, 1987). A similar message can be seen in *Three Men and a Baby* (1987) as well as the more serious Dustin Hoffman film, *Kramer vs. Kramer* (1979).

It appears also, more subtly, in Neil Jordan's much-hailed *The Crying Game* (1992). When Dil, the undoubtedly sensual, pivotal character of the film, suddenly reveals that she is anatomically male, it is not clear what we are meant to understand. The idea that sexual identity is natural seems to be subverted here, but the idea of the natural is affirmed in the twice-told parable of the frog and the scorpion: given a reasonable pledge of safety, a frog starts to carry a scorpion across a lake; halfway there, the scorpion stings the frog. As both drown, the frog asks the scorpion, 'Why?' The scorpion's answer is that it is in his nature to sting. 'It's in my nature' is also the answer the film's hero, Fergus, gives when asked why he behaves with kindness. Yet if we focus on Dil, whose gender identity is not coincident with her biological sex, explaining the self's 'nature' does not make sense. It would seem that it is only the feminine which is constructed – and in this case, literally by and for men, since in Dil we again see a man playing a woman's role more engagingly than any conventional woman in the film.[3]

Among the exceptions mentioned above, one of the most intriguing is Ridley Scott's *Thelma & Louise*. By presenting a close reading of this film, I hope to illuminate what is at stake in the disputes among feminists about biological and social construction, equality and difference, autonomy and community. My aim is to articulate a quality of the key characters that helps us transcend the binary oppositions that so frequently trap feminist thought. Drawing on the work of Bakhtin, I will call this quality that of 'emergence' or 'continuous becoming'.

Bakhtin introduces the idea of emergence in an essay on the *Bildungs-roman* or novel of education (1986). One source of his interest is the possibility this genre provides for presenting 'man in the process of becoming'. In most novels, Bakhtin argues, the hero is a constant, and all other qualities of the text are potentially variable; setting, social position, fortune can change, but 'in the image of the hero itself there is neither movement nor emergence' (1986: 21). In contrast, the novels of education present heroes in the process of becoming, of continuously learning and thus transforming.

Among the relatively rare novels with emergent heroes and heroines, Bakhtin insists on a further typology: he identifies five types of novel of emergence, respectively distinguished by (1) idyllic-cyclic time development (innocence and infancy to old age and wisdom); (2) life or experience at a school; (3) biography and autobiography; (4) adherence to a narrative structure based on a specific pedagogic process (for example Rousseau's *Emile*); and (5) the linking of historical with individual emergence. The last type is the one most admired and carefully analysed by Bakhtin. In the rare instances of it man 'emerges along with the world, and he reflects the historical emergence of the world itself. He is no longer within an epoch, but on the border between two epochs, at the transition point from one to the other' (1986: 23). For Bakhtin, Rabelais's *Gargantua and Pantagruel* stands as the purest example of this novel of emergence, where we see man growing in national-historical time.

Films, in contrast to novels, are, by definition, about movement. We talk of 'movies' and 'motion pictures' because the most distinctive quality of the cinema is movement. A still is so-called precisely because it does not move. The movement of other dramatic media is still or regressive in contrast to the predilection of film to transform images and the objects and persons they represent (see Keyssar, 1991). The film's use of transformation in a sense 'animates' Bakhtin's idea of emergence.

A key convention of cinema is that the particular world of each film has its own temporality. Many of the most meaningful instances of film not only present a person emerging but assert the inseparability of an individual's becoming from national-historical time. Jean Renoir's *Rules of the Game* (1939), Chaplin's *Modern Times* (1936), all of Stanley Kubrick's films, but especially *Barry Lyndon* (1975), Altman's *Buffalo Bill and the Indians* (1976), Coppola's *Apocalypse Now* (1979) and *The Godfather Parts I and II* (1971 and 1974) demonstrate how powerfully film can work within Bakhtin's guidelines. Each of these films is distinguished by a particular historical context, yet each transcends historical time and periodization.

In these films it is literally man we see 'growing in national-historical time', for in all cases the emergent figures are male. *Thelma & Louise* exemplifies an alternative narrative, one in which women in the process of emergence challenge social and cultural expectations on the subject of gender. *Thelma & Louise* focuses our attention on a pair of women and the importance of their relationship to their development as persons. The structure of the film is much like that of the male buddy films of the 1960s and early 1970s (e.g. *Easy Rider* [1969], *Butch Cassidy and the Sundance Kid* [1969], *Brewster McCloud* [1970]): following a brief set of establishing scenes, a journey propels the narrative line, and calamitous and humorous events are strung along the way. Only here, the key characters are women, and there is no doubt this makes a difference.

The film begins with a black and white landscape shot of a rocky hill in mid-range, with the sky above and a road down the centre. A few seconds into the film, black and white gradually transform to colour. The big open sky, the denaturalizing appearance of colour photography and the well-known iconography of the road are immediate clues to our reading of this film. The physical power of the broad and unfenced land as it meets the endless sky has always been one key to the American Western film: it is out there, on those endless hills and plains, that Americans have traditionally envisioned a freedom in isolation. The road is a revision of that symbolism, the sign of the intrusion of civilization, forever pushing back the frontier. It also indicates the replacement of the horse with the more limited and limiting automobile, that encumbrance of 'civilization'. Yet while the road is a reminder of constraints, it is also a sign of mobility, of change and possibility. And it is those possibilities of the landscape and the road, the possibilities of freedom and of escape, that shape the Western film genre and orientate the viewer at the beginning of *Thelma & Louise*.

In obvious contrast to this invitation to the open Western landscape, the next shots of the film introduce the lead characters in frames that emphasize their different but equally stifling confinements. The camera finds Louise (Susan Sarandon) working as a waitress in a crowded and noisy diner. We hear her comment, '. . . limits your sex drive', to a customer, and then we watch her make a phone call to another woman, whom she identifies as Thelma (Geena Davis). A radio blaring over the ambient talk at the diner creates a layered soundtrack, reminiscent particularly of the films of Altman. Scenic fragments and blatant parallel editing in the film's opening scenes prepare the viewer for the narrative that will unfold, as does Louise's voice saying something about 'going'.

The initially omniscient camera cuts to Thelma in a kitchen on the phone with Louise. After calling her husband, Darryl (Christopher McDonald) for breakfast, Thelma tells Louise, 'Better hang up.' Darryl's growly entrance line, 'Haven't I told you not to holler like that?' conveys the habits of this relationship. We watch Thelma help Darryl put on his watch and listen to her try – 'Hon?. . ., Hon. . .' – to ask Darryl's permission to go away for two days with Louise. Thelma never gets the request out, but Darryl does not hesitate to tell her that he may not be home for dinner. 'Funny thing,' Thelma comments, 'how so many people want to buy carpet on a Friday night.'

From the start, blue-eyed and honey-haired, Thelma looks like 'all things nice', but she turns out to be as much spice as sugar. No sooner has Darryl left than Thelma calls Louise back to ask what clothes to bring. A series of parallel edits reveals each woman packing, dressing, looking into the mirror. However, the congruences suggested by these cuts is countered when Louise arrives to pick up Thelma. In trousers, with bright lipstick and a scarf to match, Louise is at once attractive and sensibly dressed for the proposed trip in a convertible to a mountain cabin. In contrast, Thelma is dressed for a Saturday night date in an ornamented denim outfit that opens to a low-cut, matching top; she also has enough luggage for a week-long cruise. Louise makes a light remark, then gets out of the car and takes a photograph of her and Thelma, pressed tightly together to get in the frame. The relationship will endure differences over trivialities like luggage.

Louise's picture-taking requires that she awkwardly extend one arm to hold the camera, while she pulls Thelma close with the other. The gesture marks the first moment of change in the film. Thelma has literally emerged from the house where she has been kept in obedient servitude by Darryl. Her first step towards becoming an independent person is marked by her revelation to Louise that she did not ask Darryl's permission but left him a note on the microwave, an admission that suggests both her new claim to control her own life and her fear of facing Darryl. While Louise has brought a camera to shoot with, Thelma casually reveals that she has brought along Darryl's gun. Louise is stunned, but the viewer should not be. The gun may not belong in Thelma's world as Louise knows it, but it does belong, indeed is necessary, to the film's participation in the genre of the Western.

In Western movies, the gun plays a double role. It signifies and assures independence from the law, and it is an obvious phallic symbol. As Robert Warshow has suggested, the gun is one of the few things the Western hero owns (his horse and one set of clothes are the others) and 'guns as physical objects, and the postures associated with their use, form the visual and emotional centre of both types [Western and gangster] of films' (Warshow, 1975: 135). In the Western, the gun derives its symbolic position from its shape, its 'ejaculation' of bullets, its destructive power, and its usual association with men.

Guns have been carried before by American women, but a woman cannot carry a gun casually in an American film. When Beryl Kane uses a gun in George Cukor's comedy of gender transformations, *Adam's Rib* (1949), to shoot at her husband and his mistress, it is crucial to the viewer's understanding of gender roles in the film that we see Beryl's incompetence with the weapon. Beryl remains a woman to the extent that the gun appears foolish in her hands, as foolish as would be a phallus under her skirts, as foolish as the moustache we later see on her face. The gun's relation to the phallus is equally important to the tragic narrative of Arthur Penn's *Bonnie and Clyde* (1967): when Bonnie first meets Clyde she caresses his gun in a way that suggests it is not only the gun she desires, and later when she uses a gun – a machine-gun – her own androgyny is so explicit that we are to believe it exacerbates Clyde's impotence.

Thelma's first contact with Darryl's gun as she puts it in her bag is as wary as that of Beryl Kane in *Adam's Rib*. But the gun is essential for our impression of her as both an adolescent tasting her first bite of freedom and a woman taking on the power of men. Extending this impression, Thelma takes off her jacket, smokes a cigarette and impetuously insists to Louise that they make a 'quick stop' at the first roadhouse they encounter. Eager to maintain Thelma's high spirits and reluctant to take on a peremptory role, Louise agrees. Here occurs Thelma's second emergence.

Inside the roadhouse, Thelma naively returns the advances of a stranger named Harlan, who appears to Louise and the viewer as obviously 'on the make'. When, after being plied with drinks and spun into confusion dancing, Thelma goes outside to clear her head, Harlan follows and immediately begins to maul her. He not only ignores Thelma's resistance to his assault but is enraged by it. He hits her when she pleads with him to stop, and then hits again when she reminds him that Louise will be missing her. Roughly pressing her against the trunk of a car, he makes to rape her, all the while yelling at Thelma to 'shut up'. From the depths of the darkness we suddenly hear Louise's voice: 'Let her go.'

Louise's words are reinforced by the gun in her hand. Holding the gun to Harlan's head, Louise speaks in a violent and coarse manner, a voice different from any we have heard previously in this movie, in order to force Harlan to let her friend go. He obeys but protests that they were 'just havin' a little fun'. 'In the future,' Louise angrily informs him, 'when a woman's crying like that, she ain't havin' any fun.'

Harlan starts to leave, but, unwilling to lose the exchange, he insults Louise and makes a vulgar remark about how he should have continued the rape. 'What did you say?' Louise demands. When another expletive is the answer, that is the end of talk for Louise. She whirls to face Harlan's retreating back, raises and straightens her arm in a gesture of conviction, and shoots Harlan dead. Thelma appears behind Louise, noting the obvious: 'Oh my God, Jesus Christ, Louise, you shot him.' After a long moment gazing at Harlan's body, Thelma acts on Louise's command to get the car, and the two women charge off, with Thelma driving wildly, straight into traffic. Louise cannot resist a parting, belated warning to Harlan: 'Watch your mouth, Buddy.' These words are, of course, the classic monosyllabic cliché of the tough guy. More specifically, they echo the threat-within-a-command that so often calls attention to the authority of Western heroes.

This pivotal scene recalls Aristotle's notion in the *Poetics* of a peripety (reversal) of the key characters' situation. The two women had set out for a carefree weekend, a few days without the men who constrain their lives. The drive itself was part of the fun; before the roadhouse episode, they drank, they talked, they revelled in their new-found liberation. Louise's killing of Harlan reverses the situation entirely. Having watched Thelma's emergence from obedient housewife, we have now witnessed the transformation of Louise from self-assured worker to enraged and unhesitating avenger. Now their journey becomes an attempt to escape, not from their men or their daily burdens, but from the law.

As outlaws, the predicament of Thelma and Louise again invokes the Western. At the same time, the film renegotiates the terms of that genre. Louise's shooting of Harlan is ambiguous in both its legal and moral status. Like the traditional Western hero, Louise shoots Harlan for the sake of honour, not from necessity. When a Western hero does what 'he's gotta do' (defending the weak, leaving those he loves, and standing alone against the mob, as well as shooting), he is acting on his own private code of ethics. Like many Western heroes, Louise acts in a way the law cannot condone, and, like many Western heroes, her past may motivate her act but is never fully known by others. However, there is a key difference: Thelma and Louise become outlaws because of a dilemma unique to women. One of them has killed a man who verbally assaulted her and tried to rape her friend. What this woman has 'gotta do' is prompted simultaneously by something private in her soul and by the exigencies of, as Bakhtin puts it, the particular 'national-historical moment' in which Louise finds herself. Louise kills Harlan for herself but also for every woman in the audience who has been powerless in the face of a man's attack.

The replacement of male hero-outlaws by female ones is significant also for the structure of the film. First, in contrast to the classical peripeties, the peripety is here followed by episodes that extend and clarify the meaning of the change of fortune in the lives of the protagonists. By occurring early in the film rather than in a climactic finale, conventional relations of adventure, revelation and turning point are reversed. Second, whereas in conventional Westerns as well as in classical tragedy and some conventional comedy, the episodes of the drama reveal fragments of the character that culminate in an unveiling of a stable 'true' self (Keyssar, 1977, 1984), here there is no single true Thelma or Louise to be revealed. For the women leads of this film, the recognition of a true self is replaced by continuous transformation. Thelma's decision to take a vacation with Louise and Louise's shooting of Harlan are pivotal moments that launch the beginning of a process of becoming.

At each of the subsequent stops on their journey, the intervention of a man catalyses the continuous emergence of Thelma and Louise, but it is always Thelma and Louise, not the men they encounter, who metamorphose as they go. At a motel which is their first stop after the roadhouse, Louise and Thelma fight about calling the police. While Thelma, on Louise's orders, sunbathes at the motel pool, Louise takes charge and telephones her friend Jimmy to ask him to wire her money which she will repay from her savings. Jimmy agrees.

Back on the road, Thelma asks Louise where they are going, and Louise explains her plan to go to Mexico. When Louise asks if Thelma will join her, Thelma says she does not know. Louise is angry at what she sees as Thelma's inconstancy; she insists that Thelma understand that 'Things have changed. Everything's changed.' But Thelma's commitment is demonstrated when she calls Darryl a few minutes later: Darryl commands that she return that evening and Thelma rebuffs him in no uncertain terms.

On the road again after their phone calls, the importance of Thelma and Louise's friendship to their respective transformations is vivid. In the car, they quarrel, sing, drink, reflect, plan, laugh and cry. Despite its threatening underside, their spirit of abandonment has at times an appealing, contagious quality for the viewer. And for the characters it means a growing intimacy and trust. It is in this spirit that Louise, who does most of the driving, asks Thelma to find a route on the map to Mexico that will not go through Texas. 'You know how I feel about Texas,' she reminds Thelma. 'You never told me what happened there,' Thelma replies. Louise answers enigmatically, 'If you shoot a man with his pants down, you don't want to be caught in Texas.' One possible reading of Louise's words is that in Texas she once shot a man who was trying to rape her. Not until much later is there again a mention of Texas, but the shadow of this secret now is subtly present.

The journey is punctuated by a series of episodes, each of which contributes to the emergence of Thelma and Louise in presenting them with challenges not unlike the tests requisite to the education of epic heroes. The first occurs when they stop at a motel in Oklahoma City with the expectation that Jimmy's loan will have arrived. The money is there, but so is Jimmy. This sets up the temporary separation of Thelma and

Louise. Parallel editing is deployed again: we see Louise struggling to find an appropriate mode of relation with this man who now claims to want to take care of her, while in another room we see Thelma naively yielding to the advances of J. D., an attractive young man she persuaded Louise to pick up on the road, of whom they know nothing except he is 'going back to school'.

The night Louise spends with Jimmy is analogous to Thelma's night with the hitchhiker. In each relationship we see the proximity of violence and sexual passion. However, the device of parallel editing also accentuates the differences between the two relationships. Jimmy and Louise have hardly closed the door when Jimmy vents his rage at Louise's refusal to explain her situation. If, for a moment, Jimmy seemed a tempting alternative for Louise, he seems less so when he starts throwing furniture in the motel room. This is, nonetheless, a complex relationship: Jimmy has brought Louise not only the money she requested but also an engagement ring, something she apparently once wanted but now rejects. 'It's time to let go of old mistakes,' she tells him. Louise is less solicitous and more aloof than she has been in the previous scenes with Thelma; she does not confuse her gratitude to Jimmy for bringing the money with her attraction to him, nor with nostalgia for the less troubled past of a few days before. Louise is emerging as a mature and independent woman who knows what she must do. As if in respect for that emergence and for the vulnerability of the relationship between Jimmy and Louise, the camera denies us a view of their night together. At breakfast the next morning, Jimmy insists that Louise keep the ring as a simple gift, and they both look pained as he departs. At this point, Louise is closer to being the inscrutable Western hero who does what she has 'gotta do' than any other woman in film.

Thelma, in contrast, is incautious in her dealings with J. D. 'I'm just a wild woman,' she tells Jimmy as she leaves him and Louise, and that is what we see her trying to be after she lets J. D. take refuge from the rain in her room. At one point during their boisterous foreplay, J. D. removes Thelma's wedding ring. Thelma's acquiescence, following Louise's refusal of Jimmy's engagement ring, suggests a rejection of marriage common to the two women. There are differences, however: Jimmy offers Louise a ring, first as a symbol of attachment, then as a gift without obligation. In sharp contrast, J. D.'s removal of Thelma's ring seems a manipulative attempt to delude her that release from the world's obligations is a mere matter of choice. In retrospect, we can also read the ring scene in Thelma's room as a set-up for petty theft.

A second motel sequence shows the next steps in Thelma's and Louise's emergence as mature women. At breakfast next morning, Thelma tells Louise about her sexual exploits with J. D. It so surpassed other experiences of lovemaking that she is euphoric hours later. So much so, in fact, that Thelma has unthinkingly left Jimmy's loan, given to her for safe-keeping, in the room with J. D. She and Louise rush back to Thelma's room but, predictably, both the money and the con-man hitchhiker are gone.

The loss breaks the mutual warmth and intimacy Thelma and Louise had enjoyed for a moment over breakfast. Louise's immediate reaction is despair. She rebuffs Thelma's apology and contention that things will 'still be OK' and reclaims the role of the realistic adult. 'None of this is OK,' she declares, and then asks rhetorically what they are going to do for money and gas. Thelma, initially, has no concrete answer. Louise is now so dejected that she is paralysed in her knowledge of the difficulties mounting around them. But Thelma, apologetic and sobered, now does what *she* has 'gotta do'. She stops whimpering, commands Louise not to worry, pulls her out to the car, and, for the first time, takes control of the journey. Now it is Louise who desolately leans her head on her hand as Thelma did after the attempted rape and killing.

Thelma, however, has miles to go before she fully becomes Louise's partner. In the traditional Western film, if the male hero has a partner at all, the partner and the relationship are fixed, a given in the narrative. In the new Western, and in the buddy films of the 1960s and 1970s, there is often tension between the men at some point in the narrative, but this tension is resolved by mutual recognition or acceptance of their bond that transcends the differences of the moment. In this feminized Western, however, the transformation of individual identities, rather than the acceptance of immutable personas, is intrinsic to the evolution of the relationship between Thelma and Louise. The parallel editing that structures the film at the beginning and that recurs whenever Thelma and Louise are apart, is not characteristic of conventional Western movies and confirms both the link and the tension, the similarities and the differences, between the two women. This, in turn, adds an emphasis uncommon in the Western genre.

Thelma takes responsibility for her and Louise's survival in her own dramatic way. The previous night, J. D. had enacted how he deployed his skills as a robber. Thelma exploits her new knowledge by holding up a small rural store. The film accentuates the event of Thelma's market robbery by distinguishing it cinematically from the rest of the movie. As Thelma exuberantly describes the hold-up to Louise, the film cuts to a grainy black and white videotape recorded by a security camera at the store, and watched by the police, the FBI and Darryl. What they see is Thelma playing the role of robber with charm and assurance. Like the hitchhiker whose script she is following, she is a disarming thief, but unlike him, she is also genuinely compassionate. She apologizes for the discomfort she is causing the people in the shop and tries to minimize the fear she inspires. One of the many ironies that now begin to emerge is that the more Thelma lets go of the conventional Barbie-doll stereotype of woman, the more attractive she appears as a person.

Thelma's emergence as a competent outlaw is presented to the viewer as a liberation with a catch. Until now, as the police remind the two women on the telephone, Thelma had not actually broken the law. Thelma now joins Louise in the ranks of criminals; she is, perversely, freed of her innocence by her crime. She can now continue without question with Louise. When we next see Thelma and Louise on the road, Louise is driving, the top of the convertible is up again, and the two women are so attuned to each other that they can finish each other's sentences. They are moving less towards a destination than away from what Thelma gleefully calls 'the scene of [their] last crime'. With their hair blowing in the wind, they are free women.[4]

The film's use of the security videotape, however, limits the pleasure the viewer might have in watching Thelma and Louise enjoy their freedom. Hitherto, the dominant points of view have been, indirectly, those of Thelma, Louise, or 'woman', and this gives power to the women in the film as power has, more conventionally, been given to men. Most of the shots in the first half of the film are medium or medium close-ups of one or both women or of what they are seeing, minimizing the more usual cinematic treatment of the women's bodies as objects. Indeed the absence, in the important road scenes, of a man or men whose gaze is appropriated for the spectator is so striking that the film might be characterized in terms of a dominant, indirect female point of view (Pasolini, 1976: 554–8). Even an early cut to the scene-of-the-crime sequence, after the departure of Thelma and Louise, divides point of view between the local chief detective and a woman, the waitress who served Thelma and Louise at the road-house. In the neon-lit chaos of the parking lot where Harlan's body has been found, the waitress insists to the detective that Thelma and Louise did not kill Harlan. Although we know she is mistaken, her view is given credence by her appealing personal presence and her claim of authority in judging people from her experience as a waitress.

The video and the men watching it take us back to the more conventional, voyeuristic perspective of film. The FBI and the police, who are now based in Darryl's living-room, are controlling the images of Thelma and, by association, of Louise. Our gaze, too, is now that of these male figures of authority. The juxtaposition of the images of free women on the sunlit road with the dark room where the men are screening the video is a reminder of the pervasive power of men as voyeurs and of the extent of the male gaze (see Mulvey, 1989). We are reminded that these women's freedom is more limited than the images of them on the road suggest.

Thelma and Louise have been under surveillance well before the robbery is recorded on videotape. Moreover, men have appeared before in the world of this film, but until now men have either been victims or they have been marginalized by both the camera and the characters, of interest only in relation to the ongoing construction of Thelma and of Louise. They each represent different forms and degrees of chauvinism and stereotypical male behaviour towards women. Together, they present the male 'other' as seen by women, and together, in this film, they are the enemy. Even Jimmy, the only one of the men who might be emergent, whom we learn from Louise is changed from the past, remains constant before the movie spectator.

Thus our glimpses of these male authorities, though relevant to the plot, seem annoyingly arbitrary and intrusive. Perhaps we are meant to resent these cuts as the unwanted but inevitable intrusion by men into the women's world, but it is equally likely that these early inserts of male characters and their points of view are distracting because they are a relic of previous filmmaking and out of keeping with the manner of the film.

After the video scene, the various officers of the law gain power and prominence as vectors of the film. A young, unnamed FBI agent is always attached to some form of surveillance technology; Max, the big, vain FBI agent in charge, is an arrogant misogynist. It is he who tells Darryl, 'If she [Thelma] calls, be real nice, like you really miss her. Women love that. . .' In contrast, there is Hal Slocum, the local chief detective who repeatedly attempts to constrain the destructive impulses of his fellow police and FBI agents; Slocum sees the personal histories of Thelma and Louise, including Louise's experiences in Texas, as relevant to the crimes that Thelma and Louise have committed. While most of the men in *Thelma & Louise* can only think of the women as sexual objects to be used or abused as men see fit, Hal's behaviour among his colleagues, and on the telephone with Louise, suggests that he perceives Thelma and Louise as both persons and victims.

That the man in charge of the investigation of our heroines should be sympathetic and understanding underscores the theme of *Thelma & Louise* – that we emerge in relation to others, not autonomously. It is in interaction with others – both men and women – and in empathy for others, that Thelma and Louise keep becoming. Thelma cares about Louise, Louise cares about Thelma, and this mutual caring contributes to their joint consciousness of personal transformations. Pointing a gun at the head of a policeman who stops them for speeding, Thelma is apologetic. 'I swear, three days ago neither one of us would have ever pulled a stunt like this,' she tells him as she and Louise force him into the trunk of his car.

The transformations we witness are also not clearly mediated by what we think of as typically male or female behaviour but by a kind of mischievousness that may be a terrain where gender is less relevant than in daily life. A maverick quality in both women is especially evident in a scene near the end of the film where Thelma and Louise take revenge for the lewd gestures of a truck driver by seducing him off the road as if to comply with his sexual suggestions. Recalling for the viewer the earlier scene with Harlan, Louise requests an apology from the truck driver for his insulting behaviour. When he does not comply, Louise first shoots out the truck's tyres, then Thelma joins Louise and together they fire at the immense oil tank his truck is pulling. As with many moments in this film, the sexual symbolism is so blatant that the image is simultaneously funny and troubling. The vulgar truck driver, silhouetted against the huge exploding tanker, is hysterical in his helplessness. This is a scene that divides viewers primarily along gender lines: women tend to cheer and laugh; men tend to be angry at Thelma and Louise and at the women laughing in the audience. *Thelma & Louise* celebrates such acts as signs of female power and female 'bonding'. We are meant to applaud the camaraderie of their effort as much as the act itself. We are also reminded of modern Westerns, such as *Butch Cassidy and the Sundance Kid* and *Bonnie and Clyde*, in the symbolic castration of the truck driver.

On the road, away from the men in the film who variously threaten their freedom, Thelma and Louise become increasingly committed to moving on together. In the intimacy of shared experiences, it is not only the law on their tail but their own new senses of self that propel them onward. 'I feel awake,' Thelma declares not long after hearing that she and Louise are being charged with murder. 'I don't ever remember feelin' this awake. Know what I mean?' Louise answers affirmatively, and imagining the future, she proclaims, 'We'll be drinkin' margaritas by the sea, Mamasita.' This exchange is poignant if we assume that the two women understand that a happy ending is a fantasy they need to uphold as long as they can. But the ambiguity allows the film to avoid a melodramatic ending.

The actual ending of *Thelma & Louise* no more resolves the narrative than it answers the social issues of gender conflict raised by the film. At the climax of a traditional chase sequence, complete with police cars crashing into each other, a stone bridge appears on the road ahead. In their convertible, Thelma and Louise can pass under the bridge, but the police, in their top-heavy sedans, cannot. The brief respite from the noise and chaos of the chase allows Thelma and Louise to acknowledge their friendship. 'You're a good friend,' Thelma tells Louise, and Louise responds, 'You too, sweet, the best,' followed by the quip, 'How do you like the vacation so far?' Thelma remarks that she guesses she 'went a little crazy'. But Louise disagrees; instead, she suggests, Thelma has for the first time been able to express herself honestly.

Their sense of safety and solitude is quickly dashed by the sudden ascent from the canyon of a helicopter carrying Hal and Max. And now on the barren ground behind them appear hundreds of police cars that to Thelma look like an army, or as this is a revisionist Western, like both cavalry and Indians. But here the cavalry are not arriving at the last moment to save the good guys; the police cars figure as the stereotypical Indians, pressing our heroines to the edge of the cliff, seeking not to save but to capture or kill them. An amplified male voice commands Thelma and Louise to turn off their car engine and place their hands in plain view. 'Anything else,' the disembodied voice warns, 'will be considered an act of aggression.'

Once again, the terrible is also funny here because the force of the hundreds of police cars that have gathered to capture Thelma and Louise is so out of proportion to the situation; surely it is not just as outlaws that Thelma and Louise are such a threat. On Thelma's urging, she and Louise do not give themselves up but 'keep going' – they back their car up and deliberately drive it off the cliff towards the great cavern of the Grand

Canyon that lies before them. We watch their worldly goods fly away, we catch a glimpse of Thelma's hand pressed on top of Louise's hand on the gear stick, and the final pre-credit frame freezes on the car floating, horizontally, high above the canyon floor. The film then cuts to a montage of frames that recall key moments in the film, while a country ballad provides the refrain, 'You're a part of me and I'm a part of you.'

Many viewers were unhappy with the ending of *Thelma & Louise*. The women's action seems heroic to some, pathetic and wrong-headed to others. Many argued that we are seeing an all too familiar representation of women as victims. I do not think this can be the whole or even the best account of the film and its ending. Western films are, after all, replete with scenes in which the heroes are cornered by the bad guys and, against all odds, jump off the cliff, escape the enemy and make it through to some undefined future. A possible ending, therefore, would be one in which some form of woman-power enables Thelma and Louise's escape.

I have in mind something like the ending of Arthur Hiller's *Outrageous Fortune*, a film with a cult following among feminist academics but with nothing like the reach of *Thelma & Louise*. The power of *Outrageous Fortune* is rooted in the pleasure for some viewers in that rare event, a feminist victory. Two women, Lauren (Shelley Long) and Annie (Bette Midler), begin their relationship as competitors in a drama class. They soon discover that they are also competing for the same man. By the end of this outrageously theatrical melodrama, the two women are friends, and one of them, Lauren, is running for her life from Michael, the lover in question who turns out to be a Russian spy. In the final chase sequence of the film, Michael pursues Lauren from one clifftop to another, bringing the audience to a site remarkably similar to the one from which Thelma and Louise make their exit. But while Thelma and Louise reject the male-empowered world that surrounds them by driving themselves onwards and off the cliff, Lauren and Annie take a different tactic. Running barely a step ahead of the threatening Michael, Lauren comes to a series of stone pillars, each with an increasingly wide and deep gap between it and the next. Finally, one leap after another, Lauren arrives at the edge of a canyon apparently impossible to jump. Nonetheless, she leaps and, magically, makes it across the gulf. Behind her, Michael attempts to follow but fails. He clings to the cliff face, begs for help, and finally falls to his death. Lauren looks down and gloats triumphantly, 'Nine years of ballet, you asshole!' Nearby, Annie cries joyously, 'You did it, you did it!' Still on the cliff, a cross-fade transforms Lauren, Annie and several other women into the cast of *Hamlet*, with Lauren, centre-cliff, playing the prince himself, and Annie playing Gertrude.

The appeal of the ending of *Outrageous Fortune* is clear. Women triumph; they are not victims. And, as the coda suggests, once Lauren puts her training to use, she can play any role, including Hamlet. Transcendence of the limitations of gender can be learned.[5]

Outrageous Fortune and *Thelma & Louise* have real parallels. In both films, autonomy, so hailed by many feminisms, is achieved through community with others. Much like Thelma and Louise, Lauren and Annie struggle with (and for) their own individual desires for a time, but become increasingly bound to each other, confirming the importance of friendship for women-becoming-women.

It could be argued that the theme of becoming is not abandoned at the conclusion of *Thelma & Louise*. Merle Hoffman (1991) has reported the appearance of buttons reading 'Thelma and Louise Live', and perhaps these are an expression of a survival fantasy, like the end of *Outrageous Fortune*. Or more specifically, as Hoffman also suggests, the message that Thelma and Louise live may be the ultimate challenge to patriarchy, 'the triumph of life over death, the oppressed over the oppressor, gender justice and Amazonian immortality' (1991: 19). On this view, the power of *Thelma & Louise* is that of a threat. Women are waking up and not liking the ways men treat them. As Thelma tells the highway patrolman who stops them for speeding, and whom they then capture, 'You be sweet to them [his wife and children]. My husband wasn't sweet to me and look at what happened.'

Perhaps we do not have to remake the ending of *Thelma & Louise* to believe that they live, nor have recourse to the idea that their spirit lives, which is what I think the button intends. After all, Thelma and Louise go off the cliff, but we do not see them crash; in fact, they do not crash in the world of this film, but freeze in the thin air of movie magic well above the canyon bottom. This might mean that the ending of *Thelma & Louise* is more like the ending of *Outrageous Fortune* than might appear.

To get a sense of the importance of this, picture a film in which the audience actually sees the crumpled car at the bottom of the canyon with the torn bodies of Thelma and Louise hanging from it. *These* would be victims, dead. And being dead, it would be much easier to pronounce on them, and indeed to dismiss them. It is not irrational to assume that Thelma and Louise die. But I take 'Thelma and Louise Live' to mean that they are literally left in the air; viewers continue to think about them and talk about them, and Thelma and Louise therefore continue to emerge, to become. And, becoming, they must remain somewhat unknown. They can no longer be understood as essentially anything, including essentially woman.

Bakhtin speaks of the positive effects of what he calls 'novelization' of other genres in terms of 'dialogization, laughter, irony, humour, elements of self-parody' and most important for him, 'an indeterminacy, a certain semantic open-endedness, a living contact with the unfinished, still-evolving contemporary reality (the open-ended present)' (Bakhtin, 1981: 7). Most Hollywood films are defined by the fact they are closed, ended, complete. That this is not the case with *Thelma & Louise* suggests a subversion of the medium, as well as the subversion of gender. As Bakhtin puts it:

Human nature is no longer man's own private affair [when] he emerges along with the world and [he] reflects the historical emergence of the world itself. . . . This transition is accomplished in him and through him. What is happening is precisely the emergence of a new man. (Bakhtin, 1986: 23)

And, we hope, a new woman.

Notes

I wish to thank Anise Keyssar Strong and Tracy B. Strong for their generous help with this chapter.

1. Among academics, historian Joan Scott is usually given credit for drawing the distinction between sex and gender. The distinction does not always function in the same way outside of academia as it does within, as is illustrated by Congressional hearings in 1993 to consider the nomination of Judge Ruth Ginsberg to serve as a justice of the Supreme Court. When queried by the Senate Judiciary Committee about her use of the term 'gender', Ginsberg testified that she had begun to use the term on her secretary's suggestion. The word 'sex' was confusing for predominantly male audiences whose 'first association of that word is not what you're talking about'. The word 'gender', the secretary explained, served to 'ward off distracting associations'.

2. Stephen Jay Gould (1992) has emphasized both the unanticipated and leap-like nature of cultural and biological change and the difficulty in distinguishing between biological and social causes. We should perhaps stop wasting time on futile attempts at such distinctions.

3. This is similar to the message of . . . *Jimmy Dean*, except that in Altman's film becoming a woman is a matter of painful reflection and a search for identity, assisted by the efforts of other women. In *The Crying Game*, in contrast, Dil's disrobing tells us little about Dil the person and much about the filmmaker's desire to shock. No matter what we learn of Dil's anatomy, the character remains unchanging.

4. I am thinking particularly here of Doris Lessing's use of the term 'free women' in chapter headings of *The Golden Notebook* (1972).

5. I am indebted to Elizabeth Minnick for calling my attention to *Outrageous Fortune*.

References

Bakhtin, M. M. (1981) *The Dialogic Imagination*, trans. Caryl Emerson and Michael Holquist, ed. Michael Holquist. Austin: University of Texas Press.

Bakhtin, M. M. (1986) 'The Bildungsroman', in *Speech Genres and other Late Essays*, trans. Vern W. McGee, ed. Caryl Emerson and Michael Holquist. Austin: University of Texas Press.

Butler, Judith (1987) 'Variations on sex and gender: Beauvoir, Wittig, and Foucault', in Seyla Benhabib and Drucilla Cornell (eds), *Feminism as Critique*. Minneapolis: University of Minnesota Press.

Derrida, Jacques (1984) *The Ear of the Other*, trans. Peggy Kamuf. New York: Schocken Books.

Foucault, Michel (1980) *Herculine Barbin, Being the Recently Discovered Memoirs of a Nineteenth Century French Hermaphrodite*, trans. Richard McDougall. New York: Pantheon Books.

Fox-Genovese, Elizabeth (1991) *Feminism without Illusions*. Chapel Hill: University of North Carolina Press.

Fox-Genovese, Elizabeth (1992) 'A response to Nicky Hart', *Contention*, 1(2).

Gilligan, Carol (1982) *In a Different Voice*. Cambridge, MA: Harvard University Press.

Gould, Stephen Jay (1992) *Eight Little Piggies*. London: Jonathan Cape.

Hart, Nicky (1992) 'Procreation: Part Two', *Contention*, 1(2).

Hoffman, Merle (1991) Untitled piece on *Thelma & Louise, On the Issues*, Winter.

Keyssar, Helene (1977) 'I love you. Who are you? The strategy of drama in recognition scenes', *Proceedings of the Modern Languages Association*, March.

Keyssar, Helene (1984) *Feminist Theatre. An Introduction to the Plays of Contemporary British and American Women*. London and New York: Macmillan.

Keyssar, Helene (1991) *Robert Altman's America*. New York: Oxford University Press.

Lessing, Doris (1972) *The Golden Notebook*. London: Michael Joseph.

Mulvey, Laura (1989) *Visual and Other Pleasures*. London: Macmillan.

Pasolini, Pier Paolo (1976) 'The cinema of poetry', in Bill Nichols (ed.), *Movies and Methods*, Vol. 1. Berkeley: University of California Press.

Waller, Marguerite (1987) 'Academic Tootsie: denial of difference and the difference it makes', *Diacritics*, Spring.

Warshow, Robert (1975) *The Immediate Experience*. New York: Atheneum.

10

Why Multiple Personality Tells Us Nothing About the Self/Mind/Person/ Subject/Soul/Consciousness

Ian Hacking

London, Saturday, 25 March, 1843. From the fact that the philosophy of the human mind has been almost wholly uncultivated by those who are best fitted for its pursuit, the study has received a wrong direction, and become a subtle exercise for lawyers and casuists, and abstract reasoners, rather than a useful field of scientific observation. Accordingly, we find the views, even of the most abstract metaphysicians, coming into frequent collision with the known facts of physiology and pathology. For example, that 'consciousness is *single*' is an axiom among the mental philosophers, and the proof of *personal identity* is made by those gentlemen to rest chiefly on the supposed universality or certainty of that allegation. But what would they say to the case of a somnambulist who evinced what is regarded as double consciousness – the operation of the mind being perfectly distinct in the state of somnambulism from its developments in the wakeful condition? With reference to such an individual, the proof of his personal identity must rest with others, not with himself, for his memory in one state takes not the smallest cognizance of what he thought, felt, perceived, said, or did, in the other. (Wakley, 1842–3: 936–7)

This passage is drawn from an editorial penned by Thomas Wakley, once longtime editor of the *Lancet*. How do things stand one and a half centuries later? The symptoms, diagnosis, aetiology and social role of the condition have all changed. It is now common to speak of multiple personality disorder (MPD), although the name is about to change again. In the 1994 *Diagnostic and Statistical Manual* of the American Psychiatric Association *(DSM–IV)*, the term has become 'dissociative identity disorder' (DID). One thing, however, remains the same. From Wakley to the present, multiple personality has been seen as a great natural experiment for the study of the mind. Taylor and Martin (1944: 297) end their classic survey by quoting Francis Bacon on experiments of light and adding: 'Cases of multiple personality are natural *experimentum lucifera*.' And Ernest Hilgard, the great student of hypnotism, wrote in the same vein that 'overt multiple personalities . . . appear to be rather rare experiments of nature' (Hilgard, 1977: 24, cf. 18).

I believe multiple personality cannot be seen as a 'natural experiment' in this way. In my view, the progress of the disorder in history, and its ups and downs, at most teaches us something about what people are prepared to say and do, and how they are willing to interact with people of unsound mind. It also informs us about realms of behaviour that express deep distress. If these cases are natural experiments, they are not nature's revelations of the vagaries of the human mind. They are trials of a community whose central figures are the experts and their patients, though the circle quickly widens to include families, employers and the institutions of law and order. Indeed, thanks to media exposure today almost everyone encounters the phenomenon. Our culture will not touch the truly mad; gone are the days when the cruel show at Bedlam was an entertainment. Instead, we like to feast our eyes on the oddly dysfunctional, on people with bizarre yet manageable mental disorders. As a result, multiple personality has assumed a very public place in North America. Thus multiple personality is not a natural experiment, but an experiment on the community. And it promises to teach us more about the role of our conception of the mind in our social arrangements, than about the mind itself.

I argue that multiple personality shows nothing *direct* about the mind. That is, it does not furnish evidence for any substantive philosophical thesis about mind (or self, etc.). The phenomena may nonetheless *illustrate* some claim about the mind that is held for reasons independent of the phenomena. If so, would not the phenomena be supporting evidence for the philosophical claim? No. I maintain that they furnish no evidence at all. They are only illustrations. The line between 'evidence' and 'illustration' is hard to draw, because the sheer fact that there is a real-life illustration can seem like evidence. But at least for twentieth-century authors, the doctrines that are illustrated have roots in principles unrelated to multiple personality, and unsupported by its existence.

I argue my case by citing philosophers. I shall ignore the clinicians of MPD – a wide-ranging assortment including physicians, psychiatrists, psychologists, social workers, nurses and therapists. To favour philosophers over clinicians may be to pass over the cake for the crumbs in exactly the way that Wakley implied. But the theoretical views of the clinicians of multiple personality must be discussed in another context. Our philosophers do at least differ from the lawyers, casuists and abstract reasoners whom Wakley despised. They are concrete reasoners who have taken pains to learn what there is to know about multiple personality.

Before proceeding, let us examine the phenomena themselves. Outlines of the history of multiple personality disorder are available in many places, starting with Ellenberger's classic (1970). My own version is outlined in Hacking 1992 and 1995. Hence the briefest of sketches will suffice here. I shall describe two sets of symptoms: the classic double consciousness that Wakley had in mind, and multiple personality as it presents itself 150 years later. With those raw materials in hand, we shall turn to our philosophers.

Brief history of the phenomena

The first well-known detailed report of a case of double consciousness dates from 1791. It is no accident that the period coincides with the first great wave of hypnotism, that is, Mesmer's animal magnetism. This was the topic of every great Parisian salon, and it was also much discussed on the streets. Though two French medical commissions – one headed by Lavoisier and counting Benjamin Franklin among its members – denounced animal magnetism in 1785, mesmerism continued to flourish underground. It was never officially repudiated in Germany, its original homeland, and it was here that our first double consciousness was reported in full. A hypnotized person seemed to have two consciousnesses, one during the magnetic sleep, and one while awake. The mesmerized state knew about the normal state, but not the other way around: there was one-way amnesia. Hypnotism was often described as artificial or provoked somnambulism, in contrast to spontaneous somnambulism. ('Somnambulism' did not mean mere sleepwalking, but a repertoire of waking actions undertaken in a state of trance.) The language of the magnetizers was applied to the spontaneous somnambulists, who were said to have 'double consciousness'. Hence Wakley's terminology.

American cases began to appear early in the nineteenth century. The best known was Mary Reynolds of Pennsylvania, whose correspondence, in both states of mind, has been preserved. In Britain there was a steady trickle of cases; when one of them achieved some notoriety, or was used to illustrate some general theory about the mind, a cascade of similar reports would follow, some recalled simply from the notebooks of doctors who wrote in to say, 'One of my patients was like that too'. On occasion the phenomenon was associated with the two halves of the brain; some speculated that it resulted from imperfect communication between the two hemispheres, and that a consciousness resided in each one. (See Hacking, 1991b for a detailed survey of double consciousness.)

The phenomenon of 'double consciousness' is now largely forgotten. During the 1870s the term was often replaced by 'double personality', or even 'doubled life'. The whole person – her life, not just her awareness – was deemed to be split. Then 'double personality' became 'multiple personality'.

The change from consciousness to the whole personality began with a celebrated French patient, Félida X, described in detail in 1876. A veritable torrent of French multiples then followed until the end of the century. This upsurge was not an isolated event. The 1870s experienced a great revival of French enthusiasm for hypnotism, both in medical circles, concerned with therapy and the study of the mind, and in the populace at large, attracted by its thrill value. This was also the epoch of *la grande hystérie* made famous by Charcot. During the 1880s Pierre Janet invented the generic labels *désagrégation* and *dissociation* to cover splittings of self, mind, consciousness and personality. He urged that every case of hysteria was at bottom a 'splitting of consciousness'. However, this view was eventually eclipsed by Freud's conceptions (though his initial perceptions were similar to those of Janet – hardly surprising since both counted Charcot among their *maîtres*). And by the end of the century multiple personality was losing its two chief supports: hypnosis, in which interest was waning, and hysteria, the symptoms of which were dissipated into other diagnoses. Psychoanalysis was waiting in the wings to treat some of the patients who might otherwise have developed dual personalities.

By 1900 the scene had moved to Boston, where Morton Prince had two patients who attracted immense popular attention. He fought something of a rearguard action against other movements in abnormal psychology, such as psychoanalysis and behaviourism, and although cases of multiplicity continued to be reported in the United States after Prince, they lost all theoretical interest. Today's popular knowledge of multiple personality reaches back only as far as 1957, when two doctors published a sensational multibiography, *The Three Faces of Eve*, later made into an eyecatching movie. Eve was an anomaly, however, until the 1970s, when there arose a new multiple personality movement of unprecedented vigour. In 1973 another book-and-film, *Sybil*, captured the new spirit – many personalities, and a background of child abuse.

Just as the French wave after 1876 was bound up with hysteria and hypnosis, so the American epidemic that began a hundred years later was tied to child abuse. In 1980 multiple personality disorder became an official diagnosis of the third edition of the *Diagnostic and Statistical Manual* of the American Psychiatric Association (*DSM–III*). During the subsequent decade an enormous number of cases were reported in North America. An International Society for the Study of Multiple Personality and Dissociation was established. A journal, *Dissociation*, began to appear quarterly. Many specialized clinics were established. All this provoked a vast amount of opposition. Even today, mainstream psychiatry is inclined to doubt the very existence of multiple personality disorder. Sceptics believe that multiple personalities are a product of the clinic and of media hype. There are nevertheless many clinicians who have plenty of patients with all the official symptoms of MPD, which in 1980 were as follows:

> Within an individual, two or more distinct personalities exist, each of which is dominant at a particular time.
> The personality that is dominant at any particular time determines the individual's behaviour.
> Each individual personality is complex and integrated, with its own unique behaviour pattern and relationships.

The 1994 criteria for the renamed 'Dissociative Identity Disorder' are quite similar, though somewhat more sceptical. They speak of the 'presence', rather than the 'existence' of personalities. There is a firm insistence that there be some degree of amnesia – 'alters' do not recall what other alters did. And the name change is itself designed to play down multiplicity, to suggest that multiple 'personalities' are just fragments. It is implied that the problem is one of lack of integration; there are not too many personalities, but too few, not even one.

Symptoms then: double consciousness

A typical patient afflicted with double consciousness had two states, one vivacious, one inhibited. There was one-way amnesia, the cautious, proper person having no memory of the gay and merry one. In the famous case of Mary Reynolds, two-way amnesia was at issue. In her second state she had to relearn skills such as writing and playing the piano. Most of these patients were young women, although older men were also reported. Men more commonly had 'fugues': a man, perhaps about to be married or in mid-life crisis, would disappear for some days or weeks, and would even take up a new personality in another town, with no memory of his previous existence. The switch between states occurred suddenly, with a brief spasm and short trance-like condition intervening. Occasionally a third personality manifested itself. Alters not only had different memories, mannerisms and skills, but they were also said to look different, especially in the cast of their eyes.

Félida X was a seamstress. Unlike Mary Reynolds she suffered from one-way amnesia, but she could tell when she was about to have a switch and wrote notes to her other self so that she could continue her work without interruption. The typical subject, however, was engaged in the occupations of the parlour. A woman would be reading aloud, have an attack, proceed to play music; when she came to, she would resume reading at the very sentence where she left off. Michael Kenny (1986) suggests that in the United States the double was commonly of strict Protestant upbringing, and that the lively alter personality provided a way of acting out her suppressed potential or fantasies. There is also a steady undertow of sex. Multiples, including Félida, would conceive and even bear children in their second, more liberated state; they would deny, in the first state, that they were pregnant and had no memory of sexual relations.

Really florid symptoms were seldom described, apart of course from the alternating of consciousness itself. That changed in 1875, when hysterical presentations were standard in France; all the famous multiples were hysterics, with various types of partial anaesthesias and paralyses which would switch from state to state. It became standard practice to describe the horrible 'uncaused' bleeding, tortured sleep and racking pains that the patients would from time to time experience. Then, as now, there were prototypical cases of double or alternating consciousness. But there were many cases at some distance from the prototype. Take, for example, some cases familiar to Wakley in 1843. He published his editorial on 23 March; on 28 February at a meeting of the Royal Medical and Chirurgical Society, a number of cases were discussed and immediately reported in the *Lancet*. We are told of a fourteen-year-old boy who had fits of uncontrollable bulimia which lasted for days; he did nothing but eat and sleep. When he came to, he had no recollection of those events. No other justification for speaking of double consciousness was given. There was a man who seems to have had no amnesia, but who had two completely co-conscious selves, one of which persecuted the other. There is mention of bulimia patients who believe they have a 'gnawing devil' within them. Only one prototypical case emerged, where: 'In one state of consciousness this patient was capable of learning and saying things which she was quite incapable of doing in her other state. In one condition she was pert and impudent, in the other modest and retiring.' She was severely constipated; her cure resulted from 'some attention to the stomach and alimentary canal' (Wilson, 1842–3: 876).

Pert and impudent, modest and retiring. That is the template of double consciousness, only barely retained in modern multiple personality. I shall accentuate the change in prototype by moving from the distant to the immediate past.

Symptoms of the 1980s: MPD

I noted above that MPD became DID in 1994, and the symptomatology will no doubt change again. During the 1980s, the emphasis was on populations of fairly fully developed alternative personalities or 'alters'; in the 1990s talk is more about 'fragments' and their integration.

During the 1980s, in the clinics of therapists who believed in multiple personality, the alters were almost never two in number. A dozen person-alities were common; in some samples twenty-five per individual was the mean. People with over a hundred alters were reported, although in these cases fewer than twenty would regularly assume 'executive control'. There is a standard theory on the cause of the trouble. The splitting of persons is a response to childhood trauma, nearly always childhood sexual abuse. We should remember that although there was a nineteenth-century cruelty-to-children movement, what we now call 'child abuse' came to the fore in 1962, with widespread publicity about battered baby syndrome. Only in about 1975 was physical abuse taken to include incest, and later a very extended concept of incest that included fondling (Hacking, 1991a). Most sensitive clinicians realize that a patient should not be forced to recall past events that are terribly painful. Nevertheless, one standard form of multiple therapy today encourages the patient to recall the details of the (taken for granted) incidents of child sexual abuse when she is ready for them. There is also a tendency to elicit a great many alters, on the grounds that each of them will be connected to yet another repressed memory of trauma.

Since so many alters emerge during therapy, the personality structure is rather different from what it was a century ago. There are still amnesias, though they may be only partial. Periods of lost time are a standard warning sign of multiplicity – the main, public, personality is replaced by an alter, whose activities are forgotten later. You can learn a lot about contemporary culture from the life of a multiple. For example, some alters like to go shopping for clothes to express themselves, so a multiple will have distinct wardrobes, containing clothes that other alters, and the main personality, if there is one, have no knowledge of. There are commonly vicious, cruel alters, evil even to the point that they will threaten suicide in order to murder other alters. There are also helpful alters. Child alters are common. Indeed, now that child sexual abuse is the known cause of multiplicity, they have become standard. Most alters are elicited in therapy, where every alter is given its own name, though recently with so much media discussion of the topic, people have begun to discover their alters on their own. The alters of a single individual vary in age, race, sexual inclination, and even sex. That is, a person whose body is of one sex may resolutely claim the opposite physiology, rejecting all evidence to the contrary.

Multiples often report, in private, hearing other alters talk from within their heads. These argue with each other, snarl, console, and sometimes leave for 'another place' where they cannot be heard. It is wise not to admit this in a hospital or to a standard psychiatrist; if you must say it, insist the voices are inside you. Otherwise you will be diagnosed as schizophrenic and drugged accordingly. Whatever one's view on the controversial topic of schizophrenia, MPD is entirely distinct from it. As one psychiatrist in the multiple movement has said, the voices of schizophrenics are crazy, but the alters of a multiple are not mad. (Unfortunately the still popular expression 'split personality' leads lay people to confuse the two conditions.) Unlike schizophrenia, multiple personality does not respond to any known cocktail of psychotropic medications.

Diagnosed multiples typically work in service industries – including teaching and nursing – and are better educated than average. Those who are aware of their condition now commonly say 'we' rather than 'I', at least in the company of other multiples and friends. At work, alters can be a nuisance, for one may take over when you're talking to your boss or a client. Thus multiples develop strategies (a bit like maintenance alcoholics) to cover up the gross gaffes committed by misbehaving alters. Older multiples who wear glasses – a great many do – find they need different prescriptions for different personalities, and will carry several pairs around with them. Some clinicians believe that physiological or biochemical differences are associated with switches from one alter to another. However, there is no good evidence that these differences are even as great as occur during changes of mood in people thought of as normal and healthy.

Interpretations

Positivism

Before 1875 almost all the philosophical discussions of double consciousness were conducted by physicians. In Britain and America there was a canonical group of 'mental' textbooks by men trained in the Edinburgh medical school. These treatises on the human mind, psychological, medical and philosophical, have their origins in Locke, Hartley and Hume. The Scots medical men provide the most reliable sequence of cases of double consciousness in Britain, but they present the cases as curiosities. There was little philosophical speculation. The situation changed in 1876, at least in France, when Félida appeared upon the scene, and doubling became a fascination for French physicians, neurologists and philosophers. Indeed, psychology began to emerge in France as an independent profession, neither philosophical nor medical, in the light of discussions of alternating personalities. There would be no chair of psychology at the Collège de France, said Pierre Janet, second holder of that chair, were it not for the humble Félida (Janet, 1906: 78).

That powerful intellectual figure, Hippolyte Taine, had reflected on a few famous cases, such as 'the lady of Mac Nish' none other than Mary Reynolds, reported for Europe by a Scottish physician, Robert MacNish. Taine reasoned that

> Our images, by connecting themselves, make up a group which in literary and judicial language we call the moral personality. If two groups are distinctly severed, so that no element of the one calls up any element of the other, as in the case of the lady cited by Mac Nish, there are two moral personalities in the same individual. (Taine, 1878, I: 156)

In 1875 the great lexicographer Emile Littré, founder of *La Philosophie positive*, published a piece on double consciousness in that journal. He collected a variety of cases from medical literature, ranging over autoscopy, depersonalization and much else. His target was not medicine but metaphysics. 'Theology by revelation and metaphysics by intuition attribute personality to a soul which uses the brain like an instrument' (Littré, 1875: 334). He rejected, on philosophical grounds, the idea that a person is 'a primordial principle from which the other psychic properties flow'. He thought that he could illustrate his argument by citing disorders of personality. Directly after he published, Félida came to light.

For about twenty years thereafter French philosopher-psychologists of a positivist and republican stripe were much taken with multiple personality. Janet's predecessor in the chair of psychology, Théodule Ribot, argued that the traditional, neo-Kantian French school of philosophy insisted upon a transcendental ego, whose existence was proven by theology or metaphysics. The wave of multiples that struck France proved there need be no one transcendental ego, but only an empirically formed self built from memory, experience and an evolving sense of self-awareness. And multiples, he argued, proved that one individual could have more than one of those selves. 'Members of the old school,' wrote Ribot, 'accuse us of filching their *moi*' (Ribot, 1881: 98). That was in his book *Maladies de la mémoire*, subtitled 'An Essay in Positive Psychology'. I have described elsewhere how the positivists were fascinated by a few classical multiple personalities, and how they used them in their battles with metaphysicians and theologians (Hacking, 1986b: 80–4). There is no doubt that these men believed that multiple personality showed something quite profound about the human mind. They used it to bolster an essentially Lockian associationist theory of the mental. Ribot argued that diseases of the memory followed an absolutely constant 'law of regression'. As disease, injury or age impaired memory, one lost the most recent associations. To this Janet gave the name *dissociation*, which to this day is central in diagnoses of the 'dissociative disorders'.

Men such as Ribot and Janet used multiple personality to argue for their philosophical doctrines. But we have a grave problem here. For the patients all too readily fit a certain pattern already described by the philosophers. As soon as Littré said what he wanted, Azam produced the very case, with just the right phenomenology. Then there were dozens. Which came first, the philosophy or the patients? The philosophy. I have used this as a specially striking case of what I call 'making up people' (Hacking, 1986a). What we see here is less a disorder that shows us something about the self/mind/person/subject/soul/consciousness, than one whose phenomenology is sculpted to fit a prior philosophical position.

William James

James's *Principles of Psychology* (1890a) includes an incisive review of the literature on what he called 'alternating personality' in a chapter entitled 'The Consciousness of Self'. Following Ribot, he took alternating personality to be primarily a disturbance of memory, since in these cases one personality knew nothing of another personality expressed by the same body at earlier times. (It is important to ask why we should think of alternation as a disorder of *memory*. It is not as if the person with alternating consciousness has in any ordinary sense forgotten something [see Hacking, 1994]. Yet as we saw, amnesia has been restored to the criteria for multiple personality, or rather dissociative identity disorder, in a way that suggests we may have forgotten how memory got into our conception of multiplicity in the first place.)

James is a model for all philosophers of mind. He records alternating personality as a phenomenon, but lays no great weight on it for his theory of consciousness. It is a disturbance, for which one might hope to obtain a physiological explanation (he cautiously mentions some already in circulation), but no philosophical conclusions are drawn.

This is not to say that he did not follow events. His 1896 Lowell lectures were closely in touch with the work of French students of multiple personality, especially Pierre Janet. These lectures have recently been reconstructed (Taylor, 1982). In the fourth, 'Multiple Personality', James is fascinated by reports of what psychiatry now calls 'dissociative fugue', in which an individual compulsively travels, often assuming a new identity, and, when he recovers, has little or no memory of what he did on his travels. James had interviewed the famous American case of the Revd Ansel Bourne (James, 1890b: 269; cf. Kenny, 1986) and was aware of the epidemic of fugues in France, which started in 1887 and continued for about a decade (the epidemic is described in Hacking, forthcoming). He was especially familiar with the famous Bordeaux patient, Albert Dad—, and with cases reported by Janet and Fulgence Raymond, Charcot's successor and Janet's chief at the Salpêtrière. A most common name for this group of disorders was *automatisme ambulatoire*. In France it was *contrasted* with alternating personality. This is in part because it was typically men who suffered from fugue, while women tended to split. Ambulatory automatism, as it were, filled the gender space left vacant by multiple personality. James, in contrast, took ambulatory automatism to be the very prototype of multiple personality, if Taylor's reconstruction of the lectures is correct: 'As a class, the four types of alternating personality all appear to be instances of ambulatory automatism' (Taylor, 1982: 74). Nevertheless, while James followed up cases of both multiple personality and dissociative fugue reported in the literature, both popular and scientific (cf. the extensive 'Notes' to Taylor, 1982), he seems to regard these as complex psychological phenomena and does not draw inferences about the human mind or soul, except that it is difficult to understand.

A. N. Whitehead

The Philosophy of Organism presented in *Process and Reality* (1928) demands long periods of absorbed study. I hope I shall be forgiven by Whitehead's admirers for the following superficial mention of a few paragraphs.

Recent cognitive science sometimes speaks of 'the society of mind' – a phrase used as the title of a popular book by Marvin Minsky. Whitehead was more daring. He thought that everything that we commonly think of as an entity is a society. An electron is a society of electron occasions. 'Our cosmic epoch is to be considered as a society of electromagnetic occasions' (1928: 141). Indeed, 'the point of a "society", as the term is here used, is that it is self-sustaining. . . . To constitute a society, the class-name [the name for the entity or type] has got to apply to each member, by reason of genetic derivation from other members of the same society' (p. 137).

All organisms are, a fortiori, societies, but some of them are special. Whitehead had many fine things to say about the idea of a person in *Process and Reality*, including this:

> in the case of the higher animals there is central direction, which suggests that in their case each animal body harbours a living person, or living persons. Our own self-consciousness is direct awareness of such persons. There are limits to such unified control, which is indicated by dissociation of personality, multiple personalities in successive alternations, and even multiple personalities in joint possession. (p. 164)

From Whitehead's perspective, multiple personalities are all too easy to come by.

> What needs to be explained is not dissociation of personality but unifying control, by reason of which we not only have unified behaviour, which can be observed for others, but also consciousness of a unified experience. (p. 165)

Whitehead was *au courant* with the phenomena of dissociation, and convinced of their clinical reality. He used multiple personality to illustrate a thesis, not to argue it. No phenomenon known to Whitehead constitutes evidence for Whitehead's cosmology. This is the normal relationship between the philosophy of mind and multiple personality. The philosophy has a ready-made slot for the phenomena of multiple personality, but does not in fact gain support from them. No detail of the phenomena known to Whitehead is explained or predicted; the structure of multiple personality disorder is totally independent of Whitehead's cosmology.

Daniel Dennett

In the paragraph from which I have just quoted, Whitehead also wrote that 'It is obvious that we must not demand another mentality presiding over these other actualities (a kind of Uncle Sam, over and above all the U.S. citizens)'. Humphrey and Dennett (1989) take a similar position. They observe how a termite colony can appear to act as with a single purpose, even though each termite is doing its own thing. Here what seems like collective agency does not need a master supervisor. Indeed, they maintain that 'most systems on earth that appear to have central controllers (and are usefully described as having them) do not' (1989: 77). Humphrey and Dennett are inclined to use this fact as a partial model of what it is to be a person – a being with many subsystems. But how to characterize sheer personhood? They offer an analogy – which recalls Whitehead's just quoted: none other than the USA. We can speak of America's characteristics, its brashness, its Vietnam memories, its fantasy of being forever young. But there is no controlling entity that embodies these qualities. 'There is no such thing as Mr American Self, but as a matter of fact there is in every country on earth a Head of State' (p. 78). The American president is expected to inculcate and represent national values, and to be 'the spokesman when it comes to dealing with other nation states'. A nation, our authors conjecture, needs a head to get on reasonably well as a nation. Note the contrast with the Uncle Sam analogy that Whitehead urged us to avoid: Uncle Sam is not a US citizen, but the president is.

The point of Humphrey and Dennett's peculiarly American analogy is this. What we think of as a person is in fact many subsystems. It is nevertheless possible to have one subsystem that is crucially important in various ways, including the ways in which it has relationships with other people. It does not furnish 'central direction', to use Whitehead's phrase. Nor does it even have 'executive control', to invoke the corporate image favoured by many clinicians. It is rather a chief representative for the public view of a collection of subsystems. The analogy suggests a way to think about multiple personality. There are several functioning, or malfunctioning, subsystems that take turns as representative, particularly in dealing with distinct aspects of the system of subsystems.

Humphrey and Dennett do not advance a full-blown philosophy of mind. Instead they proceed to address the question that, in my experience, everyone asks: is multiple personality real? The background philosophy, however, can be found in Dennett's subsequent book, *Consciousness Explained*, where personality disorder is once again described as one 'of the terrible experiments that nature conducts' (Dennett, 1991: 419).

What do such experiments teach? As is well known, Dennett is sceptical about the very idea of the self. His theory of consciousness seeks to discredit the view that, as Dennett satirically puts it, where selves are concerned it's 'All or Nothing and One to a Customer' (1991: 422). Dennett offers MPD to illustrate how his own theory challenges the traditional view. On the same page he also mentions a tale of two twins aged forty who are never apart; they continue each other's sentences, and perform acts jointly. Here we have one person with two bodies – Fractional Personality Disorder! Significantly, the power of 'FPD' as an illustration does not depend on whether the report of such twins is true. What is important is that Dennett's view of the person allows such a description to make sense. In his *Remarks on the Foundations of Mathematics*, Wittgenstein observes that if a picture of an experiment is just as compelling as the actual experiment, then the event depicted is not really an experiment at all. It is not as experiments that FPD or MPD inform Dennett's philosophy of mind.

Certainly the old double consciousness and the recent forms of MPD are no surprise to Dennett. But their relationship to his theory seems similar to their relationship to Whitehead's cosmology. What Dennett finds astonishing in these cases is not the existence of multiplicity, but something which has nothing to do with his philosophy of mind: the horrendous conditions in which some children grow up, and which, according to MPD clinicians, lead the children to dissociate.

> These children have often been kept in such extraordinarily terrifying and confusing circumstances that I am more amazed that they survive psychologically at all than I am that they manage to preserve themselves by desperate redrawing of their boundaries. What they do, when confronted with overwhelming conflict and pain, is this: They 'leave'. They create a boundary so that the horror doesn't happen to them: it either happens to no one, or to some other self, better able to sustain its organization under such an onslaught – at least that's what they say they did, as best they recall. (Dennett, 1991: 420)

Patients have been diagnosed with double consciousness or MPD for two centuries now. Contrary to what is often said, diagnoses were not uncommon before 1970, although the frequency was nowhere near as great as at present. But patients began to say what Dennett says they say only recently. Today they all say it, or at least suspect that they ought to say it. It is how they learn to describe themselves in therapy. They do not recall themselves dissociating so much as various horrendous experiences in the persona of a number of alters. A patient is often said to be in denial if she does not produce the recollections of the monstrous acts imposed upon her. 'No such thing ever happened' is not an admissible outcome of therapy for florid multiplicity. When the events are recalled, she will also, in therapy, be able to understand why she split, telling the story that Dennett reports in the above quotation.

Do not misunderstand me. I am not saying that the recollections are false, a theme of the False Memory Syndrome Foundation, founded in 1992, and by the end of 1993 claiming 10,000 families as adherents. I am not here quarrelling with the theory that florid MPD is virtually always the result of an implicit dissociation that occurs in childhood, usually as a response to familial evil and betrayal of trust. I am speaking only to the phenomena. I emphasize that what patients say about themselves has changed radically in the past two decades.

Dennett speaks of '*the terrible experiments that nature conducts*'. What exactly are these experiments? The events consist of a patient in therapy, often lasting several years, coming to say the things she says. The 'experiment' is so strongly controlled that if she does not say those things, she may even be released from therapy for being too resistant, for denial. The question is not whether children are abominably treated or whether they will grow up with grave psychological difficulties if their childhood is vile. The question is: is the subsequent prototypical MPD behaviour one of nature's experiments? Or is it rather the way in which a certain class of adults in North America will behave when treated by therapists using certain practices, and having certain convictions?

Let us imagine an experiment, not performed because it is unethical, but about whose outcome we can make confident predictions. It began, let us say, five years ago. Two easily hypnotizable patients who score highly on various quiz-tests for dissociation, had as similar life problems as we can find in psychiatry. Both know about MPD from the media; each suspects she is a multiple. In a major Canadian city are two prominent psychiatric establishments, Institute N and Clinic Y. Doctors at N (for No) never diagnose multiple personality. Clinicians at Y (for Yes) treat many multiples. By random assignment we place one patient for assessment at N, and the other at Y. Both establishments treat their eligible patients without charge, as they are covered by government-funded health insurance. At N, a patient professing multiplicity is asked to produce her health insurance card. 'What is the name on that card?' 'Danielle Martin.' 'Then that is the person we are going to work with.' If the patient stays, she does not evolve into a multiple. But at Y, Martina Robinson, the parallel patient, ends up exactly as Dennett describes. Danielle behaves very differently from Martina. Each establishment bad-mouths the other. Each predicts that the other's patient will relapse. The focus of our experiment, then, is not the natural, but the social: it is an experiment in clinic—patient interaction.

This thought experiment follows real life all too closely. Disturbed people who stay in multiple clinics often develop multiple personality; those who stay in traditional psychiatric institutes do not. Without the right cultural setting there is virtually no multiple personality behaviour. In the right cultural setting there can be plenty. I am confident that a great many children suffered untold terrors in the 1920s. To exaggerate slightly, only one of them, Eve, grew up to be a multiple. A great many children with comparable experiences in the 1950s are multiples today, being treated by MPD clinicians. The multiplicity is not literally iatrogenic, viz. created by clinicians. Rather certain features of unhappiness will, in a favourable climate, ripen into multiplicity. That multiplicity is real enough. The therapeutic question is not about reality but about how to heal. Should we agree with Institute N and protect the patient from the MPD/DID climate? Or should we hold with Clinic Y that only in such a climate can the patient be truly cured? These reflections on the reality and treatment of the phenomena are not far from those of Dennett and Humphrey themselves. They try to defuse the issue of whether multiple personality is 'real' and persuade the reader that there is at least real multiple behaviour.

My disagreement with Dennett is about the value of MPD to the philosophy of mind. For him, MPD reinforces his challenge to the idea of an essential unitary self. I suggest that it does nothing of the sort. The patients who behave in the way he describes all work with clinicians who are firmly attached to the multiple personality movement. During the past twenty years this has involved a strong commitment to many alters and to child sexual abuse as the cause of dissociation. The MPD clinicians are certainly against the idea that seems prevalent in Institute N, that every patient comes equipped with a unitary self that has gone awry. But how does this support Dennett's theory? It shows only, I think, that he has people in the clinical world who agree with his scepticism about the necessity of a unitary self.

Nothing I have said in any way calls into question Humphrey and Dennett's lucid and probing investigation of the multiple movement. Nor does it contest any of the fundamental tenets of Dennett's philosophy of mind. They stand on their own, and that is my only point here. MPD may furnish a graphic illustration for Dennett's philosophy, but nothing in the detailed phenomena of present-day multiple personality teaches us anything about his theory of subsystems. His philosophy is no more supported by the phenomena of MPD than is Whitehead's.

Stephen Braude

Stephen Braude's book, *First Person Plural: Multiple Personality and the Philosophy of Mind*, was published in 1991, the same year as Dennett's

Consciousness Explained. Braude dispels a tempting myth. I have been urging that multiple personality has nothing to teach the philosophy of mind. But at least it seems inconsistent with ideas like that of a transcendental unity of apperception, a metaphysical soul, or a necessarily unified self. To that extent it seems, as both Ribot and Dennett have maintained, that MPD must support, however weakly, any position antagonistic to transcendental, metaphysical or religious unity. However, Braude invokes MPD *against* what he calls Dennett's 'colonialist' view where:

> there is no ultimate psychological unity, only a deep and initial multiplicity of subjects, 'selves' (or, for those smitten with recent work in cognitive science and artificial intelligence) 'modules' or subsystems within a person. (Braude, 1991: 164)

Starting with almost exactly the same suppositions as Ribot, Braude concludes that there must be a transcendental ego. There must be something that holds the alters together, that explains their overlapping skills, and that enables them to interact when they become co-conscious. There is some prior unified self in which this mental theatre is engaged.

There are two obvious ways in which to argue for underlying unity. The weaker starts from a possible aim of therapy. The multiple personality clinician (in Clinic Y, say) usually tries to integrate the alters, producing one whole person with one range of clothes in the closet, no lost time, and no embarrassing or destructive behaviour from antagonistic alters. One way to do that is to find the real personality, and to merge all the other alters into that. The fragments of the troubled patient must be made co-conscious and collaborative. In the end the dissociates become associates. This seems to lead us to the idea of an original person who has to be uncovered and restored, an original that split.

However, Braude rightly argues that there need be no original person who split and whom therapy must reclaim. Janet may have modelled the word 'dissociation' on 'association'. Dissociation was thought of as a falling apart of what had earlier been put together by association. And Ribot certainly thought of therapy as trying to cure 'reversal', a splitting or 'dis-association' that undoes unification step by step. Cure would proceed by reversing reversal, putting the self back together again, reassociating. It would be finding the original true self, which is still lurking there, under all the cacophonous alters. This is a picture of cure that is no longer current among clinicians. It is wisely rejected by Braude.

Braude takes another tack to argue for unity. He makes more distinct uses of the various characters of my title than do most authors. For example, he distinguishes between *self, consciousness, subject* and *person*. He is willing to say that a multiple has a number of different selves. Multiples are genuinely different from most people. They have distinct 'centres of apperception'. That means that they have several 'mes'. Each me has a fairly ordinary collection of beliefs, memories, hopes, angers and so forth; each me ascribes these beliefs itself to its own 'I' in the first person: Braude calls these beliefs 'indexical'.

Multiplicity is thus quite unlike our everyday experiences of mild dissociation, e.g. that of commuters who drive to work listening to the car radio. They drive safely and efficiently, and get to the parking lot on time, but usually arrive with no memory of anything that happened en route. But in such a case there is no indexicality, no subsequent 'me' with a cluster of memories, traits and feelings associated with the trip to work. Similarly, Braude argues that there are not separate centres of apperception in hypnosis. Psychic mediums, in contrast, may have several distinct centres of apperception. They go into trances. They speak of beliefs, memories and feelings in a thoroughly indexical way, associating different selves with the different voices that speak through them, the voice of your grandmother, Zoroaster, etc. Braude is therefore inclined to take the *disorder* out of MPD: mediums resemble multiples, but they are not suffering from a disorder in need of treatment. They are just unusual.

Thus far, Braude is using novel terminology, drawn from current semantic theory, for quite old-fashioned descriptions of multiples. His use of words like 'indexicality' has a logical rather than a practical focus. His idea is that the way multiples use pronouns – including a reference to themselves in the first person plural, 'we' – reflects an underlying epistemological stance that differs from other types of dissociation.

So, like Dennett, Braude is glad to say that there is more than one self per multiple person. However, Braude also notes that the alters of one individual have a lot of overlapping basic skills. They usually speak the same language (though there have been some European multiples whose alters really did speak different languages). They can walk and cross the street and tie their shoelaces; even those rare multiples who do have to do much relearning retain nearly all their ordinary skills. The skills affected are those that are originally rather ostentatiously learnt, such as penmanship, or piano, or Greek, skills that are themselves manifestations of a desired social mobility. The multiple can still engage in small talk, make change at the grocer's, ride a horse or drive a car. Of course a child alter may be unable to do some of these things, but they are precisely the aspects of the grown-up world that the patient is trying to avoid. The child alter preserves, say, the skills needed to cross a busy street. Braude concludes that there is a transcendental unity of apperception underlying the various distinct centres of apperception the multiple picks out with the indexical 'I'.

It is not clear how successful Braude's argument is against Dennett, who has protested against Braude's characterization of his position (Dennett, 1992). Dennett does not portray a multiple as several subsystems, each of which mysteriously has the same street-crossing capacity as every other. On the contrary, there may be a subsystem that handles street-crossing for this body, a body variously represented, at different times, by different subsystems, each of which collaborates with the vast majority of street-crossing and business-conducting subsystems. To continue the tired metaphors, it is entirely natural on Dennett's picture for the several alters to use the same automatic pilots.

The important point, however, is that Braude invokes the same data as Dennett to argue in Kantian style for a transcendental ego. Of course, while Kant's unity has to do with the thought, 'I think', that must accompany all of my thoughts in order that I have knowledge of an objective world, one is hard pressed to work that trick for multiples. So Kant and Braude agree on the conclusion – a transcendental ego – but differ on the argument for it. I shall leave the merits of Braude's argument to the reader. (Though I think that what helps keep all those 'mes' going for a patient in a clinic or a medium in a séance is not the indexical use of 'I' to refer to distinct centres of apperception. It is instead the practice of assigning names to the alters that are elicited. I would replace Braude's importation of technical semantics by some down-home reflections on the use and abuse of proper names.) Here I would emphasize only how loose the argument is at the joints. Ribot and Braude start with essentially the same phenomena. From these data Braude wants us to wriggle our way to his conclusion, that there is a fundamental, prior and perhaps transcendental ego. Ribot wanted us to reach the opposite conclusion, that there is no such thing. I believe, not that one or the other is correct, but that multiplicity does no more than illustrate their theses, which must be argued on other grounds. MPD adds nothing but colour to the arguments, and furnishes no evidence for them at all.

Kathleen Wilkes

Wilkes's *Real People* (1988) takes a very different tack. She writes in the tradition of ordinary language philosophy, which aims at conceptual analysis. On this view, our familiar concepts are articulated by the usage of words. We can study concepts by looking, not only at what we actually do say, but at what we would say in various circumstances. Concepts that snugly fit the sorts of things that usually happen may break down when applied to weird events: sufficiently strange happenings may leave us speechless. For the ordinary language philosopher, when we notice that happening, we have learnt something about the bounds of application for our ideas. Philosophers in this tradition are therefore fascinated by questions of 'what would we say if. . .' and are prone to invent imaginary cases that seek to push our concepts to the limit. The problem of personal identity is a particular favourite domain of philosophical fiction. Wilkes, however, takes issue with this penchant for 'bizarre, entertaining, confusing, and inconclusive thought experiments':

> To my mind, these alluring fictions have led discussion off on the wrong tracks; moreover, since they rely heavily on imagination and intuition they lead to no solid or agreed conclusions, since intuitions vary and imaginations fail. What is

more, I do not think that we need them, since there are so many actual puzzle-cases which defy the *imagination*, but which we nonetheless have to accept as facts. (Wilkes, 1988: vii)

To this end, Wilkes invokes multiple personality disorder. However, we must be wary of talk about 'the facts' of these cases. I know of one clinician, important in his day, who lied about the conclusion of his treatment of a once-famous multiple (whom Wilkes does not use) (Hacking, 1991c). This is a salutary reminder that 'the facts' may not be exactly as they stand in the case record.

Consider a multiple whom Wilkes considers at length: Morton Prince's patient, Miss Beauchamp. What are the facts of her case? Prince's prodigiously long book, *The Dissociation of a Personality* (1906) does not tell us that his patient married a colleague of his who became a society psychiatrist at Palm Springs. Nor does it tell us about a shadowy Mr Jones, probably Beauchamp's first husband, or a famous scene of Gothic horror that precipitated Beauchamp's crisis. She was an assistant in a madhouse during a thunderstorm, when Jones appeared on a ladder at the window. All this happened the day before a trial for 'the crime of the century' opened in the next village, none other than that immortalized in verse: 'Lizzie Borden took an axe / And gave her mother forty whacks / When she saw what she had done / She gave her father forty-one' (see Rosenzweig, 1987). So is truth stranger than fiction? Or do such cases represent, not imagination superseded as Wilkes implies, but imagination heightened?

These strange supplements to Prince's report do not, of course, challenge the account of multiplicity. But our confidence in the distinction between fact and fiction is further shaken by the case of Eve, also cited by Wilkes. Eve's tale was told by her doctors in 1957 in *The Three Faces of Eve*. In 1958 Evelyn Lancaster (still a pseudonym) herself gave us *The Final Faces of Eve*, which was pretty much the same story. Then in 1977 she revealed herself as Chris Costner Sizemore, and came out with *I'm Eve*, radically challenging her earlier therapy, and producing no fewer than twenty-two personalities and a lot of abuse that she experienced as a child. And in 1989 Sizemore published *A Mind of My Own*, a New Age work showing how the original three faces of Eve were actually trans-life experiences, i.e. reincarnations. The three books, of 1958, 1977 and 1989, are, we might say, the three faces of Eve.

And what of the famous Sybil of 1973, which in many ways inaugurated the modern multiple movement? In his book *Doubles*, the literary critic Karl Miller wrote that,

Every life is made up, put on, imagined – including, *hypocrite lecteur*, yours. Sybil's life was made up by Sybil, by her doctor, when she became a case, and again, when she became a book, by her author. Sixteen selves were imagined, but it is not even entirely certain that there were as many as two. (Miller, 1987: 348)

Of course, 'real' fiction is full of multiple personalities. Robert Louis Stevenson wrote the most famous tale, of Jekyll and Hyde, while corresponding with Janet. Charles Richet, clinician, physiologist, Nobel Prize winner, wrote a fictional multibiography in the *Revue des deux mondes*. The fiction of the double runs through the romantic movement: Hogg, E. T. W. Hoffman, Dostoevsky's Mr Golyadkin, and a host of others. Take James Thomson in 'The City of Dreadful Night' (1874): 'I was twain / Two selves distinct that cannot join again'. If Thomson is too tormented and too little read, take Dickens's *Edwin Drood*: 'two states of consciousness which never clash, but each of which pursues his separate way as though it were continuous instead of broken'. And on and on. Some 500 playwrights submitted scripts for the play of Prince's book! (Moore, 1938). The winning play, *The Case of Becky*, directed by David Belasco, ran for six months on Broadway, and was made into a silent movie. Are we dealing with docudrama, or drama doc? And multiplicity furnishes the story for a spate of thrillers in the present decade. That is a fitting return to the plot of the first English detective novel, Wilkie Collins's *Moonstone* (1868).

Wilkes is well informed about these stories and as sceptical as I am. Her analysis is scrupulous (though it has recently been challenged, on grounds of a philosophical theory of reference, by John Lizza, 1993). However, her confidence that here we encounter 'real people' seems misplaced. After all, the whole language of many selves had been hammered out by generations of romantic poets and novelists, great and small, and also in innumerable broadsheets and *feuilletons* too ephemeral for general knowledge today. Prince knew exactly how to describe his patient so that she would be a multiple. Is it any wonder that scanning his interminable report we conclude that there are several persons in one body? This is not a test of language against real people, but a consequence of how the literary imagination has formed the language in which we speak of people, be they real, imagined or, the most common case, of mixed race. When it comes to the language that will be used to describe ourselves, each of us, as Karl Miller already implied, is a half-breed of imagination and reality.

Epilogue

Wilkes's insistence that she is discussing real people has a salutary effect, for it makes us think about imaginary people. Dennett spoke of real-life horror stories, but the imaginary people are part of an older tradition of terror. In 1843, the editor of the *Lancet* invited philosophers of the human mind to attend to medical facts, but the imaginative reflection on medical facts was already in place. Dostoevsky's Mr Golyadkin, of 'The Double' (1846), would have been diagnosed by a clinician of the time as suffering from autoscopy, a strange state in which the patient seems to be accompanied by his double, whom he observes, but with whom he is unable to interfere. It has been associated with epilepsy, from which Dostoevsky suffered and which he made a central theme of his work. Dostoevsky probably did use medical gossip in composing the story, for autoscopy was being reported at the time in German periodicals. But it does not follow that he thereby reveals anything direct about the human mind or personal identity. Rather, it gives us yet another uncanny sense of the ever-changing human condition, its distress, incompetence, inadequacy, self-contempt, vanity. Those are all old words, crafted by preacher, moralist and storyteller alike.

As with Dostoevsky's 'The Double', so with the barrage of clinical reports about multiple personality in the past quarter-century. The behaviours that are today lumped together under MPD or DID are various; we cannot say that those modest victims of nineteenth-century double consciousness suffered from late twentieth-century multiple personality disorder, or dissociative identity disorder. We might wonder whether there were two or three disorders, or just one that was culturally adapted and renamed. This sounds like a medical question, whose answer requires us to know more than we do about the human mind. But all we should conclude is that from time to time in European and American milieux there are some very troubled people interacting with their cultural and medical surroundings. They cast, perhaps, a distorting image of what their communities think it is to be a person. We can learn something, perhaps a great deal, about how a group at a certain time represents the self; that would be the philosophical lesson to draw from the varieties of multiple personality. It is not, however, a lesson about the mind or the person or the self, thought of as objective entities about which we wish to know more. If it is a lesson for the philosophy of mind, it is a lesson about what we in the European tradition have called the mind. That mind is a figure in our social arrangements.

Note

I thank Professor Millie Bakan of York University for directing me to Whitehead. I am grateful to comments from Stephen Braude, Daniel Dennett and Kathleen Wilkes; I apologize to Professor Braude for any misrepresentations of his position that may remain.

References

Braude, Stephen (1991) *First Person Plural: Multiple Personality and the Philosophy of Mind*. London: Routledge.

Dennett, Daniel C. (1991) *Consciousness Explained*. Boston: Little Brown.

Dennett, Daniel C. (1992) Letter to *London Review of Books*, 9 July.

Ellenberger, Henri (1970) *The Discovery of the Unconscious: The History and Evolution of Dynamic Psychology*. New York: Basic Books.

Hacking, Ian (1986a) 'Making up people' in Thomas C. Heller, Morton Sosna and David E. Wellbery (eds), *Reconstructing Individualism*. Stanford, CA: Stanford University Press.

Hacking, Ian (1986b) 'The invention of split personalities', in Alan Donagan, Anthony N. Perovich and Michael V. Wedin (eds), *Human Nature and Natural Knowledge*. Dordrecht: Reidel.

Hacking, Ian (1991a) 'The making and molding of child abuse', *Critical Inquiry*, 17.

Hacking, Ian (1991b) 'Double consciousness in Britain 1815-1875', *Dissociation*, 4.

Hacking, Ian (1991c) 'Two souls in one body', *Critical Inquiry*, 17.

Hacking, Ian (1992) 'Multiple personality and its hosts', *History of the Human Sciences*, 5(2).

Hacking, Ian (1994) 'Memoropolitics, trauma and the soul', *History of the Human Sciences*, 7(2).

Hacking, Ian (1995) *Rewriting the Soul. Multiple Personality and the Sciences of Memory*. Princeton, NJ: Princeton University Press.

Hacking, Ian (forthcoming) 'Les Aliénés voyageurs: how dissociative fugue became a medical entity', *History of Psychiatry*.

Hilgard, E. R. (1977) *Divided Consciousness. Multiple Controls in Human Thought and Action*, 2nd edn. New York: Wiley.

Humphrey, Nicholas and Dennett, Daniel C. (1989) 'Speaking for ourselves', *Raritan*, 9.

James, William (1890a) *The Principles of Psychology*, 2 vols. New York: Holt.

James, William (1890b) 'Notes on Ansel Bourne', in *Essays in Psychology*. Cambridge, MA: Harvard University Press, 1983.

Janet, Pierre (1906) *The Major Symptoms of Hysteria*. London: Macmillan.

Kenny, Michael (1986) *The Passion of Ansel Bourne*. Washington DC: Smithsonian.

Littré, Emile (1875) 'La Double Conscience: fragment de la physiologie physique', *La Philosophie positive*, 14.

Lizza, John P, (1993) 'Multiple personality and personal identity revisited', *British Journal for the Philosophy of Science*, 44.

Miller, Karl (1987) *Doubles: Studies in Literary History*, 2nd edn, corrected. Oxford: Oxford University Press.

Moore, Merrill (1938) 'Morton Prince, M.D., 1854-1929: a biographic sketch and bibliography', *Journal of Nervous and Mental Diseases*, 87.

Prince, Morton (1906) *The Dissociation of a Personality*. New York: Longmans & Co.

Ribot, Théodule (1881) *Diseases of Memory: An Essay in the Positive Psychology*. London: Kegan Paul, Trench & Trubner, 1906.

Rosenzweig, Saul (1987) 'A psychoarchaeological key to Morton Prince's classic case of multiple personality', *Genetic, Social and General Psychology Monographs*, 113(1).

Taine, Hippolyte (1878) *De l'intelligence*, 3rd edn, 2 vols. Paris: Hachette.

Taylor, Eugene (1982) *William James on Exceptional Mental States: The 1896 Lowell Lectures*. New York: Charles Scribner's Sons.

Taylor, W. S. and Martin, Mabel F. (1944) 'Multiple personality', *Journal of Abnormal and Social Psychology*, 39.

Wakley, Thomas (1842-3) (Unsigned editorial) 'Double consciousness', *The Lancet*, (1).

Whitehead, A. N. (1928) *Process and Reality*. Cambridge: Cambridge University Press.

Wilkes, Kathleen V. (1988) *Real People: Personal Identity without Thought Experiments*. Oxford: Clarendon Press.

Wilson, John (1842-3) 'A normal and abnormal consciousness, alternating in the same individual', *The Lancet*, (1).

Index

abortion, 7
activity, 59, 68, 78, 85
Adams, H., 21
agreement, 11, 30, 33, 36–7, 38, 45n.4
Altman, R., 143, 145, 157n.3
ambulatory automatism, 168
androgyny, 128, 129, 130, 133
animal magnetism, 161
Aristotle, 14, 69, 82, 109, 148
'Asiatic despotism', 72–3
assertion/assertibility, 33, 36, 37, 45n.2
atomism, 4, 9, 14, 104–5
Austin, J.L., 22, 64
autonomy, 15, 125, 128, 130, 136
   in politics, 119–20
autoscopy, 177–8

Bacon, F., 159
Baker, G., 11, 34–5, 39–44
Bakhtin, M., 8, 15, 16, 144–5, 148, 156–7
Barbin, H., 140
behaviourism, 10
Belasco, D., 177
beliefs, 20, 22, 49, 50, 173–4
Berdyaev, N., 72, 81
Bildungsroman, 144
biological determinism, 77, 78, 80, 85
Block, N., 64
Blok, A., 90
Bogdanov, A., 89, 90
Bolshevism, 13–14, 72–3, 75–6, 78, 84–100
Bourne, A., 168
Braude, S., 172–5
Bruner, J., 6, 10
Butler, J., 8, 15, 132, 134, 135, 141

capitalism, 12, 68, 70–1, 86, 87
Carey, S., 24
Cartesian self, 2–5, 6–8, 10, 31, 43
categories/category system, 24–5, 52–7
Chaplin, C., 145
child abuse, multiple personality and, 164, 165
Chodorow, N., 15, 130, 141
class struggle, 71–2, 87

cognitivism, 10, 63
collective consciousness, 59
Collins, W., 177
communal goals, 109
communication, 57, 64
   envelope theory of, 51, 56
communism, 12, 68, 70–1, 73, 81, 85–7, 89–93, 95–7, 99
communitarianism, 8–9, 96, 134
   critique of liberal subject, 14, 103–21
   dialectical, 14, 15, 124–6, 130–1, 134, 135
   language (Wittgenstein), 11, 31–45
   linguistics (Whorf), 12, 47, 52–7, 62–4
comprehensive doctrines (Rawls), 108
computationalism, 48–9
conceptual role semantics, 64
Condorcet, M., 84
consciousness, 5–6, 12, 59, 77, 81, 159
consistency, 38, 42
constructionism/constructivism, 8–9, 15, 20, 129, 132, 140–5
constructivism (art), 89
contextualism, 10, 18, 19
Coppola, F., 145
correctness, 10, 11, 31, 34–9 *passim*
Crying Game, The (film), 143–4
Cukor, G., 147
cultural convention, 52–60, 63–4
cultural difference, 97
cultural perspective, 18–28
cultural practices/values, 53, 57, 58
'cultural revolution', 93
custom, 30

Dancy, J., 43
death, 13–14, 84–100
Deborin, A., 82n.3
democracy, 115–16
Democritus, 67
Dennett, D., 26, 169–72, 173–5, 177
Derrida, J., 143
Descartes, R., 2–4, 7, 9, 82, 84, 85, 123
Dickens, C., 177
disenchantment, 40

dissociative identity disorder, 159, 162–3, 164, 178
Dostoevsky, F., 70, 75, 82n.1, 177–8
double consciousness, 16, 161, 163–6, 170
Dunn, J., 21, 26

ego boundaries, 130
egocentrism, 26–7
empiricism, 4, 48–52 *passim*, 65
Engels, F., 71–2, 73, 77, 79, 85, 86–7
Epicurus, 67
epistemological individualism, 44, 123
epistemological rationalism, 128
epistemology, 4, 19, 27, 31, 76, 79
Erenburg, I., 75
essentialism, 15, 97, 124, 137
ethic of care, 131
ethical individualism, 123–4, 128, 130
'ethno-anarchism', 97
experience, 19, 30, 31, 49, 57

False Memory Syndrome Foundation, 171
Feldman, C., 26
Félida X, 161, 163, 166
feminism, 7, 8, 14–16, 123–57 *passim*
femininity, 127–33 *passim*, 137
Feuerbach, L., 86, 88
Field, H., 64
Fillmore, C., 22
film, 15–16, 140–57
Firestone, S., 132
Fodor, J., 11–12, 48–52, 62–4
folk psychology, 19, 20
form of life, 30, 33, 37, 39, 44
Foucault, M., 1, 125, 127, 133–4, 135, 140
Fox-Genovese, E., 141–2
frames of reference, 56–7
Freud, S., 69, 82, 162
functionalism, 64
funerals, 91
Fyodorov, N., 88, 96

Geertz, C., 53
gender
    neutrality, 128, 129, 130, 132
    social construction, 15–16, 129, 132, 140–57
gendered self, 14–15, 123–37
Gilligan, C., 1, 8, 15, 131, 141
Godbuilding movement, 88–9
Goodman, N., 20
Gogol, N., 96
Gorbachev, M., 75, 81
Gorky, M., 72, 88
Gould, S.J., 157n.2

grammar/grammatical rules, 22, 24, 41, 54–5
Grushin, B., 80
guns (in films), 15, 146–8

Hacker, P., 11, 34–5, 39–44
Harman, G., 64
Hart, N., 141–2
Hegel, G.W.F., 59, 67, 69
Hegelianism, 78, 79
hero-outlaws (women), 15–16, 143–57
Hilgard, E., 159
Hiller, A., 143, 155
Hilton, J., 84
historical materialism, 78, 79
Hobbes, T., 9, 20, 31, 48, 51–2, 96, 99, 123, 126
Hoffman, E., 177
Hopi, 12, 53, 54–6
human agreement, 11, 30, 33, 36–7, 38
human essence, 68–9, 85
human individuality, 13, 77–8, 80
Humbolt, Baron von, 107
Hume, D., 4, 7, 48, 49, 166
Humphrey, N., 169–70, 172
Husserl, E., 82
Huxley, A., 84
hypnotism, 159, 161

idealization, 58–60, 63–4, 77, 80
identity politics, 97
Ilyenkov, E.V., 6, 8, 12, 13, 45n.1, 58–60, 64, 67, 80
immortality, 13, 85, 90–6, 98, 99
incommensurability, 56, 57, 65
indexical beliefs, 22, 173–4
individual, contrasted with self, subject, 126–7
individual rights, 1, 9, 104, 110–13
individualism, 1, 4
    epistemological, 44, 123
    ethical, 123–4, 128, 130
    liberal, 14, 123, 126, 128–31, 134–6
    libertarian, 104, 110–14
    methodological, 9, 123, 126, 128
    moral, 101, 103
individualist semantics, 11–12, 47–52, 62–4
individuality, 13, 28, 77–8, 80, 96–7
infinity, 87
information processing, 10, 48–9
instrumentality, 10, 22, 23, 28
internal relations, 35, 39
internalization, 5, 12, 61–2, 128–9
interpretation, 19, 23, 33–4
intersubjectivity, 10, 21–2, 23, 26–8
irrealism (about self), 8

Jakobson, R., 24, 94–5
James, W., 167–8
Janet, P., 161–2, 166, 167, 168
Jordan, N., 143
justice, 116–21
  as fairness, 14, 103, 105–10, 114–15
justification, 38
justification conditions, 33, 37

Kant, I., 7, 69, 123, 126, 175
Keil, F., 24
Kenny, M., 163
Khrushchev, N., 75
Krasin, L., 92
Kripke, S., 11, 31–3, 34, 35, 36–9, 45n.3
Kristeva, J., 133
Kubrick, S., 145

labour, 68–72, 85–7, 94, 98, 99
language
  communitarian linguistics, 52–7
  community view, 11, 30, 34–9
  culture and, 20–2, 53, 57–8, 63–4
  games, 38, 125
  innate mastery of, 42
  internalization of, 12, 61–2
  meaning and, 10, 20–2
  natural, 22, 48–51, 53, 58, 64
  philosophy of, 11–12, 45n.2, 47–65
  solitary language user, 11, 30–1, 35, 40–5
  thought and, 10, 11, 47–9, 58, 60–5
  of thought, 12, 46n.8, 48–9, 56–7
Lenin, V.I., 77, 79, 80, 87, 88
  cult of, 92, 95
  tomb of, 13, 91–6, 98
Leontiev, A., 5–6, 65n.5
Lessing, D., 157n.4
Levinson, S., 53
liberal individualism, 14, 23, 126, 128–31,
  134–6
liberalism, 14, 103–21
libertarian individualism, 104–7, 110–14
linguistics, 12, 52–7
Littré, E., 166, 167
Locke, J., 4, 7, 9, 20, 31, 48, 49, 51, 52, 123,
  166
Landau, M., 25
Lucy, J., 56, 63
Lunacharsky, A., 89, 92
Lyotard, J.-F., 125

machine language, 12, 48, 49
MacIntyre, A., 1, 8, 14, 105, 116–21
MacNish, R., 166
Macpherson, C.B., 126

Malcolm, N., 11, 31, 33–6, 38, 39, 41–3,
  45n.3
Malevich, K., 91
Malthus, T., 100n.1
Mamardashvili, M., 80–1
Marx, K., 1, 9, 12–13, 59, 67–82, 85
  conception of self of, 68, 71–2
  early v. late, 79
  philosophical anthropology of, 68–9, 85–6
  as philosopher, 67–71, 72, 78, 85–6
  as political activist, 71–2
  in Soviet ideology, 73, 75–6
Marxism–Leninism, 73, 81
Marxist feminism, 129
masculinity, 15, 128–33 *passim*
Masing-Delic, I., 85
mass nouns, 54
Mayakovsky, V., 88, 90–1, 95
McDowell, J., 45n.5
meaning, 10, 11, 18–19, 62
  agreement and, 36–7
  causal theory of, 49–52 *passim*
  cultural perspective, 10, 18–28
  scepticism, 32–3, 36–40, 45n.3
  signs, 31, 39, 40
  social theory of, 64–5
  use theory, 12, 18, 37–8, 40, 42–3, 64
meaningful behaviour, 39–40, 42–3
means-ends relations, 22, 23
Medin, D., 24
mediation/mediated activity, 12, 61–2
memory, 30, 48, 61, 97, 171
  amnesia, 161, 162, 163, 164, 167
mental representations, 2–3, 12, 47–51,
  53–63, 64
mental states, 5, 7, 32, 43, 49, 52
'Mentalese', 49–50, 52, 63
mesmerism, 161
metaphysics, 19, 52–5, 58–60, 64, 133
methodological individualism, 9, 123, 126,
  128
methodological solipsism, 52
Mill, J.S., 123, 126, 128, 135
Millar, G., 24
Miller, K., 176, 177
Millett, K., 8, 15, 129, 130
mind, 31, 48–9
  multiple personality and, 159–78
  representational theory of, 48
Minsky, M., 168
modernism, 89
monuments, 90–1, 96, 98, 99
moral development, 103, 131
moral obligation, 99–100
moral values, 107–8, 110–12, 119

More, T., 84
multiculturalism, 97
multiple personality, 16, 159–78

narrative, 10, 22, 23, 24–6, 28
natural language, 22, 48–51, 53, 58, 64
natural memory, 61
naturalism, 40
nature-nurture debate, 77–8, 80
Nechaevism, 72–3, 82n.1
neo-Aristotleanism, 110, 119, 121
New Economic Policy, 94
Newton, I., 21
Nietzsche, F., 20
nihilism, 90
normativity, 14, 32, 36, 107–10, 113
    of meaning, 10, 22–3, 28, 40
Nozick, R., 14, 104, 110, 112, 113, 114

object-relations theory, 130
objectification, 68, 79, 85–6
objectivity, 20
ontology, 6–8, 14, 19, 20
original position (Rawls), 14, 105–6, 108
ostensive definition, 30
other minds, 4, 43
Outrageous Fortune (film), 16, 143, 155–6

Paris Commune, 72
Pasternak, B., 95
patriarchy, 128, 129–30, 131, 136–7
Pavlov, I., 78
Pears, D., 46n.7
Peirce, C.S., 28n.3
Penn, A., 147
perception, 48, 49, 50–1, 52, 53
perestroika, 75, 81
perfectionism, 96
personal identity, 16, 96
perspectivalism, 20
phenomenology, 27, 32
philosophical anthropology, 44–5, 68, 85
philosophy
    of language, 11–12, 47–65
    Soviet, 12, 13, 67, 69, 76–7, 80, 81–2
Piaget, J., 65n.6
Plato, 82
Plekhanov, G., 72, 88
pluralist society, 108, 110, 118
Polan, A.J., 87
political liberalism, 109, 118–9
political theory, social self in, 14, 103–21
politics, 8–9, 14, 87
    finitude and, 13, 96–8, 99
positivism, 20, 165–7

postmodernism, 4, 8, 14–15, 125–7, 132–3,
    135–7
power, 125, 126, 129, 133–5
primary goods, 115–16
Prince, M., 162, 176, 177
private language argument, 11, 30–4, 35, 42
problem-solving, 26
proletkult, 89
Prometheanism, 84, 89, 93, 98
property, 7, 70, 71
propositional attitudes, 49
propositional system, 10, 23, 24–5, 28
prototypes, 24
psychoanalysis, 126–7, 132–3, 135, 162
'psychophysics', 63
public justifiability, 108–9, 116

radical feminism, 129
rationality, 20, 38
Rawls, J., 14, 104, 105–10, 114-16, 118–19
realism/reality, 10, 38
    about self, 8
regularity, meaning and, 42–3
Renoir, J., 145
resurrection, 88
Reynolds, M., 161, 163
Ribot, T., 166–7, 173, 175
Richardson, R., 92
Ricoeur, P., 26
rights (of individual), 1, 9, 104, 110–13
Robin, R., 94
Rosch, E., 24
Rousseau, J.-J., 126, 144
rule-following, 10–11, 31–7, 39–40, 41
rule-scepticism, 32–3, 36–40, 45n.3

Sandel, M., 14, 105
Shchedrovitsky, G., 80
schizophrenia, 165
science, 20–1
science fiction, 90
scientific materialism, 78–9
Scott, J., 157n.1
Scott, R., 143
Searle, J., 22, 64
'second signal system', 78
self
    Cartesian, 2–5, 6–8, 31, 43
    -creation, 134–5
    cultural perspective, 18–28
    -determination, 111
    -development, 78, 112
    gendered, 14–15, 123–37
    -interest, 99
    mortal, 13–14, 84–100

self *(cont.)*
    multiple personality and, 159–78
    ontological status of, 6–8, 126–7
    Soviet, 12–13, 67–82
    -understanding, 105–7, 109–10, 114,
        120–1, 127
semantic theory, 11–12, 47, 48–52, 62–4
sensation, 30, 31
sense-datum language, 31, 43
sex/gender difference, 132–3
sexual division of labour, 129, 132
Shelley, M., 100n.5
Shklovsky, V., 91
signs, 31, 39, 40
Sizemore, C. Costner, 176
Sloterdijk, P., 95
social being
    in Russian Marxism, 12–13, 67–82, 86
    Wittgenstein's view, 10–11, 30–45
social construction of gender, 15–16, 129,
    132, 140–57
social constructivism, 8–9, 20
social contract, 9, 14, 104–10
social engineering, 13
social good, 115, 117
social justice, 120
social order, 117–18
social practice, 42–3
social theory of meaning, 64–5
socialism, 67, 70, 88–94, 96, 99
socialist realism, 13, 93–4
socialization, 5, 62, 71–2, 106, 128–30, 131,
    133, 136
solitary language user, 11, 30–1, 35, 40,
    41–5
Soloviev, E., 80
somnambulism, 159, 161
speech, 12, 22, 26, 31, 39–40, 52, 62, 78
Stalin/Stalinism, 13, 73–5, 80, 82n.3,
    93–5
Stampe, D., 49–50
Standard Average European languages, 12,
    53, 54–6
Stites, R., 90, 91, 93
subject, contrasted with self, individual,
    126–7
subjectivity, 4, 8, 20, 27, 31, 125–7, 131–7
    passim
surrogate motherhood, 7
symbols, 10, 50, 52
syntactic rules, 10, 24

Taine, H., 166
Tamas, G., 97
Taylor, C., 8, 14, 20, 104–5, 110–14, 125

Taylor, E., 168
Thelma and Louise (film), 15–16, 143, 144,
    145–57
theories, 24–5
Thomson, J., 177
thought
    language and, 10, 11, 47–9, 58, 60–5
    language of, 12, 48–9, 56–7
    mediation and, 12, 61–2
thought experiments, 16, 41–2, 175–6
time, 44, 54–5
'tokening' of symbols, 50, 52
tools, 60–1
totalitarianism, 67
Toulmin, S., 20
traditions, 117, 118–19, 120
training (rule-following), 34, 42
transcendental anthropocentrism, 11, 38–40
transcendental ego, 7, 16, 166, 173, 175
truth, 38, 41
truth conditions, 33, 45n.2
Tumarkin, N., 100n.4

understanding, 19–20, 27–8
universal forms/universality, 78
use theories (of meaning), 12, 18, 37–8, 40,
    42–3, 64
utopia/utopianism, 13–14, 84–8, 98–100

veil of ignorance (Rawls), 105, 108
voluntaristic individualism, 135
Vygotsky, L., 5–6, 8, 45n.1
    dialectical approach of, 12, 58–64
    on memory, 65n.5
    philosophy of language and, 11–12, 47–65
    social theory of meaning and, 64–5

Wakley, T., 159, 160, 161, 163
Walzer, M., 14, 105, 114–16, 117, 120, 121
Watson-Verran, H., 53, 65n.3
Weill, C., 143
Whitehead, A., 167–9, 170
Whorf, B.L., 12, 52–7, 62–4
Wiles, P., 85
Wilkes, K., 175–7
Williams, B., 100n.1
Winthrop, J., 21
Wittgenstein, L., 1, 6, 10–11, 30–45, 64, 170
Wollheim, R., 99
Wollstonecraft, M., 15, 128

Yaklovlev, A., 81

Zamyatin, E., 89
Zinoviev, A., 81